Advance Praise for *Rediscovering America*

"*Rediscovering America* is not only genuinely entertaining to read, but it is also deeply important! I learned many things from reading it and am already excited to share them with anyone I meet. Scott Powell has provided a fresh overview of America, revealing many things we all must know if we are to keep this republic! Please read this book!"

—Eric Metaxas, #1 *New York Times* bestselling author of *Bonhoeffer, If You Can Keep It*, and *Is Atheism Dead?*

"Scott Powell reminds us in the current age of uncertainty that without national commemorative holidays, shared reverence for our founding customs and traditions, and some sense of collective gratitude to past generations, a huge, increasingly divided, diverse, and often volatile American democracy simply cannot endure."

—Victor Davis Hanson, The Hoover Institution, author of *The Dying Citizen*

"If you understand that human beings are flawed (the Founders did), then you understand (and marvel) at what a moral achievement America is. The Left wants to denigrate that achievement. Scott Powell won't let them get away with it. Read his powerful, inspiring, and concise new book and reaffirm what you always knew— America is an exceptional nation."

—Dennis Prager, Founder of PragerU, syndicated radio talk show host, and bestselling author of *The Rational Bible*

"Scott Powell's delightful book, a luminous retelling of the great American saga through the stories behind its holidays, will be for many Americans a vehicle for recovering a deep appreciation of our profoundly unique and virtuous heritage. In his hands, the stately procession of those holidays, from Columbus Day in October to Constitution Day in September, are made to open us up to our past—a past that is already a part of us. Like the elements making up a great liturgy, the elements in our procession of holidays help us to find ourselves again, and recover the faith and hope that animated the creation of our nation in the first place."

—Wilfred M. McClay, Professor of History, Hillsdale College, and author of *Land of Hope: An Invitation to the Great American Story*

"It's always a good time to rediscover America. Our country's story is a history of great men, monumental achievements, and what may appear, even to skeptics, as providential interventions. Scott Powell has had the good idea of telling America's story by focusing on our national holidays, and how they came to be—stories that tell American readers why they should be grateful to those on whose shoulders they are fortunate enough to stand."

—Michael Barone, Senior political analyst, *Washington Examiner*, Founder and longtime co-author, *The Almanac of American Politics*, Author, *Our Country: The Shaping of America from Roosevelt to Reagan*

Rediscovering AMERICA

*How the National Holidays Tell
an Amazing Story about Who We Are*

Scott S. Powell

A POST HILL PRESS BOOK
ISBN: 978-1-63758-159-9
ISBN (eBook): 978-1-63758-160-5

Rediscovering America:
How the National Holidays Tell an Amazing Story about Who We Are
© 2022 by Scott S. Powell
All Rights Reserved

Cover jacket design by John Cote,
JC Creative Services

Post Hill Press
New York • Nashville
posthillpress.com

Published in the United States of America
1 2 3 4 5 6 7 8 9 10

CONTENTS

*   *   *

To all those who are or have been in military service
and to those who gave their lives for the American
cause of liberty and justice

*   *   *

PROLOGUE

*What this book is about and what it's
not, and why you should read it*

Rediscovering America is like no other book because of its approach to the central issue of our time—that our country is now in a fight for its life. A hydra-headed war of ideas is being waged by enemies of America to undermine our heritage and divide our people so as to bring an end to life in our constitutional republic as we and generations before us have known it. This book was written to defeat these enemies of our republic by equipping readers from every walk of life to get connected to the great accomplishments and the arc of redemption that punctuate and define our history. Americans of different generations who shared a similar greatness of moral vision and believed in the beauty of freedom and equality sacrificed their all so that this nation might be protected, guided, and healed. We are called to do no less.

Many readers will find the stories in the narrative inspire them like a call to action. Most will find that the book transcends the history genre. Almost every chapter has elements of the spiritual and self-help genre with many stories of successful and inspirational figures. Other readers have commented that *Rediscovering America* actually provided a transformational experience by connecting them with the greatness of a purpose-driven past, where individuals accomplished amazing things, and affirmed their own self-worth by making life better for so many others.

In short, *Rediscovering America* is much more than a history about people who came before us. To the extent we are shaped by what our forebears did to contribute to and form our present world, this is a book about the here and now. It may be a bit trite, but there is no denying that we stand on the shoulders of great people who came before us. And this book reveals the variety of virtues that made those people successful, which in turn can help you understand the qualities of character to direct or redirect your own life, calling, and journey.

Unlike many historical accounts that often exceed five hundred or more pages, this book delivers what you need to know in some 222 pages. And whether you are a descendant of a lineage that has been in America for generations or you are a newcomer immigrant, this book will tell you succinctly what has made America great, why it is irreplaceable, and how you can tap into and build on that greatness.

In spite of missteps and setbacks in America, the results have been profoundly positive over the long term—from the exploration and colonial period, the war for independence, to victory in two world wars and a cold war. The United States has survived and thrived, becoming a beacon of freedom and a magnet for immigrants seeking more opportunity and a better life. Through it all, engaged Americans have had the opportunity to gain clarity about the basis for freedom, equality, and the real meaning of progress—often more from their struggles and failures than from their material and business successes.

What you may have thought were random and disjointed events turn out to be developments, accumulation of knowledge, and transitions that make sense and explain why the ideas of America being a land of perpetual opportunity, progress, and hope are so enduring.

It's no secret that most academic historians approach their teaching and writing from a secular perspective. Few of them seem comfortable in exploring the spiritual ideas and motivations behind the movers and shakers of history, even though most of those movers left behind voluminous writings, correspondence, and diaries of their beliefs. This book unapol-ogetically explores those beliefs, for that is essential to understand what motivates people and explains their chosen course of action. In addition, the book's narrative includes the recounting of happenings that fall into the category of providential miracles—events that actually occurred for which there is unassailable evidence, but no plausible explanation for how those events happened.

In this book, you will learn the amazing story of how America's founding was entirely unique and different from that of every other nation in human history. Whereas other nations came into being from an evolution of tribes, clans, ethnic and religious groups, from royalty and blood lineage, the inevitabilities of language, tradition, geography, or from the results of war where the victors carve up the vanquished, America's founding was completely born of noble ideas: that all people of are equal value, that each has been given by God certain rights that cannot be taken away by any man or earthly authority, and that those rights combine to create and protect a thing called freedom in life.

Up until recently, most Americans have taken it for granted that they were free to pursue happiness, free to worship God, free to speak publicly of their views, and, of course, free to choose their leaders. But we have experienced a progression of events and a continuing orchestration of even more radical measures that put all of that at grave risk.

We can all now see the woke agenda, which includes destroying the American people's connection to their heritage. What started out as revisionist history being introduced to school curriculum sixty years ago has become blatant anti-American propaganda and critical race theory indoctrination. And it's been a short step from the shutdown of schools and the economy in the 2020-2021 response to the Covid-19 viral epidemic to young activists and militants tearing down and defac-ing historical monuments and engaging in the most widespread rioting, looting, and the most costly destruction of property (perhaps with the exception of the cost of the Civil War in the South) in American his-tory. Then there has been the social media companies' annihilation of people's First Amendment rights by imposing and enforcing new levels of mass censorship, blacklisting and cancellation of people—including the President of the United States—and even blocking public access to life-saving health information. And with the willfully orchestrated voting irregularities, the politicization of the judiciary, and the near destruction of the separation of powers, the United States now faces unprecedented challenges to its survival.

America has overcome many daunting challenges throughout its past, often waking up at the eleventh hour before taking action and prevailing. One would hope that there would be a consensus around protecting American citizens' freedom and saving the United States as a beacon of liberty in the world. This book was written for that reason, a bit like Paul Revere's ride to wake up and warn the Massachusetts colonists that the British were coming.

As you will discover in subsequent chapters and pages, our two greatest presidents, George Washington and Abraham Lincoln, both believed that if the United States should falter and be defeated, it would come not from an invasion from overseas, but rather from within—from party faction, moral corruption, and the internal enemies of the country and its Constitution, who would likely plot and operate inside U.S. borders, undoubtedly with the help of foreign ideologies and foreign adversaries.

May this work instill the reader with a greater appreciation for our amazing heritage and the sources of strength that have kept us free. It was Winston Churchill who took from Aristotle when he said, "*Courage is rightly esteemed the first of human qualities…because it is the quality which guarantees all others.*" Think of this book also as clarion call to help those you know to get out of denial about our enemies foreign and domestic, and push back against these forces and enemy antagonists with dispatch and courage, and proceed with the skill and cunning of the destroyers, but with none of their malice.

INTRODUCTION

Rediscovering America complements my recent book, *Dark Agenda*, that documents a vast range of political, ideological, and spiritual assaults on American institutions, traditions, and values that, if successful, would end freedom as we know it. The roots of these destructive ideological forces go back to the 19th century philosophers Marx, Engels, and Nietzsche. Early in the 20th century, Lenin advanced this radical ideological assault and pulled off the world's first Marxist revolution in Russia. Toward the middle of the century the influence of the Frankfurt School's Critical Theory and the postmodernist school—whose intellectual leaders included such figures as Theodor Adorno, Sigmund Freud, Herbert Marcuse, Michel Foucault, and Jacques Derrida—became ascendant. This collective philosophical influence had been mainly contained in academia, but in the 1960s things changed with the advent of liberation theology, the sexual revolution, and the radical anti-war and social justice movements, which were absorbed by the mainstream.

In the 21st century spiritual and ideological warfare has increased to a point where the fundamental and longstanding tenets of Judaism and Christianity have been sufficiently undermined and marginalized that fundamental institutions such as the nuclear family have been dramatically changed and weakened. At the macro level, there has been a general transformation of culture—a development that affects every

American. These forces that have led to a breakdown in shared values has also eroded law and order and made bipartisan congressional legislation nearly impossible and increasingly rare. The results have been and continue to be on display in some large US cities, which have become almost ungovernable. On the national level it's become very apparent that the US federal government institutions are now in large part dysfunctional and corrupt—operating outside of the constitutional bounds under which we the people live, and making a mockery of the judicial standard, "equal justice under the law" etched in stone over the entrance to the august Supreme Court building. Meanwhile, we the people have been forced to assimilate and live with censorship and cancel culture, which are not only unconstitutional, but simply and totally at odds with the pluralism, diversity, and tolerance that have always been hallmarks of Americanism.

One can see this on display in the US Capitol Visitor Center, which opened in 2008 as a museum and information center about the US Capitol. There, great efforts have been made to remove and cancel all references to God and faith. A vivid reproduction of the original Constitution has been "photoshopped" to remove the words "in the Year of our Lord" above all the signatures. The table on which President Lincoln placed his Bible during his second inauguration is on display—just the table, not the Bible.

I was born of atheistic parents who were members of the Communist Party in New York. While I rejected the rigidity of the Party, I spent years as a romantic revolutionary radical, being involved with countless advocacy groups and serving as editor of the radical left's leading news journal, *Ramparts*. I went through crises and struggle, but was blessed as a writer, producing bestselling books with Peter Collier on American dynasties, such as the Rockefellers, the Kennedys, and the Ford family. With the help of friends, like Peter, I worked through second thoughts about wasted years of my involvement with the destructive generation and its love affair with Marxism and all its manipulative derivatives and false fronts, and finally broke free to become an independent thinker.

I went on to spend the next thirty-five years of my life with renewed writing vigor, dissecting and documenting the dysfunction and dishonesty of the Left, authoring some twenty-eight books—many best-sellers—not including my eight-volume compendium, the *Black Book of the American Left.*

What Scott Powell has done in this book is tell the other side of the story—the adventurous, positive, and constructive stories behind American history. The framework of the book is quite unique—focusing on the extraordinary individuals, communities, events, and movements that hinge on America's national holidays. To my delight, each chapter brings alive colorful and diverse characters who turn out to be the main drivers of progress in America as well as being catalysts of underappreciated but critically important developments. It turns out that America's past is characterized by many, many remarkable events and people whose triumph over incredible odds of failure is more unbelievable and engaging than most fiction.

As I noted in *Dark Agenda*, almost all the Democratic presidential nominee candidates in 2020 were supporters of racial preferences. One candidate in particular was also an outspoken advocate of open borders, who also said that the new Supreme Court nominee, Brett Kavanaugh, a Catholic Christian, would mean if appointed, "the destruction of the Constitution." Nothing could be further from the truth. The candidate who outspokenly said these things was Kamala Harris, who is now vice president of the United States and likely to replace Joe Biden as president, when his term is up or, perhaps more likely, when he is removed from office for mental incompetence before that time.

Dark Agenda reminds the reader that censorship and the rewriting of history are the practices of totalitarian regimes. In that work and others, I have documented the growing liberal anti-religious bias in the judicial and educational systems of the United States. In the case of the latter, textbook publishers regularly either ignore or purposely omit reference to the role of religion and spiritual forces in affecting human events and history. *Rediscovering America* corrects that record in so many numerous and astonishing ways.

I also show how the absence of religion from our historical memory not only distorts how we think about ourselves, but also how it coarsens our culture and undermines our present liberties. Whereas most historians focus on the dates and places and how central figures react without reference to transcendent forces at work in the events that unfold, author Scott Powell covers the same ground with accuracy and attention to detail, but goes deeper and uncovers what can only be called a hidden hand of fortune, providence, or God at work through the key figures and events of American history over more than four hundred years.

Many of us long for the place we remember in our childhoods, but we have to face the fact that neither we nor our progeny will get that back unless we can win the ideological and spiritual battle against the new woke culture. And make no mistake, the United States is now in a fight for its life. The woke agenda is there for all to see. It includes destroying the American people's connection to their heritage by anti-American indoctrination in schools and tearing down and defacing our historical monuments and statues; destroying the First Amendment through blacklists, the cancel culture, and mass censorship; politicizing the judiciary and destroying the separation of powers. This is not only utterly antithetical to how we should be governed and live under the American Constitution, but it is in reality an introductory form of communist and national socialist totalitarian rule, the nightmare systems that cost humanity more than 110 million lives in the twentieth century. With the growing role of technology in the economy, governments and their partnerships with wealthy technology titans, and their social media and consumer tracking companies, the stage is being set for far greater destruction of the human spirit and loss of life than any previous period in human history.

Redefining America is exactly what the radical left and the Democratic Party have been working at for the last fifty-plus years. Their call "to define what kind of country we are" is an ominous agenda for Americans.

America is unique among nations in having been defined in the crucible of its creation from the Declaration of Independence and the Constitution. And that Constitution has made America a beacon of freedom for the entire world. In *Rediscovering America*'s penultimate chapter, you will get a deeper understanding of how the US Constitution came into being and how it has kept America free longer than any other nation in human history.

It took a civil war and two hundred years of sacrifice and struggle to achieve a society that approaches the ideals laid down in the Declaration. That achievement consummated by Reverend Martin Luther King and the civil rights movement in the late 1960s is now endangered by a party in regression because it's adopting identity politics and critical race theory that embody the antithesis of the ideas and principles established by the founding. Instead of cherishing religious liberty and individual freedom, the Democrats offer us a reversion to tribal loyalties, collectivist values, and secular progressive groupthink. On the domestic front they want to displace MLK's vision of a color-blind society, wherein the quality of character is paramount, with a system in which immutable origins—skin colors, ethnicities, genders, and classes—are the primary factors in judging individuals for promotion and determining what is just. Hostile to the idea of national patriotism, they seek to supplant the Constitution and subordinate America to an international socialist order that would inevitably result in a high-tech tyranny with unprecedented repression, corruption, and wholesale elimination of resistors among the people, which has been the record without exception in every nation across all cultures adopting that system in the last one-hundred-plus years.

A nation divided by such fundamental ideas—individual freedom on one side and group identity on the other—cannot long endure, any more than could a nation that was half slave and half free. It was Abraham Lincoln who rightly said, repeating the words of Jesus recorded in all three Synoptic Gospels—Matthew, Mark and Luke, "A house divided against itself cannot stand." That is as true today as it was then.

Scott Powell has made a major contribution in the research and writing of *Rediscovering America*, providing substantive reason for hope and confidence in the midst of troubled times. It may be the first book written in the history genre that lays out the progressive and redemptive course that is America's greatest legacy. Indeed you will find much to celebrate in the stories behind the American holidays.

David Horowitz
August 2021

CHAPTER 1

American History: Why Being
Connected to the Past Matters

What does it mean to be an American? Although the answer for each will likely be different because subjectivity is shaped by unique experience and understanding, almost no one would refer to the United States as "just another nation." The concept of "America" has always carried big and positive attributes. Even repressive and evil regimes indirectly pay tribute to America's unique stature in the world by singling out the United States above all other nations as the target of their greatest hatred and condemnation.

From the first settlers to today's immigrants arriving at America's shores and borders four hundred years later, the mythic sense of America as being a place of refuge and sanctuary, a land of second chances, renewal, and new beginnings, a place of unexplored frontiers with unlimited possibilities, has remained remarkably persistent, providing a unique and powerful optimism.

No one can say when exactly the modern age began, but it was clearly tied to the Reformation, the Renaissance, and the Scientific Revolution, which had their roots in fourteenth- and fifteenth-century Europe. And few would disagree that of all the countries in the world, America has the unique status of being the first modern country.

The Reformation and Renaissance set in motion spiritual and cultural awakenings as well as an unusual concentration of human genius and extraordinary wisdom that culminated in the birth of the United States in the eighteenth century. Dedicated to the rule of law, separation of powers and limited government, and accountability to its citizens whose rights were natural and God-given and thus unalienable and not subject to infringement by the state, the United States was truly a revolutionary model that subsequently influenced other nations worldwide well into the twentieth century.

The reformation of church corruption and pursuit of spiritual truth promoted by Martin Luther in the early sixteenth century had its analog with the pursuit of truth regarding the physical universe by contemporary Nicolaus Copernicus, who is credited as a key founder of the scientific revolution. Copernicus's empirical evidence and reasoning upset the prevailing geocentric view that the earth was the center of the universe with the heliocentric model that took its place—placing the sun at the center, with the earth and other planets orbiting it. It also laid the foundation for celestial navigation, enabling Columbus and successor explorers to cross thousands of miles of ocean and arrive at a predetermined destination, which facilitated the colonization of the coast that would become the first thirteen states in the United States.

Copernicus, followed by Kepler, Galileo, Bacon, Newton, and more, were key figures in the scientific revolution that expanded the frontiers of understanding the physical universe. Collectively, they gave birth to the scientific method, which became the most reliable and powerful means of pushing the envelope of discovery and invention through hypothesis testing that involved compiling and rationally evaluating empirical evidence and results to arrive at facts.

What was striking about the modern age compared with previous periods was the speed at which progress was made. Coming on the heels of the Middle Ages, which encompassed nearly seven hundred years of a feudal social order, punctuated toward the end with the bubonic plague in the mid fourteenth century, the modern age made rapid progress applying science and harnessing innovation and discovery, reviving and pursuing cultural excellence, and addressing and solving people's common needs and problems.

When one considers the appearance of the United States from a grand historical perspective—notably its rise from colonial poverty to the world's economic superpower in two hundred years—it's a bit like a production car today going from zero to sixty in three seconds. However, we can't say that this rapid material progress has been accompanied by as much in terms of spiritual and social progress. In fact, it is quite apparent that in contemporary America, there is little correlation between material wealth and abundance on the one hand and happiness and fulfillment on the other.

The American story is of course still being written, but many of its past historical accomplishments were ultimate achievements, such as the drafting of its founding principles and governing documents conceived by a remarkable group of statesmen; a Civil War that was America's most costly war, but succeeded in preserving the union and ending slavery; a civil rights movement that accomplished the ideals set forth in the Declaration of Independence and completed the work of Lincoln to make equal opportunity for blacks and minorities a reality. These acts and events represent a sort of finality, but they are also subject to being strengthened or weakened by what subsequent generations do.

While people's standard of living has been greatly improved and their longevity significantly increased, many Americans now seem oblivious to how we got here. The incredible benefits attributable to the application of both the scientific method and the spiritual truths of Judeo-Christian heritage are increasingly taken for granted at best. At worst, they are viewed as unnecessary, even obsolete. And in their place, new idols have arisen—what historian Herbert Schlossberg described in his classic book, *Idols for Destruction*.[1]

We have to a large degree lost our guiding national narrative. For about the last two and a half generations, there has been a subtle but growing assault on most of the values that were previously considered the bedrock of American society. Many older Americans today hardly recognize the country of their childhood. While technological progress has proceeded at a rapid pace, providing convenience, efficiency, and higher standards of material living, the foundational institutions of American society—the family, educational institutions, manners and civility, respect for law and order, and merit-based outcomes—have been in concurrent decline.

How is it that so many Americans have allowed institutions and norms to be undermined that were the basis for almost all our prior success? And how could this happen after the United States stood decisively with the forces of good—helping the Allied powers to win two world wars, defeating Hitler's fascism and then the Soviet Communist empire? The answers to these questions, which immediately follow, may be difficult and depressing for some readers to face. But please bear with this relatively short section so as to better understand how America got to where we are now. And be encouraged that the last pages of this first chapter and all of the following twelve "holiday" chapters will surprise and uplift you with remarkable stories that collectively tell a mind-blowing story of miracles, redemption, and hope.

First, the decline in the US has happened in large part because revolutionary ideological forces have been subtly at work to transform society from within. This has advanced slowly and broadly so as to be almost unnoticed, like mold growing behind walls or termites eating out the insides of beams and frames of a structure. Most assume that winning the Cold War meant we also defeated the Marxist ideology backing the Soviet Union. Yet a closer look at social history in twentieth-century America shows that strains of neo-Marxism have proliferated and collectively provided the central transformative ideological force shaping American culture over the last several generations and into the present.

Antonio Gramsci, the leader of the Italian Communist Party, was a leading twentieth-century Marxist theoretician who argued that the route to taking power in developed, industrialized societies such as the United States would be best achieved through a "long march through the institutions." This would be a gradual process of radicalization of the cultural institutions—"the superstructure"—of bourgeois society, a process that would in turn transform the values and morals of society. Gramsci believed that as society's morals were softened, its political and economic foundation would be more easily undermined and restructured.

Cultural Marxism was also advanced by intellectuals from the Frankfurt School, who were forced to flee Nazi Germany in the mid-1930s. Resettling in the US, members of the Frankfurt School, such as Herbert Marcuse, Theodor Adorno, Max Horkheimer, Erich Fromm, and Otto Kirchheimer, first set up shop at Columbia University, and then expanded their teaching to other elite universities such as Berkeley, Princeton, Harvard, the New School for Social Research, and Brandeis.

While the Frankfurt School was neo-Marxist, many of its adherents were less interested in economics and redistribution of wealth than in remaking and transforming society through attitudinal and cultural change. They incorporated Marxist class theory into sociology and psychology while also assimilating Freud's theories on sexuality. Thus, Marx's theory of the dialectic of perpetual conflict was joined together with Freud's neurotic ideas, creating a sort of Freudian-Marxism. The amalgam provided a broad-based critique of social problems oriented toward transforming society as a whole—something they called Critical Theory.

Although the leaders of the Frankfurt School had limited influence, being somewhat ensconced in Berkeley, the New School, and Ivy League universities, their Critical Theory ideas were considered avant-garde and received a multiplier effect through other universities, particularly as they were embraced by the teachers' colleges across the country in the 1950s and 1960s. What was perhaps unique about the cultural Marxists was their "street smarts" recognition that psychological conditioning was more effective than philosophical arguments to achieve the goal of transforming America's culture. If they could win "cultural hegemony," the acolytes of the Frankfurt School were confident that the wellsprings of human thought could be largely controlled by mass psychology and propaganda.

For them, the takedown of America would be accomplished by cultural transformation through gradual demoralization of the population and subversion of the system through infiltration rather than through confrontation and revolutionary militancy. The cultural Marxists' "long march through the institutions" in Herbert Marcuse's terms of "working against the established institutions while working in them" was focused on radicalization of the knowledge, information, and cultural institutions, with an early focus on educational institutions—both K–12 and higher education, the media and Hollywood, the law practice, and nonprofit foundations. Later, the employment targets for people of this mindset included social media and information search multinational corporations such as Google, Facebook, Twitter, Amazon, and Microsoft.

Essentially, the Frankfurt School believed that, as long as an individual believed that his reason and common sense could solve the problems facing society, then that society would never reach the state of hopelessness and alienation that they considered necessary to foment socialist revolution. Their task, therefore, was to undermine both the Judeo-Christian legacy and the foundation for rational reasoning by creating a narrative of destructive criticism affecting every sphere and institution of life, resulting in a loss of any absolute truth or meaning. This then would bring on mass confusion, demoralization, hopelessness, and destabilization of society—setting the final stage for bringing down what they saw as the "oppressive" order.

In addition to their goal of putting an end to Christianity and the nuclear family, the Critical Theory project also sought to exacerbate race relations and promote massive immigration to destroy national identity. Additional focal points in their agenda encouraged dependency on state benefits and the bending of the legal system to favor perpetrators of crime over victims. And lastly, the agenda sought to dumb down the media and school curricula, weaken teachers' authority, and condition them to deemphasize merit and embrace collectivist group think.

An important part of the Critical Theory project of total transformation of society was to break down traditional relationships between men and women by promoting and legitimizing unhinged sexual permissiveness with no cultural or religious restraint. Building on the Frankfurt School's Critical Theory, leaders of what came to be known as

postmodernism advanced the wrecking ball of the cultural deconstruc-
tion project right into the twenty-first century.

Postmodernists have had no use for tradition or any standards of
normalcy, believing that all truth is contrived illusion rather than absolute. Homosexuality and transgenderism are not only valid choices, but
are actually preferable, for they advance the destruction of the traditional
family and society. They also view the scientific method as being useless,
with facts too limiting to determine anything—making truth and error
two sides of the same coin. Thus, fake news did not arise out of reaction
to President Donald Trump, but more fundamentally as an extension of
postmodernism and its seepage into journalism schools and programs.
Postmodernists, by the way, were the first advocates of open borders,
which was also an extension of the project to destroy national identity
and undermine the democratic electoral process.

What is obviously striking is the degree to which this agenda of
breakdown and national transformation promoted by a relatively small
constituency of cultural Marxists has been accepted and infused into
the leadership and operating procedures of one of the longstanding political parties in the US—the Democratic Party. Illustrative of this was
Democrat presidential candidate flagbearer Hillary Clinton, wherein she
proclaimed to the 2015 Women in the World Summit, not long before
she launched her 2016 presidential campaign, that "deep-seated cultural
codes, religious beliefs and structural biases have to be changed." She had
previously lost her party's 2008 nomination for presidential candidate to
Barack Obama, who announced just days before he was elected, his desire
to "fundamentally transform America."

Since the US election in 2016, this breakdown has now erupted in a
new cultural and political civil war. On the one side, we have those who
have been shaped both overtly and subliminally by cultural Marxist ideology and, on the other side, we have those who find grounding, perspective, and purpose in transcendent values and honesty—predominantly
associated with Judaism and Christianity and the common sense that was
endowed by the Creator.

For some time now, postmodernists may have held the commanding heights in the culture that includes Hollywood, the media, and schools, and their corruption, intolerance, and visceral hatred manifest in the Democratic Party may have reached a Waterloo—with their actions being visible for all to see. In true postmodernist tradition, they have turned the Constitution and due process on its head with a ginned-up media presumption of guilt of their political enemies on salacious hearsay rather than corroborating evidence. They have demonized the police, while black-on-black murder rates soar and cities burn.

The left has a gift for packaging and naming their agenda in appealing ways. A growing number of intellectuals tell us that our culture and the way we live is not only postmodern, but also post-Christian, and that the need for redemption by God has been replaced by the imperatives of a secular redemption defined by political correctness. They call this new framework being "woke" and it is largely based on the one-two approach of promoting guilt among largely successful white males for their alleged biases and misdeeds, past and present, and then providing them a solution in the form of relief and through making amends and virtue signaling, attending critical race theory training, donating money, and accommodating new militant groups and minorities. But what we find is that there is simply no end to atonement, role reversals, and reparations to fix things. The solution is never the solution, but rather it's about another unstated agenda that advances the socialist revolution.

In short, the path of the new politically correct "woke" redemption has nothing to do with long-standing moral standards and everything to do with identity politics and division—race, class, gender, multiculturalism, and replacing worship of God with social justice, environmentalism, and the worship of nature.

We have come to a point where seemingly endless manufactured injustices are crowding out the joy of everyday life, stripping people of their spontaneity and their humor, and eliminating moral character as key promotion and leadership criteria. As a result, we see a new phenomenon of political leaders in various American cities undercutting civic and religious institutions, defunding the police and law enforcement, and failing to protect private property and business. On the national level, we also witness political leaders unwilling to defend the nation's borders or its historic monuments, which undermines the centrality of the nation-state and the meaning of America as a Constitutional republic, uniquely founded to protect the citizens' sovereign rule, property rights, and their unalienable rights to live freely with equal opportunity. The preoccupation with the cultural Marxist narrative has not only drained society of goodwill, but has also undermined and disparaged America's great heritage.

A counterreaction to the "woke" narrative is developing, primarily from the growing number of engaged enlightened citizens, bloggers, and some academics. One such acclaimed professor of American history, Wilfred M. McClay, has written about the mythic ways that Americans have defined their country's virtue and national distinctiveness. He reminds us that not too long ago, people had quite a number of common descriptive ways in which they thought of America.[2] A partial list includes:

- A City Upon a Hill: a biblical reference of America as moral exemplar
- An Empire of Reason: America the land of Enlightenment
- Nature's Nation: America as a nation uniquely in harmony with nature
- Novus Ordo Seclorum: Latin for America being "the new order of the ages"
- The New Eden: America as a land of newness and moral renewal
- Redeemer Nation: America as redeemer of a corrupted world
- The Nation Dedicated to a Proposition: America as a land of equality
- The Melting Pot: America as blender and transcender of ethnicities
- Land of Opportunity: America as the nation of material promise and social mobility
- The Nation of Immigrants: America as a magnet for immigrants
- The New Israel: America as God's new chosen nation
- The Nation of Nations: America as a transnational container for diverse national identities

American history is extraordinarily rich, and if we are to sort out and better grasp whether the country's virtues outweigh its shortcomings, we need to understand a bit more of the foundational background of the country, which is one of the purposes in writing this book.

For starters, the United States *is the only country in the entire history of mankind that was specifically founded on the recognition and principle that all people are created equal in value and that they have unalienable rights to life, liberty, and the pursuit of happiness.* While some of these rights were not fully realized for several hundred years after the founding, that does not diminish them, nor make these rights transitory or subject to being taken away by the state, because they come from the authority of God, the Creator. Because these were revolutionary ideas when they were first articulated in the eighteenth century founding of the United States, it's also important to identify where they came from.

Obedience to worldly authority had been the norm for almost all of recorded history until Martin Luther, a Catholic monk and theologian, proclaimed that liberty of conscience was the proper basis for religious and political life. When Martin Luther posted ninety-five theses on the church bulletin board in Wittenberg, Germany in 1517, over five hundred years ago, he probably had no idea what forces he was unleashing. At that time, Luther appeared to be either a fool or a subversive for proclaiming that liberty of conscience—individual freedom—was a sacred right that was given, sanctioned, and protected by God.

Although intending to spur reform within the Catholic Church rather than creating a schism in starting a new church, he ended up accomplishing both—bringing on the Reformation of the Roman Catholic Church, and empowering people to worship separately as Protestants. In so doing, Luther also set in motion ideas and principles that would affect citizen-state relationships in England and Europe, and then inspire and cause various peoples and groups to break away from Europe and pursue freedom of conscience in the New World.

After Luther, the next significant Christian reform movement took place in Geneva, Switzerland, where a society of Christians, often called Presbyterians, established a community under the leadership of

John Calvin, who, after Luther, probably did the most to advance the Reformation—the freedom of individual conscience, and the equal status of all people—inherent in Luther's idea of a "priesthood of all believers."

Calvin's "resistance theory," which justified the people's right to disobey unjust rule, would later find expression in the Declaration of Independence. After the American colonies won their independence, the real work of forming an effective government began with the Constitutional Convention in 1787—no easy task for the fifty-five delegates who convened in the midst of a depressed economy, rampant inflation of the Continental dollar, territorial threats, conflict over institutionalized slavery in Southern states, and even talk of secession not only by the Southern states, but also by some of the New England states.

The Constitutional Convention was not easy, with stubborn differences bringing on robust debate, occasionally evoking impasses that could have led to dissolution. By today's standards, it was a miracle that the convention delegates were of such character that they could rise to the occasion and muster the tolerance, large-mindedness, and generosity of spirit to agree on substantive terms of the new Constitution in just four months. But as good as that Constitution was (and is), it had to be ratified by the states to become law. Fear of corruption and abuse of power from a central government caused several key states, both in the North and the South, to withhold support until the Constitution was amended with a Bill of Rights—starting with the all-important First Amendment protecting and tolerating freedom of speech, press, and religion.

It could be said that the First Amendment is the most important, for it protects all the other amendments and Constitutional rule itself. Yet today, America's First Amendment is being shredded and nullified by "political correctness," and its offspring, the "cancel culture." The former restricts discussion to stereotypes and imposes a "lens" through which social, political, and historical reality is seen. The cancel culture phenomenon seeks to discredit, silence, and literally erase people and whole groups whose particular view runs contrary to the politically correct view. In addition, the meaning of words and language has been manipulated in an Orwellian sense, seemingly to facilitate the conditioning of the public to disbelieve their reason and common sense and accept alternative views for political purposes.

The tenets and framework of political correctness have largely negated the relevance of age-old moral truths, common sense, and the scientific method—all of which contribute to protecting relationships, solving problems, and facilitating progress. As a result, Americans are experiencing increasing regressive forces that are affecting economics, law, politics, and basic civility.

Shocking as it might seem, a pattern has been emerging in the US with similarities to the standard practices in communist and fascist totalitarian states, which is: to rewrite history and indoctrinate the population—and particularly the young—so as to be able to manipulate and control the future cultural and political landscape. In his novel *1984*, Orwell wrote, "Who controls the past controls the future."

In that sense, the US is closer to a future that is reminiscent of developments that led to persecution in 1930s Germany than anyone would like to contemplate or admit. The Nazi propaganda machine censored non-conforming views and sought to isolate and discriminate against Jews—a strategy intended to engender hatred and prejudice against them within the greater German population, thus setting the stage for the genocidal "Final Solution" of the Holocaust.

"Big Brother," a term still casually used to describe an all-knowing governing authority, comes straight out of *1984*. In the state that Orwell describes, all subjects are continually reminded that "Big Brother is watching you," by way of constant surveillance through the pervasive use of "telescreens" by the ruling class.

Orwell described the scope of the communist totalitarian enterprise, noting in one section of *1984* that, "Every record has been destroyed or falsified, every book rewritten, every picture has been repainted, every statue and street building has been renamed, and every date has been altered. And the process is continuing day by day and minute by minute. History has stopped. Nothing exists except an endless present in which the Party is always right."

Orwell's coining of the concepts and terms "newspeak, doublethink and thought police" are what we now experience in our woke culture of political correctness. Newspeak is the distorted reality accomplished by manipulating the meaning of language and words, while doublethink is the conditioned mental attitude to ignore reality and common sense and substitute and embrace a distorted or false narrative. The analogs of "thought police" in *1984* are now the cancellation enforcers of political correctness seen in the mainstream and social media and college campuses across the country.

Orwell explained, "The whole aim of Newspeak and Doublethink is to narrow the range of thought." Political correctness has the same goal, which may explain why its adherents are so intolerant—seeking to shut down and silence people with whom they disagree in social media and on college campuses. One has to assume that the tearing down of historic statues and monuments in cities across the United States beginning in the spring of 2020 and continuing into 2021 was done for the same reason it's done by communists when they seize power: to rewrite history and control the future.

Many assume that because the press is not state-controlled in the US, there is a long way to go before the American government has the power of Orwell's Big Brother. But what if the universities and the educational system and the major television and print media institutions embrace the groupthink that ingratiates them with the ruling elite and deep state? What if the culture shapers in Hollywood and the advertising industry on Madison Avenue follow a similar path in participating in and reinforcing the same groupthink norms? What if the rise of social media promotes a kind of groupthink conformity that effectively marginalizes and silences opposing views?

Propaganda may actually be more effective in America than in totalitarian societies because of the power of repetitive messaging—the key integral means and essence of brainwashing—from ostensibly separate and diverse private media sources within the United States. Citizens in totalitarian societies aren't as easily fooled because they know that the government controls the media and all its messaging.

Orwell's Big Brother has become a reality with the new dimension of social media and consumer giants. Google, Facebook, and Amazon are three of the largest "information companies" in the US, knowing almost everything about people's preferences through their artificial intelligence tracking that peers into people's "telescreen" computers and smartphones.

Clearly now, social media have great power to narrow the range of acceptable thought. On Facebook, those who express support of politically correct views—what is tacitly the popular majority view—are frequently lauded with thumbs up, while dissenters often remain silent to avoid being criticized, denounced, or canceled. All of which leads to what is called "the spiral of silence," which reinforces the groupthink of what seems to be the social and cultural majority.

If the United States is to remain the home of liberty, justice, and opportunity for all, it needs to focus on real threats, a key one now being the loss of freedom of speech and the assault on the First Amendment.

One of the nation's founders, Patrick Henry, was a gifted and passionate orator best known for his declaration, "Give me liberty or give me death." But his most important, substantive, and lasting contribution to the legacy of freedom was his tenacious and ultimately successful fight to have the Bill of Rights appended to the Constitution because of his conviction that the First Amendment and nine others were absolutely necessary to protect individual liberty against the inevitable abuse of power by centralized government.

Orwell reminds us today of the critical importance of the First Amendment, noting, "If liberty means anything at all, it means the right to tell people what they do not want to hear." Exactly the opposite of the current trajectory and what the woke, PC, and cancel culture crowd wants.

In sum, when history and facts don't matter—when the present gets severed from the past, when common sense gets jettisoned and displaced by woke PC nostrums, and when culture gets increasingly unmoored from its Judeo-Christian heritage of manners, moral standards, and noble inclinations—the barbarians, the hate mongers, and mobs emerge inside the gates. And sadly, the first victims are often the poorest and most vulnerable who are both dependent on and used by a warped political system, and who find little respite or escape from pervasive mass culture in decay.

History shows that the great leaps forward in progress were almost always spurred by individuals who had original ideas and the courage to challenge the assumptions of their times and contemporaries. The uniqueness of this book is its succinct presentation of the country's history focusing on the courageous people and ideas behind the most important events that shaped the country, which prompted the establishment of the American holidays. The stories behind these holidays are profoundly unique, but it also turns out that they are interconnected in deep ways. Each chapter can be read as a stand-alone story. But the sequencing and linking of chapters that make each of the holiday stories allows the book to cast new light on America's progress and redemption, which is an amazing story that many—including esteemed historians—have simply missed.

It was Yeats who said that man treasures and loves what vanishes. This book is specifically written to help the reader connect with a vanished past in order to become more fully human in the present. It is also hoped that the vignettes of history presented in this book help one feel connected with transcendent events, which enhance our sense of belonging and homecoming. It is certainly easier to face setbacks and challenges in life when one has vicariously lived through the much greater difficulties that have punctuated the lives of so many of America's leaders throughout our history. The realization that we stand on the shoulders of so many truly remarkable people who overcame insurmountable challenges should be a source of great hope.

This book will have served its purpose if, after reading it, many of you find courage and a voice to push back on the deceivers, haters, and facilitators of wokeism and communism. Maybe some will get involved in your local school board, or local, county, or state office. Perhaps some of the chapters and parts of the book will have served their purpose simply when you find your emotions and imagination stir you in new and powerful ways on the occasion of rising for the national anthem, celebrating holidays, or while visiting historic places like the Lincoln and Jefferson Memorials, and Arlington Cemetery in and around Washington, DC; the Gettysburg, Antietam, or Shiloh battlefields in Pennsylvania, Maryland, and Tennessee; Independence Hall in Philadelphia; or the *Mayflower* replica ship in Plymouth, Massachusetts—to name only a few historic sites worth visiting.

So, let the adventure begin.

CHAPTER 2

Columbus Day: Great Accomplishments
Start with Character

In thinking about the story of America as revealed in the events and people commemorated by our national holidays, it certainly makes sense to start at the beginning. And there is little dispute that the American story began with the seafaring discovery of the New World by Christopher Columbus. Columbus was the first to accomplish the feat of sailing over four thousand miles south and west across the Atlantic Ocean in the late fifteenth century. His quest was to find a western passage to the Indies and discover new lands on the way with inhabitants open to the Christian message.

Although many give him credit for discovering America, Columbus didn't actually find or set foot on land associated with what later came to be known as the United States in his first or subsequent voyages to the New World. But his feat in crossing the vast ocean inspired many successors to embark on similar voyages to cross the Atlantic and explore coastal lands, some of whom would make settlements in locations in what became the United States of America.

Additionally, many criticize Columbus for his alleged mistreatment and enslavement of natives in the Caribbean and Latin America. But it's often overlooked that the sponsorship by Queen Isabella and King Ferdinand II of Spain—whose ships were outfitted with Spanish crews—affected what happened. Columbus was alone in being an Italian from Genoa—a simple seafaring explorer and Christian evangelist—while the Spanish hidalgo crew members, numbering nearly a hundred to about two hundred on each of the four successive voyages, bore the primary responsibility for the mistreatment of natives. More about that later in the chapter.

Like some other American holidays, Columbus Day was established as an official national holiday many decades after it was recognized and celebrated by some of the states. It was President Franklin Delano Roosevelt who, in 1937, decided to formally commemorate Columbus by establishing a national holiday in his honor.

If Christopher Columbus had not been a man of character and determination with the faith and self-confidence to ignore critics, go against the crowd, and remain steadfast in his vision and his calling, he could never have accomplished what he did. He had grown up in a working-class family and his life was one of hardship, punctuated by near death and devastating failure that would have been the demise of most ordinary people.

Born in 1451 in the Republic of Genoa, a major seaport city-state in what is now Italy, Columbus faced a Mediterranean Sea full of rivalries, hostility, and sea battles. Notwithstanding those dangers, Columbus had a passion for seafaring, and took an interest in astronomy, geometry, and arithmetic associated with navigation. With a limited formal education, he felt compelled to go to sea, and enlisted as crew on various merchant ships hailing from Genoa. Early in his seafaring, on one merchant convoy to the Eastern Mediterranean, Columbus encountered the Muslim blockade that had largely brought a halt to Europe's valuable and important overland trade with the Orient. So, the seed was planted early in his seafaring career that finding a sea route to the Orient would likely have far-reaching benefits.

Having experienced the militant face of Islam at the eastern end of the Mediterranean, Columbus then decided to reorient his seafaring aspirations in a westerly direction. And when another group of merchants assembled a trade convoy of five ships led by a Flemish-flagged vessel to sail through the Straits of Gibraltar and head to England and Flanders, he jumped at the opportunity to sign on. However, no sooner had the convoy rounded Cape St. Vincent at the Southern tip of Portugal when they were besieged by a fleet of thirteen Portuguese and French ships.[3]

Being at war with the Flemish, the French led the attack and the battle that raged for the better part of a day resulted in the destruction of the five convoy ships. Columbus was slightly wounded and forced to abandon ship and jump into the sea by nightfall, five or six miles from the shore of Portugal. Between fatigue, injury, and the cold water, Columbus should have perished. But he had the will to survive, latched hold of a floating wooden oar from the remains of his sunken ship, and then somehow mustered the strength to propel himself by kicking his legs through the night and make it to shore by dawn.

Little did Columbus realize at the time, but for a seafarer with his ambition and vision, there was no better place to wash up than on a beach in Portugal. By the mid-fifteenth century, under Prince Henry the Navigator, the Portuguese had become the leading maritime explorers in Europe and had developed the most advanced systems of navigation and mapmaking. By 1420, the Portuguese had their first settlements on Madeira Island. Twelve years later, exploration of the Canary and the Azores Islands began. Pushing farther down the west coast of Africa, by 1462 the Portuguese colonized and established a trading outpost in the Cape Verde Islands, a distance of nearly two thousand miles from Portugal.

As a footnote to our story, the prominence of Portugal as the dominant exploration sea power would be demonstrated by Amerigo Vespucci and Ferdinand Magellan, whose exploration voyages came only a few years after Columbus had broken through the limitations of seafaring exploration. Both went through Portuguese training and sailed under the flag of Portugal. In 1501–1502, Vespucci demonstrated that Brazil and the West Indies were not Asia's eastern outskirts, but a separate continent described as the New World, which in 1507 was called "America" in his name. In 1519, Portuguese explorer Ferdinand Magellan would set out with a fleet of five ships to carry out the unfulfilled goal of Columbus to discover a western route and sea passage to India and the Spice Islands. Taking a course south across the equator, he discovered that passage, which also came to be known eponymously—the "Strait of Magellan" at the southern tip of South America. He then went on to become the first European to cross the Pacific Ocean. Though Magellan was killed in the Philippines in 1521, one of his ships continued westward to Spain, accomplishing the first circumnavigation of Earth.

Returning to our story of Columbus, it turns out that misfortune, loss, and near death became uniquely fortuitous for his future, as Portugal was the best place to test and further develop his navigation theories. Largely self-taught and arriving on the scene a full century before Galileo, Columbus believed the evidence he found went against the orthodox belief of his age that the earth was the center of the universe.

Up until that time, the route to India had been east over land or sailing a long and indirect coastal route south around Africa and then north and east. However, Columbus was convinced that by calculating the position of the sun, moon, and stars, he could navigate a route from Europe to India and the Spice Islands by sailing west—out of sight of land—around the earth.

Shipping out of Lisbon on various merchant and trade voyages to England, France, Ireland, and even Iceland, Columbus had the opportunity to discuss and test his navigational theories. And between voyages, while staying ashore in his new home port of Lisbon, he sought to learn the latest new breakthroughs in using navigational instruments from the Portuguese naval authorities who were at the time focused on developing advanced navigational techniques by sighting the stars. This was necessary to enable long passages hundreds of miles from land, which was required at the time for the Portuguese to continue trade with Africa while avoiding any encounters with the Spanish navy that was seeking control of the Cape Verde Islands, which had been under the control of Portugal.

In addition to having bravery and skill, Columbus was a devoted Christian who attributed his passions, ability, and vision to his Creator. He left voluminous writings, some in diary-like form, that bear witness to what motivated him to do what he did. In his later thirties, he could no longer ignore the calling to apply his navigational skills and find a trade route to the Orient.[4] Columbus wrote, "It was the Lord who put into my mind, [and] I could feel his hand upon me...that it would be possible to sail from here to the Indies."[5] But he also knew that such an undertaking would need the sponsorship of a sovereign state to charter, build, or sponsor a flotilla of sailing vessels and to commission his voyage.

In early 1484, he was able to get an audience with the Portuguese King John II to solicit support for his plan to sail across the Atlantic and find India and the Spice Islands. The king called in astronomers, mathematicians, and navigational experts to judge the viability of the proposal, but they counseled against providing sponsorship or support because they believed Columbus had greatly underestimated the distance across the Atlantic.

With his wife's death in the early 1480s and the rejection of his proposal, Columbus decided to leave Portugal in 1485 and make his next approach to Queen Isabella and King Ferdinand of Spain. However, they were surrounded by advisors steeped in a worldview stuck in the Dark Ages that included a flat earth perspective and the impossibility of there being human life on any landmass separated by a vast ocean from civilizations descending from Adam and Eve whose Garden of Eden was in the fertile crescent area that was a bridge between Europe and Asia, a region that came to be known as Mesopotamia.

Queen Isabella was open-minded and took a liking to Columbus, even granting a stipend for his travel expense, but decided to defer a decision on the proposal due to her advisors' closed-mindedness. At the time, Columbus had reconnected with his brother, Bartholomew, and enlisted his support. Bartholomew was willing to embark on a long journey to England to solicit support from King Henry VII. However, losing more than a year in travel delays—in part due to captivity by pirates—before he could reach England, he, too, ended up with rejection. Undaunted, he decided then and there to solicit the King of France. But that also came to naught.

In the end, the six years of waiting and traipsing across Europe trying to convince different monarchs to finance and sponsor Columbus's westward passage expedition met with failure. The proposed venture was considered foolhardy, and Columbus recounts in his diary that "all who heard of my project rejected it with laughter, ridiculing me."[6]

Queen Isabella had gotten wind of Columbus's trying to gain sponsorship from other monarchs and decided to grant him a generous new stipend and summon him to Córdoba with a promise of new discussions. Natural disaster, floods, and war prevented those talks from happening, while at the same time, the sultan of Egypt threatened Queen Isabella that if she did not cease her campaign to drive the Moors and Islam out of Spain, he would put the sword to all Christians in the Holy Land and destroy the Church of the Holy Sepulchre in Jerusalem.

When Columbus learned about this Islamic threat from the Queen, he not only found it unthinkable, but was affronted. So much so that he vowed to organize a crusading army complete with ships, artillery, and soldiers to rescue the Holy Sepulchre from Muslim hands. In the end, Queen Isabella was quite taken by Columbus's love and boldness for Christ, and his vision and unflagging resolution to find a trade route to the Orient in the face of repeated rejection over many years.

Few years in history have been punctuated by such pivotal events as what happened in Spain in 1492. It was in that year that Christendom, still suffering from the loss of Constantinople to the Muslim Turks forty years prior, drove Islam out of Europe and undertook spreading Christianity to new territories and people. Both were made possible by none other than Queen Isabella and King Ferdinand, who stood up to the threat from the sultan of Egypt and defeated the last Muslim enclave in Granada on the Spanish peninsula.

Now Isabella and Ferdinand—having previously rejected overtures from Columbus—had a change of heart and willing ears for Columbus, not just on account of his seafaring skills and vision for a westward passage, but also because of his persistence, bravery, and Christian character and evangelistic zeal. They decided to throw their support behind Columbus and committed to providing all the necessary financial backing for him to carry out his seafaring expedition to find a western trade route passage to India and the Spice Islands.

Columbus never doubted his vision, remarking that "there is no question that the inspiration was from God...encouraging me continually to press forward, and without ceasing for a moment..."[7] Departing from the port of Palos, Spain on August 2, 1492, with a crew of eighty-seven on three small ships—the *Nina*, the *Pinta*, and the *Santa Maria*—Columbus embarked on the longest voyage ever made out of sight of land to find the western passage to India.

No sooner had they cleared the harbor and trimmed their sails when a Spanish caravel was sighted, and it appeared to be on course to deliver a message. Learning that an armada of Portuguese warships was just over the horizon to the west-southwest, Columbus had no doubts about their intentions. According to his journal, the king of Portugal was vengeful because Columbus had switched his allegiance to Spain and had ordered warships to capture him.

With the wind having died out, and the prospect of being captured while wallowing in swells of a calm sea, Columbus directed his crew to launch the small deck boats and man the oars to tow the big ships in an effort to elude the enemy. Since the hostile Portuguese Armada was somewhere to the west, Columbus chose a southerly course, which the Portuguese would never expect him to take because it would take him deep into Portuguese "territory." In those days, territory also included areas of the sea that a nation controlled, typically around islands or coastlands under their control, and often with authority given by the Vatican. With the Portuguese having colonized both the Canary Islands and the Cape Verde Islands, the Portuguese controlled nearly a thousand miles off the upper west coast of North Africa, perhaps five hundred miles out into the Atlantic. But Columbus also knew that he would make a faster crossing of the Atlantic by picking up the westerly trade winds that started a few hundred miles south of the Canary Islands.

For many years, historians assumed that Columbus discovered the New World by sailing due west, as that was reflected in surviving extracts of Columbus's logbook that had daily entries that read "...they sailed on their course which was West."[8] But within the last twenty-five years, historical evidence has surfaced that suggests Columbus kept two logbooks. When he initially shifted course in a southerly direction, it's believed that Columbus wanted his official logbook to show a course outside of Portuguese territory to provide evidence that would support a plea for leniency in the event his three-ship flotilla was apprehended. He kept the real record of his true navigation course "in his back pocket and planned to dispose of it, if capture by the Portuguese seemed imminent."[9]

At sea for nearly two months, Columbus faced an anxious crew, who believed landfall should have been made by week four or five. After one of the delirious crew members made a false sighting of land that disappeared, the dashed expectations brought on trouble, with angry groups talking up ways of turning back. The situation became mutinous, with threats to heave Columbus over the side if he did not agree to their demands. In the modern Spanish navy, there is a saying that a single Basque is one of the best seamen, but a group of them are dangerous. Columbus could hardly restrain, let alone threaten punishment, for those planning mutiny given that there were forty of them against only one of him.

When Columbus could see that reasoning with the men on the three ships to keep the faith and continue when they were so close to making landfall was unanimously rejected, he turned to God. In a letter that has been preserved among his personal historical records, Columbus wrote that God inspired him to make a deal with his mutinous crew and stake his life on it. He asked for three more days, and if land was not sighted, the crew could do with him as they wished.

As fate would have it, finally in the early morning hours of the third day on October 12, under the light of the moon and the stars, the lookout from the ship *Pinta* gave the long-awaited signal of sighting land. Assuming it was an island to the east of India or perhaps China, Columbus had no idea that he was about to discover a new part of the world—the outskirts of a massive continent—far from the Orient.

The island that was sighted, where they went ashore in daylight some hours later, was one of the easternmost islands in the archipelago that later came to be known as the Bahama Islands. Columbus named that island San Salvador, meaning Holy Savior. Before returning to Europe, he planned to continue exploring, landing on and mapping other islands south of the Bahamas in the Caribbean, erecting on each a large wooden cross as his first order of business. There was of course no common language with the natives on any of the islands, so Columbus commanded his crew to act with love and not force. And by giving small gifts, such as glass beads, as noted in Columbus's journal, "they were greatly pleased and became so entirely our friends that it was a wonder to see..."[10]

In addition to finding a trade route passage to the Far East, Columbus was commissioned by Isabella and Ferdinand to claim new territories for the Spanish flag and to find gold. While many of the female natives wore gold ornaments, communication about where the gold came from proved difficult. Meanwhile, crew members of Columbus's expedition were enthralled with the Caribbean island paradise they explored—some forty islands. Typically, they never stayed in any one place for more than a couple of days, because of the dual quest for discovering gold and finding the passage or figuring out where exactly they were relative to the Spice Islands and India.

The first voyage and exploration of Caribbean islands by Columbus was cut short when Columbus's ship, the *Santa Maria*, went hard aground on a coral reef off the northern coast of Hispaniola and had to be abandoned. The problem of there not being adequate space for *Santa Maria*'s crewmen on the two remaining ships—the *Nina* and the *Pinta*—for return to Spain, was solved when Columbus suggested they create a fort and settlement, to which Columbus pledged he would return in a second voyage shortly after returning to Spain.

There was no lack of volunteers who wanted to stay in paradise, and thirty-nine volunteers ended up staying behind in the fort, named La Villa de Navidad by Columbus to honor Christ's birth. After Columbus and fellow crewmen were bid farewell, the *Nina* raised sail and weighed anchor to meet up with the *Pinta*. They were returning to Spain, having spent only ninety-six days in the Caribbean after their arrival on San Salvador on October 12, 1492. Columbus would undertake his second voyage six months after returning to Spain, and then make two more voyages over the next nine years, continuing his exploration and planting a larger settlement colony of twelve hundred people on Hispaniola under Spain's sponsorship.

Columbus was, like everyone, a flawed man. Some of his misjudgment about problems that would unfold in subsequent voyages could partly be attributed to the native environment, and the Spaniards' response. The Caribbean Sea is named after the Caribs, called the "cannibal Vikings of the West" by some historians. Companions and successors of Columbus encountered the Caribs, who spread terror and desolation over distant islands, where they would torture, kill, and even eat the males and keep the women as slave-wives. In response, the Spanish Crown decreed, in 1503, that all captured cannibals could be enlisted as slave-labor.[11]

To hold Columbus accountable for the chain of disasters that followed in his wake would not only be unfair to him, but it would also overlook the essence of the man. Columbus was at heart a passionate Christian believer who was both a simple but ambitious evangelist and explorer. He had a short formal education that largely revolved around seafaring and navigation skills, and his response to numerous events and circumstances encountered in his first voyage revealed that he was neither a natural leader nor a very good administrator.

In his later voyages, he was found wanting when Queen Isabella charged him to set up a colony in an alien land that required management responsibilities, such as town planning, farming, gold mining, and civil defense. Additionally, the majority of the twelve hundred colonists for which he was responsible were strong-headed machismo hidalgos. Columbus was in over his head. Unlike the dynamic but stable trading center of Genoa, from which he came, the colonial settlement for which Columbus was responsible, named after Queen Isabella, was located at an undesirable harbor that ended up becoming an unmanageable nursery of conquistadors, who lived to fight more than to engage in commerce or plant crops. And tropical diseases that took many of the colonists' lives compounded the problems.

In the end, when he returned to Spain from his fourth and last exploration voyage in 1504, Columbus was fifty-three and in poor health. Inflammation of the eyes sometimes made it impossible for him to read and he suffered agonies from gout and arthritis. He went to Seville and waited in vain for a summons to the royal court, hoping to receive official recognition, money, and prerogatives that had been promised him. Columbus managed to have a brief word with King Ferdinand in 1505, but the monarch was noncommittal, perhaps recognizing that Columbus was a dying man.

Columbus's sons Diego and Ferdinand, his brother Diego, and a few old shipmates were at his bedside when death appeared imminent the next year. A priest said Mass, and before the great explorer took his last breath, he simply prayed, "Into your hands I commend my spirit."

The passing of Columbus came just as the treasure of the New World began to flow, manifested in gilded galleons bringing as much as four tons of gold a year to Seville. It has been estimated that the Spanish Crown's original investment in the first voyage of Columbus yielded a return of 1,733,000 percent.[12] With such huge sums at stake, naturally Columbus's sons Diego and Ferdinand sued the crown for restitution of the hereditary financial rights—some 10 percent of the riches found— to which they were entitled according to the contract their father had signed in 1492 before undertaking the first voyage. They couldn't get a fair hearing, however, and decided to settle their case with recompense in the form of titles and estates.

Columbus Day has been largely celebrated because of its historical significance commemorating the discovery of the New World, which would lead to the establishment of a new nation founded on the revolutionary idea that people's life, liberty, and the pursuit of happiness were inviolable because those rights came from God and not the state. But we are getting ahead of our story. For now, we can say based on the historical record that Columbus is worth celebrating because he embodied character traits that are as meaningful and vital today as they were in his time, more than five hundred years ago.

Observing Columbus Day is to celebrate those virtues. Courage, independent thinking, creativity, persistence, conviction, having the vision to combine a worldly commercial pursuit with a spiritual calling, the recognition that great things can come out of misfortune and disaster, and expressing love as a universal language, are attitudes and qualities of character that never become outdated.

CHAPTER 3

Thanksgiving: The First and
Essential American Holiday

I t could be said that Thanksgiving is the holiday that made the other American holidays possible. Without the Pilgrims having courage, a willingness to sacrifice and risk everything, and absolute faith in their cause and calling, they never would have boarded the unseaworthy ninety-four-foot *Mayflower* to embark on a transatlantic voyage to an unknown continent. Were it not for their dream and determination to find freedom of conscience and religion in the New World, there may have never been a July 4th Independence Day or many of the other American holidays now taken for granted and celebrated every year.

Understanding the Pilgrims and Thanksgiving is essential to understanding the foundation of America because their story was absolutely unique, being one exclusively of a spiritual quest. But first, some background on the period that links Columbus with the Pilgrims.

After Columbus, the expansion of exploration and colonization of the New World in South America was very different than it would later be in North America. The Spanish explorers who followed Columbus in exploring Central and South America were driven by commercial interests and specifically a quest to find gold, whereas the explorers of North America, who largely hailed from northern maritime Europe, were motivated by spiritual as well as commercial interests, such as fishing and the fur trade.

In the century between voyages of Columbus and the Pilgrims, there were also two major developments—the Reformation and the Scientific Revolution—that affected expansion of the exploration of the New World.

The Scientific Revolution constituted what was at that time the most significant period of discovery and growth of the sciences in the whole of history. Three of the prominent scientists—Nicolaus Copernicus, Johannes Kepler, and Galileo Galilei—developed the theories of a heliocentric solar system and laws of planetary motion, which were at the heart of developing reliable positioning necessary for navigation at sea for months out of sight of land. And this was, of course, essential to advance exploration and colonization of the New World.[13]

While change and reform within Christendom started as early as the fourteenth century, it was Martin Luther and John Calvin of the early sixteenth century who drove the Reformation movement, which gave birth to Protestantism.

Luther came first and stood against all odds, leading a protest against the malpractices and corruption in the Catholic Church, after he posted his *Ninety-five Theses* on his church door in Wittenberg, Germany on October 31, 1517. Little did he know that his simple act of protest and call for church reform would trigger a worldwide movement.

The year 1517 has come to be the historic marker for Reformation for, after that time, the unity of what was medieval Christianity under the hierarchy of Catholicism ended. John Calvin broke with the Catholic Church in 1530, and his ministry built on Luther, inspired a third Reformation leader, John Knox, and strengthened the Protestant movement. He ushered in an understanding of equality and freedom of conscience for individuals, which characterized the beginning of the modern era.

Spiritually, the Reformation movement stressed the importance of the individual having a direct relationship with God—praying and reading the Bible without the intercession of the church or the state. Politically, it meant that government needed to be limited and accountable to its subjects and it specifically challenged the "divine right of kings" authority that was common in Europe.

Protestantism prompted religious revolution and spiritual revival across Germany, Switzerland, Denmark, Sweden, Norway, Holland, England, Scotland, and parts of France, causing far-reaching political, economic, and social effects.[14] As people learned of discoveries in the New World, Protestants realized that North America provided an opportunity to be free of the oppression and corruption of the Old World, and the real possibility to make a new start in life in the New World and even live out Christ's invitation to build a city on a hill that would be a light to the world.

The Reformation also meant that northern European powers with historic rivalry with Spain and Portugal—notably England and Holland—no longer had allegiance to Rome and the Catholic Church. At the same time, these northern European countries felt compelled to catch up to Spain and Portugal in terms of maritime and colonial exploration. In 1585, the first British settlement in North America approved by the Queen of England was attempted on an island known as Roanoke, named after the Indian tribe of that area in what became coastal North Carolina. However, within a few years it failed, with all inhabitants perishing and never being unaccounted for.[15] The next attempt at colonization was in 1607 at Jamestown, a place not far from Roanoke, in a region that came to be known as Virginia.

The Jamestown colony was sponsored by the Virginia Company in London, whose charter specified the spreading of the Gospel as being one of its core missions. But like Roanoke, Jamestown lacked a family unit basis, being predominantly settled by men, and it would have entirely failed without being resupplied. The colony did survive, and interestingly, the Jamestown settlers preceded the Pilgrims and their establishment of the Mayflower Compact by about a year, when in 1619, they took the first step in self-government by establishing the Virginia General Assembly.[16]

In 1619, Jamestown also became the first entry point of black African labor in North America, but that did not actually mark the beginning of slavery. The Africans introduced to Jamestown were in fact former slaves captured by the English from Portuguese slave ships, and they were traded for food and water. In that trade, the Africans were accepted by the Jamestown colonists as indentured servants, with equal status as the many English, Scottish, and Irish-born indentured servants, which meant that they would become free when their indenture or bond was completed—generally a term of four to seven years. The slave trade did later come to Virginia around 1650, but not in the time and the way of the common narrative surrounding Jamestown, which does not in any way diminish the problem or excuse the institution of slavery in early America.[17] But it's important to remember that before and right through the seventeenth and eighteenth centuries, slavery was practiced all over the world. While slavery came into America in both the Northern states and the Southern states—but proliferating more in the southern agricultural states—it became a crisis in the making for Americans whose morality was grounded in Christianity. Because slavery played a big role in shaping the economy and social order of the Southern states, it would later threaten the continuity of the nation by the mid-nineteenth century.

In 1620, the Pilgrims would arrive and establish Britain's second successful colony in North America five hundred miles north of Virginia at a place they called New Plymouth, in a region that would become the state of Massachusetts, named after the Indian chief Massasoit.

The story of the Pilgrims and the first Thanksgiving really begins in England well before Jamestown, and even before the Reformation, with John Wycliffe's 1384 translation of the Latin Bible into English—making God's word accessible to common people. Reformation in England took root in the early 1530s, but the new Church of England, later known as the Anglican Church, became entwined with the British royal monarchy, which retained some Catholic formalities, hierarchical structures, and opened the door to political influence and corruption.[18]

The Puritans were English Protestants influenced by John Calvin of Geneva and his disciple John Knox of Scotland, who objected to this residual influence of Catholicism in the Church of England, particularly the church hierarchy that ran counter to the Reformation's egalitarian assertion of a "priesthood of all believers," which simply meant that before God, all were equal. While Puritans hoped to keep the candle of true Protestant reform burning within the Church of England, there came to be a small group known as Separatists who believed reform efforts were futile and it was necessary to entirely break from a government-affiliated church.

In 1608, when King James denied the Separatists' request for permission to start their own church, they knew they were Pilgrims who had to leave England and seek refuge in the more tolerant Dutch society. The first captain they hired to transport them to Holland turned out to be a traitor and a thief who betrayed and surrendered the Pilgrims to the British authorities, which included the King's local sheriff. As a result, the first attempt at emigration not only failed, but several of the Pilgrim leaders, including William Brewster and William Bradford, were jailed for a time.[19]

The second attempt to flee England to Holland by ship was almost as disastrous. When the designated departure time came, many of the Pilgrim men, ahead of the women and children, made their way out to the contracted Dutch transport ship at anchor in a remote place on the Humber River. Unfortunately, the unusual crowd and activity of women and children who arrived at the waterfront was apparently spotted and raised concerns. It wasn't long before British authorities arrived and took them into custody before they could get away on the small rowboats positioned on the riverbank to take them out to join their waiting husbands and fathers on the nearby transport ship.[20] Seeing the British authorities were represented by well-armed infantry, cavalry, and perhaps cannons, the Dutch captain feared retaliation and gave orders to weigh anchor and hoist sail.[21]

Separation from their loved ones caused overwhelming sorrow for the Pilgrim men, but that feeling of loss would be compounded by fright within forty-eight hours. They would then face what was for all an unprecedented paralyzing fear as a ferocious storm battered the ship in the North Sea. And it went on for nearly a week, causing the ship to take on water and list.[22] As the ship began to founder somewhere between Norway and Holland, with the Dutch crew giving up all hope, shouting out, "We sink, we sink,"[23] the Pilgrims cried out to the Lord to have mercy and save them. William Bradford, who was among those in desperate prayer, remembers and records that almost immediately, "the ship not only righted herself but shortly afterwards the violence of the storm began to abate..."[24]

With a new sense of gratitude to the Almighty who protected them, those first Pilgrims finally arrived in Holland, and eventually settled down in the city of Leiden. Over the next months, they were joined by their wives and children, who had been released, and over the next few years other Separatists would also come to Leiden. Under the leadership of their charismatic minister, John Robinson, their congregation grew, quadrupling in size to some five hundred over the next ten years.[25]

The Pilgrims still identified with the culture of England from where they had come and were not entirely content. Leiden was an industrial city with a demanding and fast pace of life, and there was concern among Pilgrim parents that their children, many of whom were in adolescence, were facing moral challenges and adopting the Dutch language and customs. Furthermore, religious warfare was intensifying in Europe, and there was a possibility that the sons of the Leiden Pilgrims faced possible conscription into the army of the Protestant Dutch state that was being threatened by its neighboring Catholic states of Belgium and France.[26] The Pilgrims knew that peace in Holland might come to an end with the twelve-year truce between Spain and Holland expiring in 1621, a few years away.[27]

The Pilgrims also heard of the success that finally came to Jamestown, and the British monarchy was eager to approve additional settlements under the Virginia Company, which originally had been chartered for that purpose. Discussions within the Pilgrim community started with the recognition that going to the New World would allow them to live as Englishmen and raise their families in accord with the Bible. But for the spiritual leaders of the Pilgrims, as expressed by William Bradford, their worldview was deeper and started with the recognition that whether living in England or Holland, they would be living in the midst of sinful "Babylon." And the Pilgrims were called like the chosen people of the Old Testament to break free of the slavery in Egypt and seek out a Promised Land where they could establish a "New Jerusalem of holy living."[28]

A consensus soon emerged within the Pilgrim community to pursue voyaging to the New World. So, in June of 1619, Pilgrim leaders John Carver and Robert Cushman quietly pursued and succeeded in securing a patent from the Virginia Company. The necessary capital to secure a ship for the Pilgrims came from investors who formed a joint stock company in which the Pilgrims would have a minority stake but would also have commercial obligations to repay the investors.[29]

Finally, in July of 1620, the first group of Pilgrims departed Holland on the *Speedwell*, a small vessel that was to take them across the English Channel and rendezvous with the primary larger ship, the *Mayflower*, located in Southampton, England. The two ships then would commence the voyage across the Atlantic. But the *Speedwell* proved leaky and unseaworthy, and after two attempts to commence the transatlantic voyage, the Pilgrims had to abandon the *Speedwell*. They took her back to England, losing an entire month in the process.

Undaunted, but crowding onto the *Mayflower* as many from the *Speedwell* as they could with consideration for space and safety, the Pilgrims finally set sail from England on September 16, 1620, with 102 on board. They would be bound for the northern region under the claim of the Virginia Company, which was the area near the mouth of the Hudson River.

As summer had now turned to autumn, they faced stormier weather than they would have had they been able to stay on the original departure schedule. It turned out to be a harrowing passage across the Atlantic— one that included wild pitching and broadside battering by gale force winds and steep waves rising as much as a hundred feet from trough to crest.[30] At one point, the ferocious seas caused such a pounding that one of the ship's main beams was split. But as fate would have it, one of the passengers had brought along a "house jack" whose normal use was raising heavy timber posts and beams for home construction.[31] The *Mayflower's* main deck could have collapsed, causing the ship to flood and sink, but the jack was put in place. And with half a dozen stalwarts with adrenaline coursing through their veins, the jack was screwed, raising the split beam and providing it essential support to maintain the integrity of the ship.

There were many times when the *Mayflower* proceeded under "bare pole" or a few short reefed sails. In the end, she was blown off course from the intended destination of the established Virginia Colony to the wilds of Cape Cod. The Pilgrims knew not where they were nor how to proceed, so they beseeched the Almighty for favor in making landfall and in finding a suitable place with fresh water and fertile soil to establish a new and independent settlement.

Now in sight of land after a frightening voyage, and facing hunger from depleted and spoiled provisions, some of the secular *Mayflower* passengers were clamoring for rebellion. And so, under the direction of Pilgrim leaders William Brewster and William Bradford, the drafting of a governing agreement was undertaken to quell unrest and ensure the establishment of a unified settlement that would be acceptable to both their Christian brethren and the secular crewmen and merchant adventurers who made up some two-fifths of the 102 passengers aboard the *Mayflower.* That governing document, known as the Mayflower Compact, was introduced "solemnly and mutually in the presence of God and one another," and it was specifically referred to as a *covenant.*[32] Hebraic in origination, a covenant was understood to be an unbreakable agreement with precedents being made between God and towering figures of Jewish history—such as Abraham, Noah, Moses, and David. William Bradford had a deep appreciation of Judaism and the Old Testament, and chose to write the preface to his *Of Plymouth Plantation*—which contained twenty-five biblical passages—in the original Hebrew.[33]

After Moses led the Israelites out of Egypt, crossed the Red Sea, and journeyed on to Mt. Sinai, God made a covenant with Moses, providing

the Israelites the Ten Commandments and other laws—a necessary re-
quirement before they could proceed and cross into the Promised Land.
Similarly, every able man aboard the *Mayflower* had to sign the Mayflower
Compact before any could "cross over" and finally set foot in the New
World after their ship arrived at Provincetown at the tip of Cape Cod at
sunrise on Saturday, November 11, 1620.

As a covenant adapted to the civil need of forming a government with
laws—established "for the general good of the colony"—the Mayflower
Compact embodied fundamental principles of self-government and common consent. Thus, the Mayflower Compact established the foundation
for democratic government in America, and it is often cited as the cor-
nerstone of the US Constitution.[34] In his bestselling book, *Mayflower*,
award-winning adventure historian Nathaniel Philbrick asserts that the
Mayflower Compact "ranks with the Declaration of Independence and the
United States Constitution as a seminal American text."[35] Additionally,
it is noteworthy that the forty-one Pilgrims' appeal to the Triune God
for protection in their signing the Mayflower Compact foreshadowed
the "firm Reliance on the Protection of divine Providence" expressed
in the last sentence of the Declaration of Independence which the fifty-six delegates to the Continental Congress signed in Philadelphia on
August 2, 1776.

The fact that all the Pilgrims survived the squalid and cramped ship
quarters during the dangerous crossing of a vast ocean is no doubt partially attributable to the good fortune that the *Mayflower* had previously
been enlisted as a wine transport cargo ship. Unlike most ships, she
had a "sweet smell," from all her decks and bilges being "disinfected"
with wine sloshing and soaking from broken barrels of Bordeaux and
high-alcohol port in the many prior crossings of the sometimes stormy
English Channel.

That fortune changed once the *Mayflower*'s passengers settled in
"New Plymouth," Massachusetts in December of 1620. The first winter
was devastating, with over half the Pilgrims dying, including nearly half
the women. Four whole families perished. But it could have been worse.

It was fortunate that those Pilgrim colonists settled where they did in Plymouth, for the Patuxet "Indian" tribe, known for its aggressive warriors, who had previously lived there, had been entirely wiped out by an extraordinary plague four years previously, allowing the more friendly and approachable Pokanoket tribe to move in near Plymouth. And had there not been one among those Indians who was miraculously fluent in English by the name of Squanto, perhaps none would have survived.

Six years before, in 1614, Squanto had been kidnapped by a British fur trader and opportunist, Thomas Hunt, and taken to Málaga, Spain where he was sold into slavery.[36] Some records have it that Spanish Christian friars sprung Squanto from his chains and helped him get to England, where his plan was to learn English well enough to find a job as a translator aboard a British trading vessel coming to the New World. Squanto would ultimately execute his plan, getting to England and meeting up with John Slanie, a wealthy merchant who took him in as an indentured servant for four years.[37]

In 1619, Squanto succeeded in getting passage on a British merchant ship under the command of Captain Thomas Dermer, bound for New England.[38] Miraculously, Squanto found his way back to the area of his birth, near Plymouth, only to find that almost all of his tribe of origin, the Patuxet, had perished from an epidemic during his five years of absence in England. However, a nearby diminished Pokanoket tribe accepted him only a short time before his newfound English language skills would be called on after the Pilgrims arrived.

In fact, just four months after the Pilgrims first disembarked in Plymouth, Squanto and his friend Samoset facilitated the signing of a peace treaty between the Pilgrim colonists and Massasoit, the chief of the Wampanoag tribe, the dominant tribe in the region. That treaty kept the peace with the Wampanoags for more than fifty years.[39] At the same time, Squanto and native tribesmen would teach the Pilgrims survival skills, showing them how to hunt, fish, and plant various crops, such as corn—which was unknown to the Englishmen.

In spite of the huge loss of loved ones and community members, the Pilgrims were extraordinarily grateful for the first season's harvest—modest though it was—and decided to invite Massasoit and some of his people to a three-day-long feast, at which they would thank God not only for the harvest, but also for their survival and initial success of a diverse colony that included both Christians and nonbelievers.

No one knows for sure the exact date of this three-day event patterned after the "harvest fest" in England and also the Feast of Tabernacles in the Jewish calendar. Massasoit arrived with some hundred followers, more than two times the number of the Pilgrims, and for three days, they entertained each other and feasted.

This feast later became known as the first Thanksgiving, which we now celebrate on the fourth Thursday of November. Today many Americans—Christian, Jewish, and secular—find Thanksgiving to be their favorite holiday of the year. And for good reason beyond the joy of a feast. Thanksgiving was the first holiday of the Pilgrim forefathers, who spoke of their voyage to the New World in terms of a flight from persecution to freedom, much like the Israelites' exodus from Egypt to reach the Promised Land.

Some eighteen months after this feast, it came to be known that Massasoit was on the brink of death from an unknown sickness. Governor William Bradford immediately sent elder Edward Winslow to administer natural herbs, medicines, and prayers to Massasoit. Astonishingly, he made a full recovery within days, and remarked, "Now I see the English are my friends and love me; and whilst I live, I will never forget this kindness they have showed me."

It is noteworthy that George Washington and Abraham Lincoln were the two early American presidents—both of whom we celebrate for their unique greatness on Presidents' Day—with the strongest conviction about the importance of Thanksgiving as a national holiday. Shortly after taking office in 1789, President Washington and the US Congress proclaimed Thanksgiving to be set aside and celebrated nationally every year.[40] However, its celebration turned out to be intermittent until President Abraham Lincoln, in 1863, proclaimed a national day of "Thanksgiving and Praise to our beneficent Father who dwelleth in the Heavens,"[41] to be celebrated on the last Thursday in November.

Many years later, Congress signed into law the Holiday Act, recognizing the permanence of a paid holiday on Thanksgiving for all government employees.[42]

Times are very different than they were some four hundred years ago at the time of the *Mayflower*'s voyage to the New World. But the qualities of character that made the Pilgrims exemplary are as relevant today as they were back then. A contemporary Thanksgiving makeover might include: establishing the faith to hold on to a vision of a "promised land" no matter what; gaining the fortitude to endure hardship; mustering the courage to go against the crowd and defend the truth; embracing respect and tolerance of people of different beliefs; extending goodwill necessary for lasting peace; and renewing the predisposition to sacrifice for others and practice love and gratitude at every appropriate opportunity.

CHAPTER 4

Christmas: The Celebration of the Birth of the Savior

The previous chapter opened with the observation that Thanksgiving was the first and most essential holiday for Americans. But actually, Christmas and Easter are without a doubt more foundational to the formation of America, for if Christ had never been born and died the way he did, all of history would have been different and neither Columbus nor the Pilgrims would have received or have been motivated by the good news of salvation through Christ to explore or establish a new community with a higher purpose in the New World.

Additionally, there would never have been a constitutional government created in the way and time that it was in America, without two necessary conditions: first, the foundation of recognizing man's unalienable rights of freedom and equality that came out of Reformed Christianity and the Bible; and second, the unprecedented collection of Christian human genius that came together—rather amazingly at the same time—in the people we call the Founding Fathers. It was their extraordinary learning, faith, wisdom, temperament, and practical experience that enabled them to write and frame the Declaration of Independence, the Constitution, and its Bill of Rights. So profound was the accomplishment of the Founding Fathers that it far surpassed achievements of Periclean Athens in Greece, Cicero and the Roman Republic, or Florence under the Medicis.

The constitutional republic formed by the founders provided for and protected individual rights of freedom and independence such that America achieved material prosperity more rapidly than any other prior civilization. Additionally, that government framework enabled people to move closer to the divine image in which all people are created free and equal than they would have achieved under any prior system.

People have been motivated to flee oppression and escape persecution from the beginning of recorded history. A recurring theme in Western classical literature and in modern classics such as *Superman* and Disney originals, which revolve around the struggle between good and evil, is the need and critical role for a rescuer or savior. The ultimate rescuer and savior for mankind would be a "messiah." And history shows that it is only Christianity that has its roots and its entire reason for being in the Messiah Jesus Christ. No other religion makes the claim that it was founded by a messiah.

The Christmas holiday is the celebration of the birth of Jesus Christ, the Messiah and the most consequential person in all of human history. To begin, it's worth reflecting on a few of the unique attributes of Christ.

First, he is more historically verifiable than any other person who lived in that time and era, including such luminaries as the Roman emperors or Greek greats Aristotle or Alexander the Great.[43] Christ is the only person in history who was pre-announced starting a thousand years before he was born, with eighteen different prophets from the Old Testament between the tenth and the fourth centuries BC predicting his coming birth, life, and death. Hundreds of years later, the circumstances of Christ's birth and life validated those prophecies in surprisingly accurate detail.[44]

Second, Christ lived, and not only demonstrated his otherworldly power to heal and perform the ultimate miracle of bringing the dead back to life, but he set the absolute highest standard of love possible, both in his teachings and in the fact that he made the ultimate sacrifice for mankind by affirming his life through death to rescue and save them. As Jesus prophesied, his resurrection confirmed God's power and plan—providing "seeing is believing" evidence by bringing Jesus back from the dead and burial in a tomb to being alive, thus providing the people with living proof of who he was.[45] The New Testament provides accounts from multiple sources who witnessed Jesus firsthand after the resurrection. In fact, Jesus made ten separate appearances to his disciples between the resurrection and his ascension into Heaven—a period of forty days. Some of those appearances were to individual disciples, some were to several disciples at the same time, and once even to five hundred at one time.[46] Additionally, we don't know all the times that Jesus appeared to his disciples during these forty days, for the disciple John himself explained that the Gospel accounts were not a complete record, stating specifically that "Jesus did many other signs in the presence of the disciples, which are not written in this book."[47]

Third, no other religion teaches that God became flesh. In other faiths, God is too high and exalted to be accessible in terms of having a communion with believers. In Christianity, God had his Son born in the humbleness of a stable and had him raised in Nazareth, a small and very poor town that was one of the lowest in social status in Israel because he wanted his Son to be approachable by people from all walks of life. In spiritual paths outside of Judaism and Christianity, God is an impersonal force to obey and with whom you may be able to merge and become "one," but a two-way personal relationship of communion with God is not possible. But in the person of Jesus Christ, we see God with a human face who cries, forgives, cares, and loves—a God with whom we can have a personal and intimate relationship. Through Christ, people can experience all the dimensions and fullness of God.

For Christians, Christmas is a unique time of joy because it acknowledges and celebrates the birth of the savior Jesus, whose life, death, and resurrection make it possible for people to experience and enjoy a personal and intimate relationship with God. Jesus was born a Jew, and his teachings were built on the foundation of the covenants of the Torah and the Old Testament. And so it is that Christians and Jews have much in common and share a natural mutual affinity. It is probably not by chance that the holiday celebrations associated with Chanukah and Christmas come in close proximity or that the sacred Jewish holiday week of Passover and Christian Holy Week of Easter overlap.[48]

Early Christians in the Roman world selected December 25 for the Nativity feast celebrating the birth of Jesus—the day that became Christmas—because that day was in the plausible timespan for Christ's birth and it also fell on the date of the most important pagan festival, the birth of the winter solstice sun god, Natalis Solis Invicti.[49]

In early colonial America, the Anglicans, Lutherans, Moravians, and Roman Catholics who settled predominantly in the Middle Atlantic colonies and in the South were the first to celebrate Christmas. The Northern colonies in America, which were largely influenced by Calvinism and Puritan practices, were less inclined to celebrate Christmas in those early days. However, that began to change with the growing arrival of Christian immigrants from many lands, each with differing beliefs, customs of worship, and celebration associated with Christmas. Interestingly, colonists in Virginia were celebrating Christmas in early colonial times with food and merriment, while by an irony of history, it was actually Massachusetts—which had its roots in a stoic Puritan fundamentalism—that was the first state in America to declare Christmas a legal holiday in 1856. After the Civil War, Christmas became a US national federal holiday in 1870.

The Christmas tradition of gift giving surely goes back to the Three Wise Men, who journeyed some eight hundred miles from Persia and possibly elsewhere, and whose spiritual orientation was anything but Jewish, to present the newborn savior Jesus with gold, frankincense, and myrrh—expensive rarities that showed recognition of baby Jesus as a future king—a king not only for the Jews but for all people.[50]

Three centuries later, the tradition of gift-giving was strengthened by the figure of St. Nicholas, a fourth-century Christian of Greek origin who became Bishop of Myra in Asia Minor. Nicholas was born and raised in Patara, Lycia (a present-day coastal town in Turkey), and he inherited the estate of his wealthy parents after their untimely death from a plague.

According to history and legend, Nicholas then began giving his inherited money to the needy in his hometown, and at the same time, he felt a call to Christian service. He became a monk when he was only seventeen years old, and shortly thereafter became a priest. Nicholas was unusually gifted, for historical records reveal that he was chosen to be archbishop of Myra in Lycia when he was in his early twenties.[51]

Under Roman Emperor Diocletian, Nicholas was persecuted and imprisoned for a number of years for his faith. Once free, he went back to his calling to help the poor, and became renowned for bringing gifts to the homes of the poor and needy.[52]

One story relates that Nicholas learned of a merchant who had gone bankrupt and that creditors were seeking to take his daughters and sell them into slavery or force them into prostitution to repay the debt. Nicholas threw bags of gold through that merchant's window at night, designating that it be used to provide a dowry so each of his three daughters could marry, thus saving them from slavery or sin. When the father learned who generously gave the money, Nicholas implored him not to tell anyone, as he wanted the glory to go to God alone. This and many other stories of Nicholas's anonymous generosity inspired the custom of secret gift-giving on the anniversary of Nicholas's death in December 343 AD—310 years after the death and resurrection of Christ.[53]

Nicholas was not only kind and generous, but also extraordinarily bold and righteous. Another well-known story of Nicholas recounts his courageous rescue of three innocent men when he fearlessly grabbed the sword right out of the executioner's hand just as he was about to carry out death sentence orders issued by a corrupt governor. Nicholas was also known as a prayer warrior and became famous for having many miraculous answers to his prayers.[54]

Persecution of Christians ended with Emperor Constantine, and church history records show that Nicholas was one of 318 bishops out of 1,800 invited by Constantine from all over the Christian world to attend the First Council of Nicaea in 325 AD. The central purpose of the Council was to define and establish the relationship of God and Jesus within the Holy Trinity. Several accounts have it that when Egyptian

Bishop Arius asserted that Jesus the Son was not equal to God the Father, it so upset Nicholas that he walked across the room and slapped Arius across the face.[55]

Such abrupt behavior caused Nicholas to be temporarily removed from the council proceeding. Legend has it that he was then stripped of his bishop's garments and put in chains to keep him from further disrupting the solemn gathering. Ashamed of his outburst, Nicholas fervently prayed for forgiveness that night. Shortly thereafter, Nicholas's bishop vestments somehow reappeared while at the same time his chains fell off. When Constantine heard this, he ordered that Nicholas be freed, and thereafter Nicholas was fully reinstated as the Bishop of Myra.[56]

In the end, the Council of Nicaea rejected the argument of Arius and developed a consensus around the position that Nicholas supported, which was that Jesus the Son, God the Father, and the Holy Spirit were equal within the Trinity. Nicholas's presence at the Council of Nicaea is noteworthy, for it was likely a contributing factor to the reconciliation of a key theological dispute central to Orthodox Christianity. This was a profound development in the early church, and it made the Nicene Creed the only ecumenical statement accepted as authoritative by the Roman Catholic, Eastern Orthodox, Anglican, and major Protestant churches. To the present day, Christians all over the world repeat the Nicene Creed weekly when they stand to say what they believe.[57]

After Nicholas died, devotion to him grew and extended all over Europe and Russia. He became the patron saint of charitable fraternities and guilds, of children, sailors, unmarried girls, merchants, and pawnbrokers, although Bishop Nicholas was never officially canonized St. Nicholas. By the Middle Ages, he came to be venerated as the "people's saint" of churches, villages, and cities as distant as Fribourg in Switzerland and Moscow in Russia. Thousands of European churches were dedicated to him—one, built by the Roman emperor Justinian I at Constantinople (now Istanbul), was erected as early as the sixth century.[58]

The Saint Nicholas Christmas gift-giving story and traditions evolved over America's first two centuries. It has been widely thought to have been brought to America by Dutch immigrants to New Amsterdam (later known as New York), who pronounced Saint Nicholas's name as "Sinterklaas," that many heard as "Santa Claus," which stuck in America ever since.[59] And many Christians found it natural to integrate the Santa Claus story and traditions for children with the more substantive Scriptural basis of the Christmas celebration.

Some Christians have had a problem with including St. Nicholas and Santa Claus in their Christmas celebrations, seeing Santa Claus as a diversion and even competitor to Jesus. Yet Santa, unlike other traditions such as Christmas trees, mistletoe, and holly, is largely based on Christian principles and the example of a selfless Christian man.[60] In many ways—notably Santa's keeping track of who is naughty and nice and his generous, supernatural ways of gift-giving—make Santa Claus the ideal secular companion for celebrating Christ's birth.

Christians and Jews faced intense persecution in the Roman Empire right up until the time of Constantine. From that time on, Christianity flourished in Europe through the Middle Ages and later inspired Renaissance Art and the Scientific Revolution in Europe. The age of exploration began about this time and facilitated expanded trade and colonization, which took Christianity across the Atlantic and to Africa and the Far East.

Fast forward 450 years and we find that hostility toward Christianity is again on the rise as it was in the first few centuries after Christ died. And that persecution comes not just from people from other religious beliefs—notably radical Islamists—but also from secular progressives who now dominate modern Western culture.

Various towering intellectuals even wish that Christ had never been born. Karl Marx and Friedrich Nietzsche, who separately inspired and/ or influenced the rise of murderous totalitarian regimes in Russia and Germany, both condemned Christianity and religion in general. For Marx, "religion was the opium of the people." Nietzsche said Christianity was "the greatest of all imaginable corruptions."

Like the American Christmas classic movie, *It's a Wonderful Life*, which depicts what would have happened to a hypothetical American town, Bedford Falls, if the star of the film, Jimmy Stewart, had never been born, it is worth thinking about what the world would look like today if Jesus Christ had never been born.

For starters, if Christ had not been born, people around the world may not have agreed on how to measure time. Think how confusing it would be if different people and nations didn't count days and months in an identical manner and speak about history in years as before Christ (BC) or after Christ (AD). Christ affected history with such impact that he split time in two, dividing all human activities and events into happening before his coming (called BC) or after his coming (called AD). No one else in all of human history effected this. Christ had to have had a supernatural impact on the world for that to be accepted.

More importantly, history shows that Christianity and its Church have brought about more changes for the advancement and benefit of people than any other force or movement in history by an immeasurable factor. What is particularly surprising to nonbelieving secular-minded people are the myriad achievements made by committed Christians, which they have applauded.

Before Christ, human life was cheap and expendable all over the world. In Central and South America, the Near East, Africa, the Middle East, and the Far East, child sacrifice was a common phenomenon. Babies, particularly females—who were considered inferior—were regularly abandoned. Author George Grant points out: "Before the explosive and penetrating growth of medieval Christian influence, the primordial evils of abortion, infanticide, abandonment, and exposure were a normal part of everyday life…" After Christ, that changed in the West and particularly with the sixth century Christian Byzantine Roman Emperor Justinian whose law code declared child abandonment and abortion a crime.[61]

Human life was also cheap in the West prior to Christ's influence. In the early Roman Empire, human gladiators were eaten by lions, bears, bulls, and wild boars, or they were forced to fight each other to the death as sport for the entertainment of the masses. Emperor Nero held parties in his gardens in which entertainment would typically include torturous killing of prisoners, outcasts, and enemies by wild beasts, by crucifixion, or by being dipped in oil and ignited as human torches. But when Christianity spread in the Roman Empire and was embraced by Constantine, these practices were ended and made illegal.[62]

In ancient cultures—in India, China, Rome, and Greece—women were considered inferior and simply viewed as property of their husbands. More recently, in the last two and a half centuries, with the advent of the Christian missionary movement, the lives of women have been greatly improved. Countless female infants abandoned in China were saved from almost sure death by Christian missionaries who then protected, educated, and raised them in Christian orphanages. In India, prior to Christian influence, elderly widows were burned alive on their husbands' funeral pyres, while infanticide—particularly for girls—was practiced by tossing little ones into the sea. In Africa, wives and concubines of tribal chieftains were routinely killed after the latter's death.[63] These practices were greatly ameliorated or entirely stopped as Christianity began to penetrate and influence the respective cultures.

We all recognize today the important role that charity plays in countless ways to help people in need. But before Christ, there is no trace or record of any organized charitable effort. Institutionalized charity was basically unknown until Christians initiated and established its permanent presence.[64] The early Christians gained fame and renown by being generous to their own and to nonbelievers as well. Emperor Julian "the Apostate," the last Roman emperor to try to destroy Christianity, was dumbfounded by the love that Christians showed to pagans and even those who persecuted them. The early church grew in large part by providing a way out of Rome's harshness, bringing in converts who "turned from Caesar preaching war to Christ preaching peace, from incredible brutality to unprecedented charity."[65]

The tradition of charity continued throughout the darkest periods of the Middle Ages because of the Catholic Church. And because charity has been so intertwined with and motivated by the love of Christ, the tradition of charity gained more momentum and breadth with the Protestant Reformation. Today, widely recognized organizations such as the Salvation Army, Samaritan's Purse, and Goodwill Industries, which are Christian-based organizations with origins in the US that operate shelters for the homeless, provide disaster relief and humanitarian aid to developing countries, and also provide employment, training, and rehabilitation for people of limited employability, now have operations in nations around the world.

The rise of the concept of education for the masses has its roots in Christianity. Establishment of schools open to the public started with Christian monasteries as early as the fourth century AD. And the great St. Patrick is now credited with establishing monastery schools in Ireland, which preserved teachings, records, and traditions of ancient Greece and Rome, thus "saving" civilization, which was being overrun by conquering barbarians.[66]

In the fifteenth century, Johannes Gutenberg had a passion to see Bibles printed and made available to the public. Starting his project in France and moving to Germany, he was able to design and make a printing press that made possible, for the first time, the mass production of books—an invention that was in effect a providential preparation for the Reformation that took off a little more than a half century later. The Gutenberg printing press opened the door to providing people access to the Bible, which had previously been under the exclusive purview of the Catholic Church. After the Reformation, campaigns for literacy and education for the masses, undertaken almost exclusively by Christians, were of course greatly facilitated by book publishing.[67]

Education for the common man had its greatest impetus in the period immediately after the Reformation. Protestant leaders, notably John Calvin and John Knox, knew that if the reform movement were to survive and expand, it was necessary that there be widespread literacy at all levels of society so that people could read the Bible for themselves. Thus, Calvinism, which had a dominant impact on the colonization of America, gave a powerful impulse to popular education. In fact, within fifteen years of their arrival in New England in 1630, the Puritans passed a law requiring education for all children.[68]

Not only did the gift of lower education come from Christianity in America, but so did higher education and the universities. Of the first 120 colleges and universities founded in America before the Revolutionary War, almost every one of them had Christian origins.[69] In early America, Harvard, Yale, and Princeton universities were originally founded as seminaries, and seven of the eight Ivy League universities were originally founded for the purpose of establishing Christian-based institutions of higher learning.

Ezra Stiles became president of Yale University in 1778, two years into the Revolutionary War. He addressed the Connecticut General Assembly, saying, "Great and extensive will be the happy effects of this warfare, in which we have been called in providence to fight out, not the liberties of America only, but the liberties of the world itself."[70]

His contemporary, Samuel Langdon, was president of Harvard University during the Revolutionary War from 1774 to 1780. He went on to pastor a church in New Hampshire, delivering a sermon in 1788 during the period when the states were deliberating the ratification of the Constitution, in which he said:

> The general form of such a constitution hath already been drawn up, and presented to the people, by a convention of the wisest and most celebrated patriots in the land: eight of the states have approved and accepted it…and if it passes the scrutiny of the whole, and recommends itself to be universally adopted, we shall have abundant reason to offer elevated thanksgiving to the supreme Ruler of the universe for a government completed under his direction.[71]

Two thousand years ago, Apostle Paul was way before his time on the issue of slavery, stating in his letter to Philemon that he should receive his former slave as "a brother beloved."[72] Today, slavery is still practiced in parts of the Middle East, Africa, and Asia, but it was abolished in the Western world, and it was Christians who led the efforts in spearheading and inspiring movements for abolition—in Great Britain, Europe, and America.

It turns out that the Second Great Awakening in American Christianity was a key force in unleashing powerful currents of spiritual conviction that became an important driver in the abolition movement. And this was analogous to the spiritual role of the First Great Awakening, which assisted two important events necessary for the birth of the new nation of the United States: 1) the spiritual knitting together of the thirteen independent colonies so they could undertake the Revolutionary War; and 2) the flowering of the human genius and the inspiration of the Christian founders who produced the Declaration and framed the Constitution and Bill of Rights.

Charles Finney was perhaps the preeminent minister and leader in the Second Great Awakening in the United States. Often called the "Father of Modern Revivalism,"[73] he was deeply involved and committed to the abolition movement and frequently denounced slavery from the pulpit, even denying communion to slaveholders in his churches.[74]

In Britain, after devoting twenty years of his life to a single-minded crusade to end slave trade, William Wilberforce finally succeeded in getting parliament to pass an abolition law in 1807, a year before the slave trade legally ended in America. In the United States, in addition to Charles Finney, it was towering Christian leaders like Frederick Douglass, Theodore Parker, William Lloyd Garrison, and Harriet Beecher Stowe who led the abolitionist charge to end slavery in America, well before Abraham Lincoln became the Civil War president who saved the Union and emancipated blacks from slavery.

Healthcare for the poor has its roots in Christianity. The establishment of hospitals and universities, which accelerated through the Middle Ages, was exclusively undertaken by Christians.[75] In both the early Orthodox Church of the East and the Catholic Church of the West, Christians took to heart the teachings of Christ, who said: "I was naked and you clothed Me, I was sick and you looked after Me." The Syrian Church was the first institution to provide health care service in the East, while the Catholic Church was the first to do so in the West.[76] In 325 AD, the Council of Nicaea issued an edict requiring every cathedral to have an infirmary or hospital to take care of people on pilgrimages. In the ninth century AD, the Benedictine monastery in Salerno, Italy, founded the first and most famous medical university in Western Europe.[77]

An unprecedented outpouring of the visual arts, with the building of cathedrals and commissioning of sculptures and paintings, came about as Christianity flourished in Europe during the Middle Ages—the period from the fall of the Roman Empire (476 AD) to the beginning of the Renaissance (1350 AD). The Renaissance inspired an amazing number of even greater works of art from masters the likes of which the world has never seen since—such as da Vinci, Michelangelo, Raphael, Donatello, and Botticelli. Almost all their created images were taken from or inspired by the Bible. While it's impossible to measure, the Christian Renaissance produced more of the world's greatest and most valuable works of art than any other period, school, epoch, or place in the world by a manyfold factor.[78]

Advancing in our time frame in the achievement and legacy of progress that came out of Christianity, some may feel the United States was slow to abolish slavery and elevate women. But progress in these two spheres actually came sooner in America than most other places in the world, which was largely due to the Constitution that was drafted to provide for change and assure that the promise of equal opportunity would reach greater fullness with time.

Christian women were most influential in getting laws regarding both child labor and women's suffrage passed. Methodist Frances Willard inspired millions of Americans to support women's right to vote, which was enshrined in the 19th Amendment to the Constitution in 1920. Calvin Coolidge was the first president to benefit from the women's vote in 1922. He captured the essence of Christmas rather uniquely in an address to the American people, stating, "To cherish peace and good will, to be plenteous in mercy, is to have the real spirit of Christmas. If we think on these things, there will be born in us a Savior and over us will shine a star sending its gleam of hope to the world."[79]

The civil rights movement to establish racial equality in the latter half of the twentieth century was inspired and led by American Baptist minister Dr. Martin Luther King. And while modernity has brought impatience and a demand for rapid results, less than two generations after Dr. King led the civil rights movement, blacks in America achieved commensurate or greater success than whites in many areas and sectors of the economy—in the fields of professional sports and entertainment, as senators, House members, Supreme Court Justices, and reaching the highest office in the land in 2008, as president of the United States.

Suffice it to say that the quality of life everywhere around the world would no doubt be significantly worse today if Christ had never been born and Christianity had not become the greatest spiritual force ever to advance the care and development of people.

Many might think a savior like Jesus would be the consummate celebrity. Yet in almost every way, Jesus defied popular expectations of how celebrities should act and how a great social movement should begin and grow. With the resolve of their beloved leader Jesus, eleven of the twelve disciples were executed and put to death because of their absolute faith and commitment to God's providence through Christ. As such, the more Christianity was persecuted, the more it prospered.

Jesus Christ, being God who became man, divided history in two. He had no servants, yet everyone called him master. He had no formal education or degree, yet the educated Jews called him rabbi and teacher. Jesus had no medicines, yet he was desperately sought out as a healer. He had no army, yet emperors and kings feared him.

History shows that so many levels of human advancement were made possible by God who became man, born in a stable in the small village of Bethlehem, a speck in the vast Roman Empire. And while that empire crumbled and fell, Jesus, who had neither an army nor won any military battles—went on to become the Lord and Savior for people who believe all over the world. For, as he said, "My Kingdom is not of this world."[80]

Indeed, at the Christmas holiday, there is good reason to sing "Joy to the World."

CHAPTER 5

*New Year's Day: Necessary Endings
and New Beginnings*

Of all the holidays, New Year's Day is the oldest, dating back to ancient times. Historical records show that there were many different dates that marked the beginning of the "new year" at different points among different civilizations in the long history of man. In both ancient times and in more recent times, typically the New Year was tied to harvest; and celebration often commenced after the fruits and vegetables brought in from the orchards and fields were approved as fit to eat. But since varieties of fruits and vegetables have different harvest times during the year, there often were multiple New Year's festivals celebrated during the course of a year. Harvests revolved around the solar and lunar cycles, but there were problems that necessitated continuous calendar reforms, which included changing the lengths of months from year to year.

The Romans broke away from harvest dates driving holidays, and in 153 BC, they were the first to use January 1 as the beginning of the year. But coming up with a consistent formula for accounting for days in a year remained problematic. The old Roman calendar was inconsistent from year to year, and it became manipulated for political purposes. In 46 BC, during Julius Caesar's rule, a new calendar was introduced bearing his name—the Julian calendar—which had one basic rule: any year evenly divisible by four would be a leap year.

During the early medieval period, most Christian European countries considered New Year's Day to be on March 25, a date they connected to the spring equinox. In 1582, Pope Gregory XIII undertook reforms that brought into being our present calendar, commonly called the Gregorian calendar. It established the observance of New Year's Day on January 1st and included the method of calculating the days and months of the year with the carryover provision from the Julian calendar of an extra day every four years for leap year. The Protestant countries of northern Europe were slow to go along—even speculating that the Gregorian calendar was a Catholic plot. Finally, in the eighteenth century, the Protestants accepted the new Gregorian calendar. And that unity between Catholics and Protestants was important in influencing other countries and cultures. Leaders in Oriental countries under the influence of Hinduism, Islam, Taoism, and Buddhism then considered this new calendar the "Christian calendar." And by the early 1900s, they accepted and adopted the Gregorian Christian calendar, bringing uniformity to the world around using one common calendar.[81]

The origins of the customs that we think of as being related to the New Year date back to pre-Christian times. According to Mircea Eliade, a foremost authority on the history of religions, the New Year rites of pre-Christian man were preponderantly undertaken for the purpose of abolishing and indemnifying the past. On the New Year, creation would begin anew, and mankind would be reborn in spirit, entering into another cycle of time. There were five series of rites that accompanied the end-of-year festivals: 1) purgations, purifications, the confessing of sins, driving off demons, and expulsion of evil out of villages; 2) the extinguishing and rekindling of all fires; 3) masked processions and ceremonial reception of the dead; 4) fights between two opposing teams; and 5) an interlude of carnivals, Saturnalia, and self-indulgence.[82]

It is noteworthy that non-Christian cultures also considered confession of wrongdoing, expulsion of evil, and purification as being part of their new year rituals, which suggests that diverse people of different beliefs have independently arrived at similar fundamental biblical beliefs about the basic flawed or sinful condition of man—a sort of transcendent understanding.

It's well known that there's a great deal of excessive drinking across countries and cultures throughout the world on New Year's Eve. What most don't realize is that drunkenness is in large part a secular remnant of a rite that was once religious in nature, and that was the reenacting by people of the chaotic world that was believed to exist before the ordered cosmos was created by God, which was symbolic of New Year's Day.

New Year's Day became a time for exchanging gifts well before that custom became associated with Christianity. For instance, the Celtic-Teutonic Druids established a tradition of giving their holy plant, mistletoe, at the beginning of the New Year. That tradition was eventually brought into the Christmas tradition.[83]

It is believed that the origin of the American New Year celebration started with the Dutch in their New Amsterdam settlement—what is now Manhattan—in the first half of the seventeenth century. The Dutch were known far and wide for their love of beer and wine. When in 1664, New Amsterdam passed to English control, the English and Dutch settlers continued to live together peacefully. In fact, after surrendering control of Manhattan to the English, the Dutch persuaded the English to give up their March 25 New Year and observe it on January 1st and enjoy all the libations that went along with the holiday.[84]

We know quite a bit about the traditions of New Year celebration of the presidents of the United States because of their diaries and the historical records. On New Year's Day 1790, in what was then the capital of the United States, New York City, President Washington and the First Lady had a stream of visitors come to pay their compliments of the New Year—the vice president, governors, senators, members of the House of Representatives, and various foreign dignitaries. The second president, John Adams, held the first New Year's reception in the newly constructed but unfinished White House in Washington, DC, in 1800. The third US president, Thomas Jefferson, who was the first Democratic president, kept the New Year's tradition alive. In 1804, he opened the doors of the White House to a diversity of guests that included "the heads of departments and other officers, civil and military, foreign diplomatic characters, strangers of distinction, the Cherokee chiefs at present on a mission to the seat of government, and most of the respectable citizens of Washington and Georgetown."[85]

Abraham Lincoln was elected at a time when America was more divided than at any prior time. With the Civil War raging into the second year of the Lincoln presidency, it was far from clear whether the United States would survive as a nation. But after the Union victory at the Battle of Antietam in September 1862, with Confederate General Lee withdrawing from the field, President Lincoln felt that his prayer had been answered, providing him a clear sign to issue the Emancipation Proclamation on the next New Year's Day—January 1st, 1863. That declaration officially freed the slaves in the Southern states—symbolically cleansing the country from the national sin it had been carrying since the founding. That act that provided a new beginning also proved to be a turning point in the Civil War, with the Union forces winning the bloodiest battle thus far at Gettysburg in July that year.

Today, the New Year's Day holiday is generally associated with festivity. The revelry of partying, noisemakers, and libations on New Year's Eve is short-lived, but personal reflection that prompts New Year's resolutions to "make amends" or "turn over a new leaf" can be lasting fruit that really matters.

As we reflect on the holidays, it is entirely appropriate that Christmas and New Year's Day come in close proximity. And while most don't think about it, it's not too much of a stretch to recognize that New Year's Day is a bridge between Christmas and Easter. For the birth of goodness that is symbolic of Christmas is fortuitously followed a week later by the New Year's resolutions, the letting go of the things that need to be let go to prepare the way for renewal and regeneration, which is the essence of Easter.

One cannot get on with the new until the old is let go. There cannot be a resurrection until there is first a burial. So, in a very real way, the New Year's celebration is a prelude to Easter and the fulfillment, rebirth, and triumph of the highest good.

CHAPTER 6

Easter: The Day that Transformed the World Forever

If Christmas—the date of Christ's birth—marks the watershed of measuring time in terms of splitting calendar history into two epochs, BC and AD, then Easter marks the day and commemorates the events that transformed the world forever.

Although for many, Easter comes and goes with less anticipation and cultural fanfare than Christmas, and the Easter bunny hardly rivals Santa Claus, no Christian holiday is as important as Easter. It could be said that without Easter, Christmas would be a holiday without meaning.

Good Friday is the beginning of Easter weekend, as it commemorates the day that Christ died through crucifixion—an event of horrendous suffering that fulfilled the prophecy that the Messiah would come, suffer, and sacrifice his life to indemnify and pay for mankind's sins.

Easter Sunday commemorates the resurrection of Christ following his death, an event that settles once and for all the truth of what Jesus taught and the veracity of the miracles he performed during his three-year ministry. The resurrection of Jesus Christ is a miracle of the highest order. The resurrection changes everything. For believers, it provides a new identity in Christ whose resurrected presence provides new life.

If Jesus had just died and had not risen, he would have been just another great teacher or rabbi. There are many religions with different founders, prophets, and teachers going back thousands of years, but only one of them, Christianity, has a founder who professed to be the Messiah—the son of God—and who provided irrefutable proof by conquering death through the resurrection.

Every other consequential person of history came into the world to live. The death of other religious founders and leaders—such as Abraham, Moses, Buddha, Mohammad, or Confucius—brought an anticlimactic end to their lives and their work. But Christ came into the world as God's son in order to die and pay the price for man's sin. His sacrifice was the ultimate climax of his life, done for the benefit of all mankind—opening the way to eternal life in heaven for all who believe.

Of the four major world religions built on personalities, only Christianity claims that its founder is still alive, having overcome death through resurrection. No Jew ever believed that, after Abraham died and was interred, his tomb ever became empty. After Buddha died, no disciple ever claimed that they saw or spoke to him again. As for Mohammed and his teachings that are the basis of Islam, there is no trace of this founder appearing to his disciples or followers after he had died at age sixty-one. His occupied tomb is located in Medina and is visited by tens of thousands of devout Muslims every year.

Christ was unique in that he gave up his life as a sacrifice in order to fulfill why he came into the world. Christ set the absolute highest standard of love possible, both in his teachings and also in his making the ultimate sacrifice—giving his life to rescue and save mankind. And then to provide "seeing is believing" evidence, God brought Jesus back from being dead and buried in a tomb to being alive—resurrected—so that people would have living proof of who he was.

Easter is the oldest Christian holiday and there is a connection to the Jewish Passover tradition which commemorates the exodus of the Israelites from slavery in Egypt.[86] Many Christians inferred from the book of Mark (14:12) that Jesus's Last Supper, the night before his crucifixion, was a Seder, a ritual meal held in celebration of the Jewish holiday of Passover.

In the first few centuries after Christ's death, Easter was observed in conjunction with the Jewish Passover on the fourteenth day of the month of Nisan, which meant that it was celebrated on a different day of the week every year. This irregularity, which caused confusion, was taken up at the First Council of Nicaea in 325 AD, where it was decided that Easter should always be celebrated on the first Sunday after the full moon following the spring equinox.[87]

Once Christianity gained stature and inherited the power and wealth of the Roman Empire, its Easter celebrations became spectacular affairs with new traditions and practices incorporated with Christian interpretations. Like Christmas, the customs of the Easter celebration as we know them today incorporated a number of pagan traditions.[88]

To understand how the bunny, the eggs, and the lilies became part of our modern Easter traditions, we have to go back to about the seventh century AD when the Saxons were Christianized. The Saxons had believed in a fertility goddess—also called the goddess of the spring—known as "Eastre." Images of Eastre often included a hare and eggs. The hare's prolific breeding and eggs hatching were viewed as symbols of fertility associated with Eastre, who also was credited with heralding new life and bringing back the warm sun of spring after long winter months.[89]

The celebration of renewal and rebirth that was central to honoring this Saxon goddess Eastre was surprisingly compatible with the Christian teachings and tradition about Christ's resurrection and rebirth. And so it was that when missionaries converted the Saxons to Christianity in the seventh century AD, the celebration feast of Christ's resurrection took on the name of Easter after the Anglo-Saxon goddess of spring, whose festival was celebrated at the time of the equinox, which was in close calendar proximity to Christ's death and resurrection. With Christ's resurrection being all about new life, it was natural for the rabbit and eggs to be incorporated as symbols of Easter.[90] Early Christian missionaries may have recognized that embracing the names and customs of the local population with whom they were living would help those people accept and believe in Christianity.[91]

Easter egg hunts started in America in the 1700s. Reliable legend has it that a community of Pennsylvania Dutch became fascinated by a hare named "Oschter Haws," whom some thought was prolific in gathering eggs and rolling them together in the grass. Children began building nests for the eggs—and they also enjoyed searching for the eggs that were left behind. Oschter Haws eventually became the Easter Bunny, who is known more for the tradition of gathering eggs into nests—which evolved into Easter baskets—and hunting for eggs that would go in the basket.[92] Pennsylvania German immigrants introduced the belief and tradition of the coming of the Easter Bunny on Easter Eve, which of course was parallel to the visitation of Santa Claus or Christkindl on Christmas Eve.[93]

As for the origin of Easter lilies, many have believed and repeated the story that white lilies—which symbolize purity and honesty—prolifer-ated in the Garden of Gethsemane, where Jesus prayed in the last hours before Judas's betrayal. Legend also has it that the reason that these early blooming lilies, now called Easter lilies, came to grow with a turned-down blossom was over the sorrow that Jesus tearfully expressed in his prayers on the eve of his crucifixion.[94]

One of the explanations for the children's game of rolling Easter eggs, a tradition that was brought to America by the British, is that it was done in imitation of the stone being rolled away from Christ's tomb. The White House Easter Egg Roll started with James Madison, who was hailed as the father of the US Constitution and served as the fourth US president from 1809 to 1817.

Easter has been a very personal holiday for presidents who followed Madison. When we think of America's sixteenth president, Abraham Lincoln, we remember the tragic battlefield of Gettysburg, which was the location of his most famous speech. But it was also the place of new life and rebirth for him. Sometime after delivering the Gettysburg Address in November 1863, Lincoln confided that he had struggled with his faith, not understanding why God did not show favor for the

Union efforts through the early war years, but stated that, "...when I went to Gettysburg and looked on the graves, our dead heroes who had fallen in defense of their country, I then and there consecrated myself to Christ..."[95] Less than two years later, after the Civil War was over with victory of the Union North over the Confederate South—ending slavery and preserving the United States—Lincoln would lose his life to an assassin's bullet at Ford's Theatre in Washington, DC. That day was Good Friday, April 14, 1865.

Since Easter is the oldest and most important Christian holiday, let's now consider some of Christ's attributes that are reflected in the Easter story.

No one else in human history made the claims Jesus did to be able to deal with every last problem of the human heart. One primary reason the Bible is a perennial bestseller that outstrips the sales of every other book every year, is that it's the most complete owner's manual to the most complex creation of all—the human species. Nowhere else can one find as succinct yet comprehensive an explanation of what God's love is all about than in the Bible's Psalms and Jesus's teaching through parables.

The Gospels provide a limited account of Jesus's life before his public ministry began at age thirty, but there are a few vignettes that make it clear that his course was solitary and lonely in most of his childhood, youth, and manhood—probably a necessary preparation for his ministry of unconditional love, forgiveness, and salvation. And that ministry could only begin after Jesus endured a forty-day fast and, immediately thereafter, had to overcome three temptations while in a state of near death and exhaustion. Jesus succeeded in all these and was then baptized in the Jordan River by John the Baptist.

Once Jesus's ministry started, he became the most sought-after person in Israel. He was surrounded by people who appeared to have felt they were in heaven just being in his presence. An underappreciated quality about Jesus to reflect on at Easter is that he welcomed people whom no other religious leader of his time would have dared associate with—society's rejects, diseased lepers, reviled tax collectors, and prostitutes. By caring for outcasts and the disenfranchised, Jesus showed a radical level and standard of mercy and love never seen before. He said, "It is not the healthy people who need a doctor, but the sick. I have not come to call the righteous, but sinners, to repentance."[96] Jesus was always patient, cheerful, kind, and hailed as a messenger of life and peace. In seeing and addressing the diversity of needs of men, women, and children, he gave all the same invitation, "Come unto Me."

Many went to unusual means and ends to approach him and seek his aid. In the Gospel accounts of that ministry, no one who came to Jesus in need was ever turned away unhelped. In trying to sum up the various accounts of Christ's healing ministry, scripture paints a picture of a stream of healing power that surrounded and flowed from Jesus, enabling some to be completely and instantly healed by even touching his garment.

In his three years of ministry, Jesus actually devoted more time to healing the sick than to preaching. His compassion knew no limit, and his work was not restricted to any time or place. In fact, there is one account of his presence in Capernaum, where the multitude thronging to see, hear, and be near him was so large that the meeting house in which he was teaching was full with an overflow crowd out into the street. When some men arrived carrying a paralyzed man, they simply could not get in, so they climbed up on the roof of the building, tore out the thatch and made a hole right above Jesus and lowered the paralytic down. When Jesus saw their faith and determination, he said to the paralyzed man, "Son, your sins are forgiven…get up, take your mat and go home."[97]

Wherever Jesus was, whether on the green pastures of Galilee, by the seashore, on the roads and byways, in the synagogues, and other places where the sick were brought to him, Jesus set up his "hospital" to heal the afflicted. There were times when it appeared that he spent all day ministering to those who came to him—and he healed every last one—only to continue to heal into the evening and night to accommodate those who had to work by day. Jesus's healing was not limited to the physical body, as the fullness of his mission was to bring people complete restoration that included inner healing for the mind and soul so as to bring peace and perfection of character.

There are various accounts in the Bible where those whom Jesus healed would rejoice in their restored health as they tried out their new-found faculties. And the villagers who had known them as crippled, blind, or deaf were mesmerized by witnessing the miracle of those who were made new, and they wanted to hear from the lips of the healed their account of the power and miracles that Jesus had wrought. For those who had been deaf, Jesus's voice may have been the first sound that they had ever heard. For those who had been blind, Jesus's face may have been the first they had ever looked upon. How could they not love and give praise to Jesus for what he had done in giving them new life? Jesus brought a kind of gentle force diffusing life and joy wherever he went.

Christ's life was one of constant self-sacrifice. He had no real home in this world except for the kindness and hospitality of friends who provided comfort and a roof over his head. He took on the life of the poorest and worked among the needy and the suffering—a truly itinerant healer.

Since the Easter story revolves around the greatest miracle of healing—the resurrection—which was manifest in Jesus Christ's coming back to life three days after his final breath on the cross, it is fitting to reflect on Christianity's work in healing. Already mentioned in the Christmas chapter was an acknowledgment that healthcare for the poor and the establishment of hospitals originated with Christianity, beginning in the Middle Ages as a directive and mission of the Roman Church.

The tradition of an itinerant healer—which is who Jesus was—wasn't really taken up again and replicated until the 1800s, when a British Christian woman named Florence Nightingale, then only seventeen years old, had a "divine calling" to do God's work in taking care of the ill and injured. Against her parents' wishes, she pursued training in Germany and France and returned to London to serve in various nursing and administrative capacities. Nightingale was catapulted to fame throughout Europe and the United States by her voluntary service in the Crimean War in 1854, when she organized an expedition of thirty-eight volunteer nurses whom she trained along with fifteen Catholic nuns to serve itinerantly near the battlefields.

In the United States, heroic accounts of Nightingale were a source of inspiration for many. One of those was Clara Barton, a New Jersey school teacher who moved to Washington, DC, for a warmer climate and more opportunity. She was working in the US Patent Office at the time Lincoln was elected president in 1860. Although Lincoln did not run on a platform to abolish slavery in the South, everyone knew where he stood. And even before he was inaugurated, seven of the Southern states exercised their prerogative to secede from the Union.

While most historians designate the start of the Civil War with the South Carolina militia's bombardment of Fort Sumter, which was occupied by Union forces who refused to leave the fort and the territory of the newly independent state, there were actually no casualties in that assault. The first Civil War bloodshed came a week later in Baltimore, Maryland. When Clara Barton heard that victims were being transported forty miles by train to Washington, DC, she dropped her work at the US Patent Office and dashed over to the train station and to the Capitol building, where she threw herself into diagnosing, treating, and caring for the diverse and horrendous needs of some forty injured men. For the first year of the Civil War, Ms. Barton continued in that same vein, tending wounded Union soldiers as they were brought back from the battlefield and arrived in Washington, DC. In her spare time, of which she had little, she also collected and distributed bandages, blankets, and other supplies for the army.

But by the second year of the war, Ms. Barton decided she could best support the troops by going in person to the battlefields. Starting in 1862 and continuing for two years, her itinerant healing efforts took her to some ten different battle sites, including the gruesome battles of Antietam and Gettysburg. A woman grounded by her Christian faith and outsized courage, she always tried to serve near the front line, where there were the most casualties and where live rounds were frequently whizzing by. Ms. Barton once said, "I may be compelled to face danger, but never fear it, and while our soldiers can stand and fight, I can stand and feed and nurse them."[98] Being the first woman to serve on the field of combat—nursing, comforting, praying, and cooking for the wounded—Clara Barton was soon known as the "Angel of the Battlefield."

The significance of the work she performed during the war cannot be overstated. But remarkably her commitment to that calling continued apace after the Civil War. She went overseas, serving in Strasbourg, Lyons, and Paris, France to provide care for the wounded from the Franco-Prussian War. In May 1881, Barton had found her second calling, and decided to form the American Association of the American Red Cross, of which she was unanimously elected president.

In the Bible, Paul told the Romans that "God proves His love for us in this: While we were still sinners, Christ died for us."[99] A thousand years before the death of Christ, in Psalm 22, David prophesied about the crucifixion in graphic detail. Crucifixion was the most agonizing death penalty, so torturous that the Romans did not render that particular kind of death sentence to any Roman citizen. The pain of crucifixion, which went on for hours, was utterly unbearable. In fact, because there was nothing in the language that captured the intense torment, a new word was created to describe it. And that word was *excruciating*, which literally means "out of the cross."[100]

Perhaps Jesus could have fulfilled his mission and God's plan of salvation by dying in a less painful way—still serving as sinful man's substitute by paying the death penalty for man's sin and rebellion against God. But the ultimate agonizing pain of crucifixion was what Jesus bore to show the depth of God's love.

Once, when Jesus was having dinner with a Jewish Pharisee, a woman convicted by her own sin came to Jesus to wash his feet with her tears and hair, and then apply perfume. His host was aghast at the immoral woman's presence and the perceived waste of expensive perfume on feet, but Jesus responded that God's work was to forgive sinners, and that those who were forgiven much could then love much. On another occasion, Jesus put it this way: "It is not those who are well who need a doctor, but those who are sick. I didn't come to call the righteous, but sinners."[101]

Jesus also performed many healing miracles of a different kind. Jesus confronted evil head on and drove demonic spirits out of people dangerously possessed and abandoned by society. Early in Christ's ministry, when it was not yet time for the fullness of truth to be known that Jesus was God's son—the true messiah—demonic spirits were terrified of Jesus, knowing clearly who he was. Mark 3:11 reads: "And unclean spirits, when they saw him, fell down before him, and cried, saying, Thou art the Son of God." Luke 4:41 reads: "And devils also came out of many, crying out, and saying, Thou art Christ the Son of God. And he rebuking them, did not allow them not to speak: for they knew that he was Christ."

Christ's ministry and works were unique in still other ways. All other religions require works to achieve enlightenment and salvation. Christianity turns that on its head: Faith in Christ and all his teachings transforms the heart, from which good works naturally follow. In saying "my yoke is easy and my burden is light," Jesus presents an original, compelling appeal which even the most hardened cynic can't easily refuse.

Returning to the resurrection, it is unquestionably the most fantastic claim that Christianity makes. The Biblical record provides accounts of Jesus making numerous appearances after the resurrection, some to individuals, some to groups, some to several disciples at the same time, and once even to a crowd of five hundred at one time. Particularly noteworthy is the fact that there were no accounts or witnesses who came forth and disputed these appearances, or called it a "hoax," not a single one. Nor do we find any historical record of any witness accounts that were contradictory.[102]

Skeptics of the Biblical account of the entirety of Jesus need to recognize that there's actually far more reliable historical evidence for his life, teachings, miracles, death, and resurrection than there is evidence for any other historical figure of ancient times.

It was previously observed that no one doubts the authenticity of the life and acts of Alexander the Great, who was born some 350 years before Christ. Yet there are only two original biographical accounts of his life, which were written by Arrian and Plutarch some four hundred years after Alexander died. The manuscripts of Virgil and Horace, both of whom lived within a generation of Christ, were written more than four centuries after their deaths.[103] The copy of works by Livy and Tacitus on

Roman history and the works of Pliny Secundus on natural history, were written on average some seven hundred years after the time of the original account, with many major sections of the original manuscripts not having survived. Yet no one doubts Virgil and Horace lived and authored great poetic masterpieces. Nor do we hear questions about the authenticity and accuracy of accounts of Livy or Tacitus in chronicling the events of the Roman Emperors Augustus, Claudius, Nero, or Tiberius.[104]

Looking at the big picture, there are about one thousand times more manuscripts preserving the teachings and deeds of Jesus in the New Testament (about twenty-five thousand) than there are preserving other classical ancient works of historic figures who lived at approximately the same time, with the exception of Homer, whose *Iliad* is backed by eighteen hundred manuscripts—but that is *still less than one-tenth* the number of ancient manuscripts that back and authenticate the New Testament.[105]

We know the historical Jesus mainly through four different accounts known as the Gospels—Matthew, Luke, Mark, and John—not written hundreds of years later, but within a generation or two of Jesus's life. Matthew and John provide eyewitness accounts from their years of walking with Jesus as disciples. Mark also had eyewitness experience, although he was only a teenager when Jesus's public ministry began. Luke, the doctor, learned about Jesus from his friend Paul, the Apostle who wrote most of the Letters of the New Testament.

We can point to prophecy fulfilled by Jesus's death, burial, and resurrection; and we can read the rock-solid testimony of eyewitnesses. After Jesus had been betrayed and was facing trial, his disciples were fearful for their lives and they fled. But in the first forty days after the resurrection, Jesus appeared alive to his disciples and more than five hundred people on twelve separate occasions. His appearance and interaction with his remaining eleven disciples, also known as apostles, in different circumstances during those forty days, so transformed them that they completely and exclusively committed their lives to teaching and sharing the good news of healing and salvation from sin and dysfunction through Jesus Christ.

The events around Jesus's resurrection were so significant and were experienced by people so diverse that they could not be denied. In the book of Acts 2:32, Peter says to the other apostles, "God has raised this Jesus to life, and we are all witnesses of the fact." Paul said in a speech recorded in Acts 13:31: "For many days he was seen by those who had traveled with him from Galilee to Jerusalem. They are now his witnesses to our people."

Because of their experience with the resurrected Jesus, the apostles were in a unique position, knowing with certainty that Jesus was truly the Son of God. They had been present for the life, ministry, death, and resurrection of Jesus. If the claims about Jesus were a lie, the apostles would have known it. That's why their commitment to their testimony was so powerful and compelling. Additionally, the apostles' willingness to die for their claims has tremendous evidential value—and confirms the truth of the resurrection.

No one will die for something they invented or believe to be false. Seeing, talking to, and touching the risen Jesus transformed the apostles, who then committed the rest of their lives to educate and advocate for the truth about the message of salvation through Christ. With the exception of John, who lived, worked, and died on the island of Patmos, the other eleven apostles—including Matthias who replaced Judas, the betrayer of Jesus—died as martyrs for their beliefs in the divinity of Christ. And even the action of Judas testified to the divinity of Christ, for Judas was so convicted by his overwhelming realization that he had betrayed the Son of God, that he could not live with himself and committed suicide.

It turns out that Easter, which has its ultimate meaning through the resurrection, is one of ancient history's most carefully scrutinized and best attested events.

Easter is the commemoration of the single event that transformed the world forever—the resurrection of Jesus after his death on the cross. The resurrection is real and changes everything.

That God would send his Son to die as a sacrifice for the sin of all who would believe in him is an unbelievable gift—beyond most people's comprehension. That a resurrection and a joyous eternal life await believers is beyond anything anyone could imagine. That is the promise and essence of Easter.

CHAPTER 7

The Fourth of July: A Declaration of Independence and the Birth of a Nation

In continuing our story of America that began with the explorer Columbus and the Pilgrim settlers—before our three-chapter segue on the Christmas, New Year's Day, and Easter holidays—we will now turn to our next historically sequential national holiday: the Fourth of July, also known as Independence Day or July 4th. The Fourth of July commemorates the day the founders appealed to God and proclaimed the Declaration of Independence to the American people and the world in the year 1776. Before we get into what actually happened in that fateful year, it's helpful to explore the ideological and spiritual developments that began centuries earlier.

Without a doubt, it was the Reformation of Christianity that burst upon Europe in 1517 with Martin Luther posting his *Ninety-five Theses* on the church door in Wittenberg, Germany that was most influential in empowering people to challenge authority of both the church and the state. With time the Reformation would provide a wellspring of ideas and principles that were foundational to the American Revolution, and it's safe to say that the Reformation was a necessary condition for the American Republic to come into being.

Luther set in motion an awakening that stimulated an unusual blossoming of spiritual inspiration, human genius, and extraordinary wisdom that culminated in the birth of a new nation—one unprecedented in human history, dedicated to the proposition that its citizens had unalienable rights of life, liberty, and the pursuit of happiness. So, if there had been no Reformation, there would likely have been no United States or Fourth of July commemoration as we know them today.

With obedience to authority and class stratification having been the norm for pretty much all of recorded history, Luther appeared to be either a fool or a subversive for proclaiming that liberty of conscience and equality of all believers, regardless of class, was the proper basis for religious, social, and political life.

After Luther, it was John Calvin of Geneva and John Knox of Scotland who contributed the most to advancing the depth and breadth of the Reformation. Calvin's "resistance theory" justified the people's right to disobey unjust rule, which was the essence of the Declaration of Independence. Probably all of America's Founding Fathers had read and even memorized a brief summary of Calvin's theology contained in the Westminster Catechism because, when they were in their formative years, it was part of all the colonies' school curricula.[106] Calvin's most important work, the multi-volume *Institutes of the Christian Religion*, was cited by John Adams, Ben Franklin, Alexander Hamilton, and James Madison in their correspondence and deliberations about the Articles of Confederation that followed the Declaration of Independence on July 4th, 1776.[107]

John Knox was not only a giant in Scottish history, but also in Reformation ideas influencing both Scotland and England. More fiery than Calvin, Knox was a man of enormous courage; he openly challenged the ruling authority of Mary, Queen of Scots, denouncing her for attempting to restore Catholicism. When it was revealed that she had a role in the murder of her husband Lord Darnley, he argued on Christian principles for rebellion against, overthrow of, and execution of an unrighteous monarch.[108] Calvin's views had inspired John Ponet to write *A Shorte Treatise of Politike Power*, which also influenced Knox's argument, on Christian grounds, on the right of resistance to tyrannical kings.[109] John Adams, one of the earliest and most ardent figures advocating revolt and separation from England, a signatory to the Declaration of Independence, and the second US president, said that Ponet's work contained "all the essential principles of liberty, which were after dilated on by Sidney and Locke."[110]

* * *

Between the early colonial period and the beginning of the Revolutionary War—from the 1730s to the 1750s—a spiritual revival, known as the First Great Awakening, took place in America. Inspired and led by the preaching of Jonathan Edwards and George Whitefield, the Great Awakening was akin to a second Reformation. And nothing before it or since compares with its profound effect on Americans' thinking and feelings.[111] Cultural upheaval swept through the colonies from the North to the South, affecting how people thought about themselves individually and how they viewed social and political order.

The Great Awakening advanced spiritually what had hitherto been accomplished in the Reformation. Whereas the reformed Christian Pilgrims, Puritans, Presbyterians, Baptists, and Methodists were believers in a God who operated primarily through covenants and contracts, the Great Awakening revealed in new ways that God acted through the heart and commitment of each individual. Therefore the individual of Christian belief need not look beyond him or herself for the source of authority. This change was like a metamorphosis as it sunk in that God didn't work exclusively through kings or bishops, clergy or magistrates, but through the people themselves.[112]

The Great Awakening gave American colonists a rekindled view of their ability and their calling to interpret the will of God for themselves. They also became more democratic, believing that the church should be self-governed and more independent from state government and politics. In addition, the Great Awakening paved the way for the disestablishment of the Church of England as the official church in North Carolina and the key state of Virginia, a necessary precondition for the War of Independence from Great Britain.

John Adams, a key leader of the American Revolution, observed that ideas and attitudes determine outcomes. Reflecting back on the birth of America, he stated that, "The Revolution was effected before the war commenced…[and it] was in the minds and hearts of the people; a change in their religious sentiments of their duties and obligations."[113]

Up until this time, the colonies were largely independent and relatively disconnected from one another, which made it difficult to coordinate efforts to separate from Great Britain. But the Great Awakening revival—sustained and spread by the powerful preaching of Jonathan Edwards and George Whitefield—served to unify the colonies in new and effectual ways.

Edwards' preaching was so powerful and ignited a revival so great that bars and brothels shut down in many cities because so many turned to God and simply left their bad habits and immoral ways behind. The common thread of testimonies from people attending and listening to Edwards' message was that they felt convicted and touched by the Spirit of God at a very deep level in ways never before experienced.

Whitefield was an energetic traveling preacher, nicknamed the "Grand Itinerant," who toured the thirteen colonies seven times from the 1730s to the 1760s, preaching some eighteen thousand times to some ten million Americans.[114] Although small in stature, Whitefield had a booming voice. His friend Ben Franklin methodically calculated that Whitefield could preach to an audience of thirty thousand and be heard by everyone. When he preached to a huge crowd in Philadelphia on one occasion, it was recorded that his voice was clearly heard over two miles down the Delaware River.[115]

His open-air sermons attracted huge audiences, causing many to be awestruck and penitent with souls awakened. Some would later recognize that the Great Awakening was a kind of "dress rehearsal" for the War of Independence.[116]

Edwards and Whitefield also profoundly affected a number of the Founding Fathers, with secondary effects on many more. Samuel Adams was deeply influenced and sought a political revolution to separate the church from England's influence. Ben Franklin and George Whitefield were friends, and Franklin wrote of the profound influence that Whitefield had on him, influence that ran counter to Deism.[117] In looking back on American independence, John Adams wrote that "the Revolution involved a radical change in religious sentiments before it eroded old political loyalties. That prior change came in the First Great Awakening, energized by the preaching of the Reverend George Whitefield."[118]

The Great Awakening inspired many young men to seek training to become Christian ministers. Princeton, Rutgers, Brown, and Dartmouth universities were established to meet this need. Whitefield and Edwards both supported the establishment of the College of New Jersey to train ministers intending to serve in the "New Light" Presbyterian message that came out of the Great Awakening. When the time came for a new president at the college in 1768, they encouraged Benjamin Rush and John Stockton (who would later both become signatories to the Declaration) to recruit British Presbyterian minister John Witherspoon to become president of the college. He rose to the occasion, relocated his family across the Atlantic, and under his leadership, the College of New Jersey thrived and was ultimately renamed Princeton University.

* * *

At Princeton, Witherspoon had an unparalleled record as a leader and educator for over twenty-five years. He taught a large group of the Founding Fathers, and his graduates included a president of the United States, James Madison; a vice president, Aaron Burr; ten cabinet members; six members of the Continental Congress; thirty-nine US representatives; twenty-one US senators; twelve governors; fifty-six state legislators; thirty judges; three US Supreme Court justices; six members of the Constitutional Convention; and thirteen college presidents.[119] Suffice it to say that Witherspoon's Princeton produced many more independence and revolutionary leaders than any other educational institution in the country. Witherspoon himself may have been the source of adding the invocation of "appealing to the Supreme Judge of the World for the rectitude of their intentions" to the first draft of Jefferson's Declaration of Independence in order to give the document divine authority. In any case, Witherspoon was a signer of the Declaration and a signer of the Articles of Confederation, representing New Jersey as a leading member of the Continental Congress (1776–1782). In short, John Witherspoon was the quintessential Founding Father that most people have never heard of.

The July 4th holiday is a much more light-hearted and festive American holiday—with cookouts, parades, beach and boating parties, and fireworks—than other patriotic holidays such as Memorial Day or Veterans Day. Very few people today realize or remember how somber the occasion was when those fifty-six members of the Continental Congress signed the Declaration of Independence in 1776. They were in fact signing their death warrants as traitors to Great Britain. And at that time, Great Britain was the most powerful nation on earth, while the thirteen American colonies were poor, underequipped militarily, and relatively disunited. When the news of America's Declaration of Independence arrived in Great Britain a month or so after July 4, the British Crown declared it an act of treason, which meant that all signatories would be punishable by death.

It is a little-known historical fact that for this reason, combined with the low odds of prevailing against the British Army and Navy, the identities of the fifty-six members of the Continental Congress who signed the Declaration were kept secret by not being immediately made public. For more than six months following the Declaration of Independence on July 4, 1776, copies of the document in circulation displayed only two signatures: John Hancock, president of the Continental Congress, and Charles Thomson, secretary of the Continental Congress.[120]

Eleven years prior, starting in 1765, the British initiated new policies of taxation and quartering of British troops that created unrest with the colonists. Taxation by the British on tea imports in the colonies led to the Boston Tea Party rebellion in 1773. When British troops engaged and killed Americans in Lexington and Concord outside Boston in April 1775—dubbed the "shot heard 'round the world"—and at the Battle of Bunker Hill two months later, it was clear that a war against British injustice had begun.[121]

The Continental Congress responded to this in June of 1775, a year before the Declaration of Independence, unanimously choosing George Washington to lead the Continental Army as general and commander in chief. He was immediately dispatched to take command in Cambridge, Massachusetts, with a mission to defeat and drive the British from Boston.

At a height of six foot two with perfect posture, broad shoulders, poise, and grace of movement, Washington was an imposing figure whose very presence commanded everyone's attention and respect. But what was far more important about Washington was his steady and trustworthy character, his faith in the protective hand of Providence, his fearlessness in battle, and his relentless persistence in the cause.

After Washington arrived in Cambridge, military engagements between the two sides were limited the rest of that summer, and then into fall and winter—in part due to Washington's knack for using deceptive maneuvers that projected more power and numbers than he actually had. This culminated on the night of March 4, 1776. Washington implemented diversionary tactics of parading four thousand troops and ceaseless firing of mortars from Cambridge on the north side of Boston, while he directed the clandestine building of fortifications and the placement of a battery of heavy cannons on the south side of Boston at Dorchester Heights, a hill nearly as high as Bunker Hill with a commanding view of all of Boston, its harbor, and of course all the British forces.

When British general William Howe woke up the next morning, he was dumbfounded as to how those fortifications and formidable cannons had been erected undetected and so quickly. He began to mobilize a counteroffensive to take out the rebels' newly fortified commanding heights, but bad weather and high winds forced him to reconsider. And while there was some exchange of fire over the next few days, Howe wasted no time in organizing the British withdrawal from Boston—recognizing the higher priority and imperative to secure the city of New

York, which had far more strategic value than Boston. This was because New York controlled the entrance to the Hudson River, and the Hudson River divided all of the New England colonies from the rest of the country. As John Adams put it at the time, "New York was the key to the whole continent."[122]

Washington then marched his troops from Boston to New York to prepare for the coming of the British. Indeed, things looked grim for Washington as he considered the number of troops under his command to defend New York. Of the estimated fifteen to nineteen thousand soldiers, only two-thirds were fit for active duty. According to his intelligence sources, Washington knew that he would face twice his numbers of well-trained Red Coats under Howe's command, with more British and German Hessian soldiers coming all the time by ship.

No matter the odds against him, George Washington was a man of extraordinary faith and fearless courage. He wrote his brother on May 31, 1776: "We expect a very bloody summer of it at New York…If our cause is just, as I do most religiously believe it to be, the same Providence which in many instances appeared for us, will still go on to afford its aid."[123]

* * *

Washington wrote from his past experience, having several times witnessed firsthand the protective intervention of Providence when bullets whistled by him in the heat of battle. The most remarkable encounter had occurred twenty-one years before in a skirmish in the French and Indian War in 1755 known as the Battle of the Monongahela. Washington was serving as junior officer to then British general Braddock, and the enemy ambushed their battalion—mowing down, either killing or wounding more than half his fourteen hundred fellow soldiers. When it was over, every one of Braddock's officers on horseback—except Washington—was on the ground either wounded or killed, while Washington was on his third horse under continuous fire in the open, riding back and forth across the field to organize retreat. Washington recounted his experience in a letter to his brother, in which he wrote: "…by the miraculous care of Providence, that protected me beyond all human expectation; I had four bullets through my coat, and two horses shot under me, and yet escaped unhurt."[124]

This "miraculous protective veil" around Washington would be corroborated some sixteen years later, by the Indian chief who had instructed his warriors to train their rifles on Washington to take him down at the Monongahela ambush—but could not. The chief, who was now grand ruler of his tribes, acknowledged that he was "old and [would] soon…be gathered to the great council fire of my fathers," and he wanted to meet face to face with Washington to pay homage before he passed away.[125]

The chief succeeded in meeting up with Washington, who happened to be traveling in the territory with a Dr. James Craik and a party of hunters. Showing extreme deferential respect toward Washington, the chief recounted his eyewitness observation of Washington's inexplicable invincibility sixteen years before: "A power mightier far than we, shielded him from harm. He cannot die in battle…. Listen! The Great Spirit protects that man, and guides his destinies—he will become the chief of nations, and a people yet unborn will hail him as the founder of a mighty empire."[126]

* * *

Returning to our 1776 narrative, Washington was in New York preparing his defense in May and June of that year, when on July 6 a courier arrived to deliver a copy of the Declaration of Independence proclaimed in Philadelphia several days before. Washington was so deeply moved by the power of the Declaration's words that he ordered copies sent to all generals in the Continental Army and ordered chaplains be hired for every regiment, stating his purpose was to assure that "every officer and man, will endeavor so to live and act, as becomes a Christian Soldier, defending the dearest Rights and Liberties of his country."[127] Like the Mayflower Compact, the Declaration was a true covenant of absolute commitment, its last sentence invoking: "…with a firm reliance on the Protection of Divine Providence, we mutually pledge to each other our Lives, our Fortunes, and our sacred Honor."

From this point on, it was no longer armed confrontations to correct abuse and grievance against Great Britain, and perhaps effect a reconciliation. The Declaration had the most profound effect, changing the whole character of the war, making it clear that henceforth it would be a commitment, an all-out fight to the finish for an independent America.[128]

After the meaning of the Declaration had sunk in a few days later, Washington called a respite to his troops' battle preparations. On July 9, he announced a gathering and celebration in order to read the Declaration to his soldiers and townspeople. The crowd hustled down to what is now lower Manhattan where they could see the British ships at anchor in New York harbor, and a few rowdies took the occasion to pull down a monument to King George III and sever the statue's head.[129]

British ships kept sailing into New York Harbor through the Narrows throughout July and, by the second week in August, over 150 ships were at anchor in the harbor. It was a sea forest of masts as one gazed from lower Manhattan over to Staten Island. At that time, Washington's colonial army in New York had about eighteen or nineteen thousand men, while there were about thirty-five thousand soldiers on those British ships.

Finally, the time had come, and the British generals amassed some fifteen to twenty thousand troops on Long Island. The first shots came on August 27 and the battle that ensued was beyond anything the Americans had previously experienced. They were vastly outnumbered and utterly overwhelmed by the British, who took a thousand prisoners and killed or wounded another six or seven hundred American militia. Things looked exceedingly grim, with more British forces on the way from nearby ships anchored offshore. Washington decided retreat was the only way to save his troops to fight another day.

Under the circumstances, the odds of a successful retreat with almost no preparation time were exceedingly low, for such a maneuver required coordination of a multitude of variables, from obtaining and ferrying vessels to precise timing, and meant dealing with adverse winds and strong currents crossing the East River to Manhattan from what is now Brooklyn at the northwest end of Long Island, as well as deceiving the enemy until the evacuation was complete.

Would Washington's faith in providential intervention come through? He told no one except a few trusted direct report officers that retreat was now the plan. But that night—just as had happened in Boston—a sudden storm came up with adverse winds preventing the British navy from being able to sail and intercept the open boats ferrying the retreating Americans with great difficulty across the intense current with the eddies, swirls, and chop of the East River to Manhattan. And by morning, when winds subsided, miraculously a thick fog descended across the retreat staging area and out onto the river, muffling every sound and shrouding everything from sight. So then, with calmer conditions, the latter half of the evacuation could proceed more rapidly—totally unnoticed by the British.

Washington was one to lead out in front of his troops, but now in retreat, he stayed behind until the last man boarded the final rescue watercraft. Not a single life was lost during the rescue of more than nine thousand soldiers, and Washington is credited with orchestrating one of history's greatest feats of military evacuation of its kind. But it was made possible only by providential forces beyond his control—unnatural weather that brought stormy winds by night followed by calm seas and thick fog by day.[130]

While that retreat saved the Americans to be able to fight another day, it also led to General Howe's swift capture of the prize of New York over the next several months.

The following month, in October 1776, the British defeated the Americans at the Battle of White Plains, about thirty-six miles north of the city of New York. After that rout, the only point on Manhattan Island still held by the Americans was Fort Washington, a few miles north of the city. But that didn't last.

In the early morning of November 15, 1776, the British were joined by German Hessian soldiers, and Washington's troops were completely overwhelmed—barricaded inside of Fort Washington—with the British and Hessians firing unceasingly on them. By the time the Americans surrendered, they had lost twenty-nine hundred soldiers, nearly six times the casualties of the British and Germans. It was a military disaster and a devastating blow to morale.

Three months previously, at the outset of the New York campaign, Washington had sixteen to nineteen thousand under his command. He now left New York with only thirty-five hundred troops—having suffered three major defeats—crossing the Hudson River into New Jersey, and marching south toward Philadelphia.[131] Washington's greatest challenge now was to maintain the confidence and loyalty of his greatly diminished and discouraged troops. Desertions were on the rise and more soldiers would depart in the weeks ahead when enlistment contracts were up. But for a gallant few, nearly all thought the Revolution was lost.

Washington's faith and belief in the cause of independence sustained him, but he knew that at this point, only a decisive victory could bring about a reversal of fortune, which was vital for recruitment and funding from the Continental Congress.

Having marched his troops south through New Jersey, in early December 1776, Washington decided to encamp right across the Delaware River in Pennsylvania. Several weeks after getting established, Washington learned through intelligence sources that some two to three thousand enemy soldiers—mainly German Hessian mercenaries—were occupying Trenton, New Jersey only a few miles away. Washington had an opening and wasted no time in planning secretly for a surprise attack on Trenton to be undertaken Christmas night.

Crossing the Delaware with several thousand troops, two dozen horses, and heavy cannons would not be easy at the best of times. But that Christmas night's sleet, snow, and gale force winds made the crossing some miles upstream of Trenton next to impossible. Washington had decided to divide his troops into three different staging spots for crossing. Two of those groups found the crossing too difficult and risky, and decided not to proceed. Washington forged ahead, commandeering the many heavily laden open boats through the turbulence and ice of the Delaware. It was dangerous and slow going. As a result, they were fewer in number than what had been planned, nearly three hours behind schedule, and would lose the element of a surprise attack in the dark of predawn.

With his forces now amassed on the New Jersey side of the river, Washington led by example and instilled courage in the twenty-four hundred troops assembled, many of whom were scantily clad and even barefoot. Over the course of the three-hour march to Trenton, many suffered from frostbite and loss of feeling in fingers and toes. Two soldiers froze to death. When Washington's troops came upon Trenton in the morning light, the good fortune of surprise was still with them, for the Germans were groggy, having carried on late into the previous night of Christmas with plenty of food and drink. Within forty-five minutes, the Americans were victorious, inflicting 111 casualties and securing the surrender and capture of nine hundred prisoners. No Americans were killed and only four were wounded. Washington was extolled as a hero for an extraordinary victory. John Hancock noted it was all the more "extraordinary" because it had been achieved by men "broken by fatigue and ill-fortune."[132]

Another intelligence tip came in a few days after the Trenton victory, regarding British encampment in Princeton. Washington wasted no time in planning and executing a second successful surprise attack, outwitting his enemies again, staging a "false front encampment" with fires burning all night near Trenton, while he and fifty-five hundred patriot soldiers with their horses and cannon stole away in the dark and made their way to Princeton, New Jersey for a second surprise attack. In that battle on January 3, 1777, Washington's leading from the front was so bold that it inspired many of the locals in Princeton to spontaneously join in the routing of the British. The words of one such volunteer, utterly impressed by Washington's courage, are worth recounting. He said, "I shall never forget what I felt…when I saw him brave all the dangers of the field and his important life hanging as it were by a single hair with a thousand deaths flying about him. Believe me, I thought not of myself."[133]

Perceiving these back-to-back victories as the harbinger of more to come, and perhaps with many recognizing the power of commitment manifest in the Declaration, Hancock and the Continental Congress, also known as the Founding Fathers, authorized and saw to it that copies of the Declaration with all fifty-six signatures were posted throughout the thirteen colonies by the end of January 1777.

If we take the Declaration of Independence seriously in terms of the words selected to mobilize support for the cause, July 4th was a key moment in American history when the Founding Fathers placed everything on the line in a sacred covenant and trusted the Almighty for the results. As esteemed British historian Paul Johnson notes: "The Americans were overwhelmingly churchgoing, much more so than the English, whose rule they rejected. There is no question that the Declaration of Independence was, to those who signed it, a religious as well as a secular act, and that the Revolutionary War had the approbation of divine providence."[134]

Ultimately, what was truly revolutionary was not the military success of America against all odds in the War of Independence, achieved some five years later. Rather, it was the assertion in the Declaration of Independence that the rights of the people come from God, and not the state. And since rights come from God, they are absolute and "unalienable," and the state's governing authority is to be limited by that first principle and thus cannot infringe those rights. No other nation in history, perhaps with the exception of ancient Israel, has been founded in such a way that the sovereignty of the state was limited by unalienable rights of its people.

And perhaps, just so posterity would be reminded that the hand of God is on America, it happened that on the fiftieth anniversary of Independence Day, July 4, 1826, America's second and third presidents, John Adams and Thomas Jefferson, both of whom were key contributors in drafting the Declaration of Independence, took their final breaths and died within hours of each other. In a eulogy delivered the following month, Daniel Webster marveled at this "striking and extraordinary coincidence," and what it might suggest. He surmised that both Adams and Jefferson had been gifts from Providence to the United States. He saw in their late stage in life, aged ninety and eighty-three respectively, that their "happy termination" on the fiftieth anniversary of the July 4 Declaration were "proofs that our country and its benefactors are objects of His care." This miraculous concurrence was made even more striking five years later, with the death of James Monroe, America's fifth president, on that same auspicious date, July 4th.[135]

As it turns out, The Declaration of Independence, which we celebrate on July 4th, is not just what gave political birth to the United States, with its unique emphasis on limited government and freedom for its citizens. It was the Declaration's simple ideas put into practice that empowered the American people and enabled the nation's ascendance from colonial poverty to global superpower in a little more than two hundred years.

CHAPTER 8

Presidents' Day: Washington and Lincoln are as Relevant Today as Ever

Presidents' Day is unique among American holidays in providing the opportunity to remember and appreciate why George Washington and Abraham Lincoln—whose birthdays fall in February—were the two greatest US presidents.

While Washington was the founding father of the United States, becoming the first president in 1789, Lincoln would save the nation from division and collapse—bringing an end to the Civil War and the scourge of slavery as the sixteenth president in 1865. In short, Lincoln saved the republic that Washington made possible. And two remarkable men they were, whose wisdom and judgment are timeless and as relevant today as they were in their times many years ago.

In the prior chapter on the Fourth of July holiday, we covered some of the high points of George Washington's life and leadership through the end of 1776, when he crossed the Delaware River on a blustery, freezing, and snowy Christmas night. Leading some twenty-four hundred men and trudging some nine miles in the wee hours of the morning, he made a victorious surprise attack on the British allied Hessian mercenaries in

Trenton, New Jersey just after daybreak. Then just days later, Washington outwitted his enemies again in a second successful surprise attack against the British in nearby Princeton. Utterly amazed by Washington's courage to lead from the front with bullets whizzing by everywhere and fierce hand-to-hand combat all around, his men fought with greater conviction than ever, securing victory in less than a half-hour.

Washington's two morale-boosting victories in New Jersey were significant, but many historians also credit the American victory at Saratoga, New York in October 1777 as a source of optimism in year two of a six-year war. There, the victory of the Continental Army under the command of General Benedict Arnold and General Horatio Gates was made possible again by seemingly providential help as adverse winds inexplicably blew consistently for several months, preventing British general Burgoyne from receiving planned reinforcements. While morale and hope was raised in 1777, it would prove fleeting, for over the next four years of the Revolutionary War, American patriots would lose more battles than they would win.

Washington would be once again outmaneuvered and humiliated by British general Howe, who succeeded in the ultimate symbolic victory of marching his British troops into Philadelphia in September of 1777, literally occupying what was then America's first capital—the city of the signing of the Declaration and the seat of the Continental Congress.

And while the British were settling in, expropriating and inhabiting the homes of wealthy Philadelphians, Washington was regrouping with his sick, weary, and underfed troops, camped out in cold, dank tents during the long winter of 1778 at Valley Forge some thirty miles away. As fate would have it, there were benefits to the hardship experienced at Valley Forge. Accounts of that winter indicate that Washington, in desperation, begged the Continental Congress for more financial aid and provisions. He also beseeched God in prayer for intervention and assistance.

There is certainly no reason to doubt the story of Washington's passionate prayer in the snows of Valley Forge, as the historical records of Washington show that he was a man of daily prayer. Over one hundred different prayers in Washington's own cursive writing have survived and make up the historical record.[136]

There were five different individuals who gave an account of Washington praying at Valley Forge. The primary source—that being the written record of another's verbal account—may not meet a skeptic's threshold for believability. Nevertheless, Nathaniel Snowden's written record of the testimony of an eyewitness observer, Isaac Potts, an individual who was neither sympathetic to Washington nor the Revolutionary cause, cannot be easily dismissed. By chance, Potts had encountered George Washington alone on his knees praying loudly in the snowy woods of Valley Forge, and shortly thereafter related the eyewitness account to Snowden, who recorded it in his diary. That account of Washington's prayer at that dark hour of the revolutionary struggle depicts him as beseeching "God's deliverance of aid for the cause of the country, humanity and the world."[137]

Indeed, Washington placed everything on the line for the cause, as did the fifty-six signatories of the Declaration of Independence, citing in the last sentence of that document that "with firm Reliance on the Protection of divine Providence, we mutually pledge to each other our Lives, our Fortunes, and our sacred Honor."

Without Washington's leadership, unrelenting perseverance, and reliance on the Almighty, America's Declaration would probably have come to naught, as the record of battles shows that there were on balance more setbacks than successes against the British. But Washington's men were willing to sacrifice and press on even when their cause appeared hopeless because they saw in their general a man of moral excellence and indefatigable faith in the cause. Washington deeply cared for his men's well-being, led by example, and continuously put his life on the line—unhesitatingly charging to the front, seemingly oblivious to any fear of death. But Washington also knew when to protect his troops in retreat so as to be able to fight another day.

Washington also credited divine intervention and assistance, such as when the British, in hot pursuit of the weaker American troops, were stopped in the Carolinas by sudden flash floodwaters at the Catawba

River, and then also at the Yadkin River after the American forces had already crossed. In his 1781 correspondence to William Gordon, Washington described it this way: "We have…abundant reasons to thank Providence for its many favorable interpositions in our behalf. It has at times been my only dependence, for all other resources seemed to have failed us."[138]

Washington and the Continental Army were in fact perpetually short of financial resources. Fortunately, even before the Revolutionary War started there was a young Jewish lover of liberty being raised up, Haym Salomon, whose ancestors had fled Jewish persecution in Spain in 1492 and settled in Poland. Born in 1740, Salomon acquired a knowledge of finance in his twenties, conducting business throughout Europe, gaining fluency in six languages including French, Spanish, German, and English.[139] With Poland being invaded by Russia in 1772 and being threatened by neighboring countries on all sides, Salomon decided it time to leave, and he immigrated to England. Shortly thereafter he decided to come to the New World, settling in New York in 1775 and establishing himself as a financial broker for merchants engaged in overseas trade.

When the Revolutionary War began, Salomon identified himself with the American patriot cause, joining the Sons of Liberty. About a month after Washington's defeat and retreat in the Long Island engagement in August 1776, the British arrested Salomon as a spy. His British captors gave him a break when they learned that Salomon was fluent in German and could serve as an interpreter for the German Hessian mercenary soldiers under their command. But when the British found out that Salomon was encouraging the Hessians to desert the war effort against the Americans, he was arrested and imprisoned again in 1778—sentenced to death for treason and espionage.[140]

Having amassed some wealth, Salomon offered a bribe his jailors couldn't refuse, and they in turn helped him escape. Salomon and his family fled to the American capital of Philadelphia, where he resumed in earnest his practice as financial agent and broker. With his unique talent for deal-making and his impeccable reputation of integrity, his business flourished and he quickly became one of the most successful financiers in his newly adopted city, which got the attention of the Continental Congress and delegate Robert Morris in particular, who was responsible for funding the provisioning of Washington and the Continental Army. Salomon's reputation also led to his becoming the exclusive agent to the French consul, as well as the paymaster for the French forces in North America, and he brokered the sale of a majority of the war aid from France and the Dutch Republic through the sale of bills of exchange to American merchants.[141] In fact, Salomon is mentioned some seventy-five times in Morris's personal correspondence relating to selling bills of exchange to raise money for the Revolution.[142]

In the end, Washington's success in a few key strategic victories that kept hope alive and his will to wear down, outlast, and demoralize the British forces paid off. More than six years after he first engaged the British in Boston, the stage was set with the help of the French army and navy to deliver a final knockout blow to the British. In August of 1781, Washington had met up with French general Rochambeau on the west side of the Hudson in New York. They had decided to march their respective armies together to Virginia and attempt to trap British general Cornwallis in the coastal town of Yorktown, while the French fleet would simultaneously establish a naval bombardment front offshore.

But Washington was without funds for food, supplies, and munitions to make that 350-mile march and succeed with adequate firepower. When Washington learned from Robert Morris—the Continental Congress delegate in charge of financing the war effort—that there were neither funds nor credit available, Washington told him, "Send for Haym Salomon." Salomon promptly found buyers for various "bills of exchange" he had on the books and provided Washington the critical and timely funds for the provisioning the long march and the munitions for ultimate victory at Yorktown, Virginia, in October of 1781.[143]

General Washington had pulled off the impossible: that of leading the inexperienced and poorly equipped Continental Army to defeating Great Britain—then the world's most powerful empire and advanced military power. Washington overcame the overwhelming odds on the ground with a spiritual power from on high that combined faith in the cause of American independence with unwavering perseverance, making possible a final victory little short of miraculous. It would take another two years after the British surrender at Yorktown for the Treaty of Paris to be formalized in 1783. After the war, financial records sum up that Haym Salomon's fundraising and personal lending provided over $650,000 (more than $10 billion in current dollars) for Washington and the war effort,[144] as well as for compensation of key members of the Continental Congress, such as James Madison and James Wilson.

Toward the end of the war, the Continental Congress came to be known as the Confederation Congress and continued to be the governing body of the United States for the next eight years, up until March 4, 1789, when the Constitution went into effect after ratification by the states.

The first attempt at reforming the Articles of Confederation in 1786 failed, and it was agreed that there should be a second meeting of delegates from all the states for the purpose of drafting a new Constitution out of the Articles of Confederation. The meeting would be in Philadelphia starting on May 25, 1787, and it came to be known as the Constitutional Convention.

The Confederation Congress was also meeting in Philadelphia simultaneously with the Constitutional Convention, and its main purpose at that time was to establish governing principles for the Northwest Territories, which consisted of what later became the states of Ohio, Indiana, Michigan, Illinois, Wisconsin, and part of Minnesota. What is noteworthy is that the Constitutional Convention was barely at the midpoint of their debates and drafting of the new Constitution, when the Confederation Congress passed the Northwest Ordinance on July 13, 1787, which established the governing rules for the Northwest Territory. It outlined the process for admitting new states to the Union—carved out of that territory—and guaranteed that newly created states would be equal to the original thirteen states. The Northwest Ordinance of 1787 protected civil liberties and outlawed slavery in the new territories and states.[145] So, even before the Constitution had been drafted, a large portion of the founders had spoken out against and legislated to prohibit slavery. And although there was anti-slavery sentiment among a number of the Constitutional Convention delegates from the Southern States, it was not addressed in a substantive way, except inserting language in article 1, section 9 of the Constitution to prohibit slave trade after 1808.

Delegates to the Constitutional Convention included: George Washington, James Madison, George Mason, Alexander Hamilton, and Ben Franklin, and some fifty others, eight of whom had signed the Declaration of Independence. Washington's reputation for undaunted courage in battle, dedication to his troops, reverence for the Almighty, and the staid and confident poise of a leader preceded him to Philadelphia, and he was the unanimous choice to serve as president of the Constitutional Convention. And, not surprisingly, after the Constitution's ratification by the states, on February 4, 1789, the nation's first Electoral College unanimously chose George Washington to be the first president of the United States. He was reelected unanimously for a second term, and the American people clamored for him to stay on for a third, but the founding father knew it was time to step aside.

Washington's final gift to his country was his Farewell Address, which he called "a warning from a departing friend." Prophetic in nature, it was a penetrating articulation of the key threats to freedom and the republican form of American democracy: the failure of institutions to keep people informed and enlightened, the problems of factions and hyper-partisanship, and the decline of religious obligation and national morality. So impressive was it, that Washington's Farewell Address was more widely printed than the Declaration of Independence.[146]

That parting exposition from Washington specifically described the problems facing the American republic in the need "for enlightened public opinion," and the harm from "the alternate domination of one faction over another, sharpened by the spirit of revenge...[which] serves always to distract the public councils...enfeeble the public administration...agitate the community with ill-founded jealousies and false alarms." Washington also believed that the inner strength and morality of the nation could not be sustained without religion. On this, the Farewell Address is as relevant today as it was then, wherein Washington asked, "Where is the security for property, for reputation, for life, if the sense of religious obligation desert the oaths which are the instruments of investigation in courts of justice?"

* * *

Abraham Lincoln was born in 1809, some twelve years after Washington left office. He would be elected sixteenth president of the United States in 1860 and immediately confront the greatest crisis in American history. At that time, the nation was being literally ripped apart as a result of a growing number of Southern states asserting their rights to secede from the Union, claiming their Constitutional state rights to manage their own internal affairs—which permitted the use of slave labor—in their own way. When he took office, Lincoln knew the challenges he faced with secession, the abolition of slavery, and likely civil war, were beyond his or anyone's capability to solve.

What endears many to think of Abraham Lincoln as one of the greatest presidents is in part that he embodied the American Dream. He was almost entirely self-taught; overcame poverty, hardships, and the dangers of a frontier life; and bore the painful loss of two sons and other close personal associates, yet he succeeded in achieving the highest office in the land. But there is so much more to the story.

Born in Kentucky, Abe and his sister Sarah were still infants when their parents, Thomas and Nancy, moved to find greater economic opportunity. Just five years later, they moved again, farther west into the frontier—this time from Kentucky to Indiana. There were only three books in their one-room prairie log cabin—the Bible, the Catechism, and a spelling book.[147] Abe had little formal schooling, spending less than a year in any classroom in his upbringing, but his mother helped instill in him a love of learning, and reading the Bible was the best source. Unfortunately, they were settled in their new Indiana home for just two years when Abe's mother died of what was then known as milk disease.

Within two years, Abe's father remarried to Sally Bush, who loved her new stepchildren as her own and continued to raise them with the Bible being the center of the home and their education. This was a time when the Bible was almost universally read and was considered the reference source for society's thinking, even as life on the frontier had its share of bad actors and was extraordinarily tough for most everyone. His stepmother also helped Abe through the struggles of adolescent years by encouraging his intellectual curiosity.

Abe was a late bloomer. Being independent and more cerebral, he didn't want to follow in his father's footsteps of a career of manual labor that would exhaust him and crowd out the life of the mind. He tried many things and held many different jobs, including delivering goods on two long "float trip" voyages down the Mississippi River to New Orleans. There his eyes were opened to the dark side of human nature—from horse thieves, poker sharps, and squatters to prostitutes. But it was the inhumane practices of shackled slaves being marched out of the city toward cotton plantations that stuck in his mind.

At age twenty-two, Abe Lincoln realized it was time to strike out on his own. He decided to settle and find opportunity in New Salem, Illinois—a walk of about a hundred miles. New Salem was a small town of fifteen log cabins, and he was welcomed. Being tall and strong and having so many colorful stories from his frontier upbringing, Abe found that respect and friendship came naturally. And with his reading skills and high character, he had no trouble in finding new work opportunities, as a clerk, postmaster, storekeeper, and surveyor.

While self-taught, Abe recognized the value of learned neighbors and mentors—especially those who could loan him books. Over the course of the next few years, he borrowed every book in town and from miles around—broadening his horizons with Shakespeare, *Robinson Crusoe*, Parson Weems's biography of Washington, and Ben Franklin's autobiography, to name only a few. One of his mentors, Justice of the Peace Bowling Green, introduced him to Blackstone's *Commentaries on the Law*, and helped launch his career as a lawyer. Green also recognized Lincoln's oratory skills and encouraged him to run for public office.[148] And so it was that when he was twenty-five, Abraham Lincoln got elected to the Illinois legislature as a member of the Whig Party, which he supported because of its platform principles of growth, development, progress, and freedom.

Lincoln would be reelected three more times, and during those eight years serving in the Illinois state legislature, he met Stephen Douglas. In one of his reelection campaign speeches delivered to the Young Men's Lyceum of Springfield, Illinois on January 27, 1838, Lincoln spoke about the dangers of slavery in the United States, as the chief institutional threat likely to corrupt the federal government and destroy the United States from mob violence that could undermine the rule of law.[149]

In 1840, now living in Springfield, the capitol of Illinois, Abraham Lincoln was engaged to Mary Todd and they would marry two years later at the end of his fourth and last state congressional term.

Lincoln then set his sights on running for the 7th US congressional seat from Illinois. Though Lincoln failed in his bid in 1844, he was successful in 1846. However, he would be a one-term congressman. Having immersed himself in politics at the state and national level for fourteen years—and now having lost reelection—Lincoln was empty and despondent as he returned home to Springfield, Illinois. He recognized that politics neither satisfied his need for deep and lasting meaning, nor did it provide spiritual sustenance.

This began Lincoln's wilderness years. It became particularly difficult in early 1850 when his four-year-old son Eddie died of tuberculosis. Devastated, feeling alone, and grieving, Lincoln went back to his roots in the Bible and turned to God, who of course had been there all the time.

The greatest challenge of his life and that of the nation was still more than ten years away, and Lincoln would need further refinement and development to meet those trials. The pastor who had conducted the funeral service for Eddie, turned out to have authored what would become a classic defense of Christianity—a book in which Lincoln got immersed, and which was instrumental in accelerating Lincoln's reconnection with and development of his Christian faith.[150] In ensuing months and years, Lincoln came to realize that he met God more deeply through personal suffering, and that God cared about the fate of nations just as He did about individuals.

Lincoln returned to his law practice, which came back to life and thrived over the next few years. But when Stephen Douglas, then US senator and chairman of the Senate Committee on Territories, introduced the bill that passed into law known as the Kansas-Nebraska Act of 1854, which extended slavery into new states, Lincoln became aroused as never before. He firmly believed that Americans should not tolerate something as inhumane as slavery—which by then had existed on American soil for over two hundred years—without taking a moral stand on the issue. More and more, Lincoln reached back to the Declaration of Independence and to the book of Genesis in the Bible, wherein God created all people equal in his own image and endowed them with the unalienable rights of life, liberty, and the pursuit of happiness.

The Kansas-Nebraska Act spurred the creation of the Republican Party, formed initially to keep slavery out of the new western territories, and Lincoln felt compelled to reenter the political arena as a candidate for the US Senate in 1855. He canvassed throughout the state and his speeches got more popular attention than ever, but it came to naught as the state legislature decided the outcome for Senate candidates at that time.

Lincoln received the Republican nomination for the US Senate again in 1858 to run against Democratic incumbent Stephen Douglas. In his acceptance speech for the nomination, Lincoln declared that "a house divided against itself cannot stand" and that "this government cannot endure permanently half slave and half free." That speech was pivotal, for it revealed to the American people that Lincoln was a visionary who fully grasped the long-term impact of slavery on the nation and its people.

Lincoln then went on to challenge Douglas to a series of debates on a range of topics related to slavery that had divided the nation into hostile camps that threatened the survival of the Union. Those debates did not deliver the senatorial election in Lincoln's favor, but with transcripts being widely reprinted in newspapers across the country, they served to educate voters and set the stage for Lincoln to win an Electoral College landslide in the presidential election of 1860.[151]

On the eve of departing Springfield for the White House in early 1861, Lincoln shared with his longstanding and faithful law partner, William Herndon, "the feeling which had become irrepressible that he would never return alive."[152] Departing from the Springfield train station, Lincoln told the crowd, "I now leave, not knowing when or whether ever I may return, with a task greater than that which rested on Washington. Without the assistance of that Divine Being who ever attended him, I cannot succeed. With that assistance I cannot fail."[153]

Lincoln's inauguration on March 4, 1861, was accompanied by challenges the likes of which no other president encountered—with seven states of the Deep South having declared their independence by seceding, and the Confederate States of America being formally established with its own constitution and government and Jefferson Davis as its elected president. A month later, the American Civil War began when Confederate forces fired on Union-held Fort Sumter in South Carolina.

Although there was no declaration of war on either side, President Lincoln rejected the Southern States' rights of secession, and asserted that the position of the Union was that the Southern States were in an unacceptable state of rebellion from the United States. He stated further that he believed secession would lead to anarchy and destroy the world's only existing democracy. Lincoln's legal reasoning was that all states had pledged loyalty to each other as the United States, and that status was confirmed by each state voting to ratify the Constitution. This was debatable and the consensus of the seceding Southern States was that their legal right for separation was implicit in both the Declaration and the Constitution, and then reinforced by the debates around amending the Bill of Rights and further debates during the ratification process.

Lincoln had stated in his first inaugural address that the Federal government would not go to war unless the Confederate states initiated it. So why did the Confederates appear to have executed such a classical folly, by firing on Fort Sumter, which jeopardized their states' rights?

The Southern States' view was that Lincoln had acted aggressively towards the South before they initiated fire by ordering the sending of a perceived hostile fleet to reinforce Fort Sumter. Confederate Vice President Alexander Stephens argued that the essential truth was that "it is not he who strikes the first blow, or fires the first gun that inaugurates or begins conflict." Rather, the true aggressor is "the first who renders force necessary."[154] General Beauregard's troops did fire the "first gun" on Fort Sumter, but that decision may have been made on the basis of an imminent arrival of a hostile fleet in Charleston Harbor, which would have exposed his troops to fire from two fronts: Fort Sumter cannons at the front and the Union naval cannons from the harbor to the rear.

For Lincoln, the attack on Fort Sumter was justification for calling up seventy-five thousand men to put down the "Confederate rebellion." Regardless of fault, the die was cast and the Civil War was under way. But things did not go well for Lincoln in that first year, highlighted by a major Confederate victory at the Battle of Bull Run thirty miles from Washington, DC, in late July 1861.

There has clearly been moral mythology surrounding Lincoln, encapsulated by his nickname Honest Abe. However, when Lincoln entered politics, there were times he became a fence-straddling politician wanting to have it both ways—for instance, in favor of and opposed to racial equality—depending on the audience he was speaking to. What Honest Abe found in war politics was the need to maintain double standards on some issues such as slavery and, at other times, he retained the prerogative to suspend law and abuse power against people who exercised their free conscience in taking political positions that were opposed to his policy objectives. For instance, within a few months of the commencement of the Civil War, Lincoln ordered and carried out the arrest on August 7, 1861, of all pro-Confederate members of the General Assembly of Maryland, fearing they might possibly vote to secede from the Union. A year and a half later, when Lincoln proclaimed the Emancipation Proclamation, he did so knowing he would not enforce slavery's abolition in Maryland and perhaps other border states, allowing slavery to continue there until the end of the Civil war.

With Washington, DC, being surrounded by two states—Maryland, a border state that allowed slaveholding, and Virginia, a Confederate slaveholding state—Lincoln felt compelled to take steps to prevent Maryland from joining forces with Confederacy, which would have made the Union's capital and seat of government an island in hostile territory.

Tragedy struck Abe and Mary Lincoln again early in 1862 when eleven-year-old son Willie died of typhoid. And with the war effort in year two not going well—with defeats by Confederate forces in the Seven Days Battle of Richmond in June and the Second Battle of Bull Run in August—Lincoln found himself in a state like Washington's at Valley Forge, beseeching God for help in yet the deepest valley of his life.

Lincoln acknowledged that Confederates prayed to the same God that he and the Union forces prayed to. But he struggled with the uncertainty of why, so far, the Almighty was permitting the bloodbath to continue with more favor being shown toward the South.

It was barely a year and half since Lincoln proclaimed in his first inaugural address that he "would act to preserve the union," but also "not interfere with the right of each state to order and control its own domestic institutions...." But with a baptism by fire since the moment he had stepped into the White House, he now was brought to his knees imploring God's help.

And through his prayer life, that help came, and Lincoln had an epiphany of moral clarity, realizing that it was not enough to win the war, put down secession, uphold what was then law, and preserve the status quo of tolerance of slavery in the Southern states, as he had stated in his first inaugural address upon taking office. He realized the simple truth that God could not bless the Union's war efforts unless the goal was aligned with God's will and announced to all. It was analogous to the founders' recognition that the Declaration was a necessary spiritual condition to win the War of Independence.

As the middle of the year 1862 approached, Lincoln felt called to act on this by issuing an Emancipation Proclamation to abolish the legitimacy of slavery. But Lincoln also knew that such a decree needed to come at the right time, just as the founders knew that a delay in the release of the fifty-six-signature Declaration was necessary—so as not to appear rash or as an act of desperation, but rather when their side was showing strength. On July 22, he told his cabinet, "I made a solemn vow before God that if General Lee were driven back from Pennsylvania, I would crown the result with the declaration of freedom for the slaves."[155]

It turns out that Lincoln did not have to wait very long. In early September, Confederate general Robert E. Lee planned a military campaign with his able subordinate commanders Jackson and Longstreet to gain decisive victories against divisions under General McClellan in the Union home turf territory northwest of Washington, DC, Lee's battle plan was to divide up his fifty-five thousand Confederate troops under his direct command on that campaign so as to capture Union supplies at Harpers Ferry, while others crossed over the Potomac from Virginia to Maryland in separate divisions and converged on the anticipated main battleground between the town of Sharpsburg and Antietam Creek.

In one of those "miraculous accidents" of history, one of the Union soldiers under McClellan's command who had camped in the same field that Lee's troops had passed through only days before spotted a peculiar hand-folded small parcel on the ground. He picked it up, only to find a copy of Lee's battle plan orders folded and tied around three cigars.

That intelligence—immediately passed up the chain of command—enabled McClellan to change the Union battle plan and redeploy forces to isolate and neutralize the separated divisions of Lee's army, which prevented them from reinforcing the Confederates in what would be the main Battle of Antietam.

The bloodiest battle to date with over twenty-two thousand casualties, Antietam proved to be a victory for Lincoln and the Union forces, for it blunted Lee's invasion of the North and forced his withdrawal to Confederate Virginia. It was also a key early turning point in the Civil War—preventing the British and French from recognizing the Confederacy.[156] But perhaps most importantly, it was an answer to Lincoln's prayer, signaling it was time to make public the Emancipation Proclamation to abolish slavery. And so it was that, after the Emancipation Proclamation was signed into law on January 1, 1863, things on the ground began to change.

The next major battle was at Gettysburg, Pennsylvania, which took place July 1–3, 1863. Lincoln's cabinet members were anxious and implored him to take refuge for personal safety and flee the White House and Washington, believing that Lee would turn the Confederate Army on

Washington after winning in Gettysburg, which was only sixty-five miles away. But Lincoln was so confident of a favorable outcome from divine intervention that he stayed in the White House with both relative peace and confidence in the outcome of that mammoth battle. And victory for the Union at Gettysburg did come.

By mid-1863, Union victories in Gettysburg, Pennsylvania, and Vicksburg, Mississippi, confirmed the new triumphant trajectory that would bring an end to the long and agonizing Civil War, saving the Union and ending the scourge of slavery. Gettysburg, the bloodiest battle with over fifty-one thousand casualties, had a huge impact on Lincoln, who acknowledged, "When I went to Gettysburg and saw the graves of thousands of our soldiers, I then and there consecrated myself to Christ."

Early in his presidency, Lincoln often said that the duration of the Civil War was in God's hands. But in the Gettysburg Address, he left no room for doubt about the final outcome, that America would "have a new birth of freedom and that government of the people, by the people, for the people, shall not perish from the earth."

Lincoln was more uniquely gifted than Washington in his ability to combine poetic wartime rhetoric with sound policy. He eloquently linked the preservation of the Union with the emancipation of slaves and, perhaps even more significantly, with the larger cause of human freedom in the world. Lincoln's speeches were so succinctly moving that they would be memorized by generations of American schoolchildren. In the words of the great twentieth-century political philosopher Walter Berns, Lincoln's rhetoric made him the American counterpart of "what Shakespeare was for the English or Homer for the Greeks."

Union forces had decisive victories across the Southern states in the latter half of 1864. An end to the Civil War was now in sight, which contributed to an overwhelming reelection of Lincoln in November that year. In Lincoln's second inaugural address on March 4, 1865, we see a wartime president transformed, displaying yet another profound dimension to his character, captured in his closing words: "With malice toward none; with charity for all," he said, "let us...bind up the nation's wounds; to care for him who shall have borne the battle, and for his widow, and his orphan—to do all which may achieve and cherish a just and lasting peace among ourselves, and with all nations."

Confederate general Robert E. Lee surrendered the following month on April 9, 1865. Five days later, on Good Friday, a bullet from the gun of assassin John Wilkes Booth killed Lincoln at Ford's Theatre in Washington. Perhaps it was in some way providential that Good Friday was Lincoln's last, for some forty-four years later, the greatest literary figure in the West, Leo Tolstoy, called Lincoln "a Christ in Miniature." Sadly, Lincoln's death deprived an exhausted and broken nation of the benefits of a second term from a man transformed by God and the war, who, in spite of earlier compromises and inconsistencies, emerged as a spiritual giant of compassion and reconciliation. The nation desperately needed the magnanimous leadership of Lincoln for Reconstruction, but it was not to be.

In Washington, as the founder of the United States, and Lincoln, as its savior, we are confronted with flawed men who made mistakes, but whose remarkable qualities of character were so formidable that they became part of the essence of what we call "American exceptionalism." Both presidents would readily admit that it was not their abilities that made the difference, but rather their faith, trust, and reliance on God that gave them their strength and opened the way for ultimate success.

What is also noteworthy is that both Washington and Lincoln agreed that America's greatest threat to its sovereignty as a Constitutional Republic would not come from a military threat from a foreign power. Rather, America's downfall would come from within.

We mentioned how Washington's Farewell Address was prophetic in nature in describing the three sources of peril to liberty and the American Republic that are as relevant now as they were then: the failure of citizens to be well-informed; internal division because of party factions and hyper-partisanship; and the decline of religious obligation and national morality.

Lincoln said, "If [danger] ever reach us it must spring up amongst us; it cannot come from abroad. If destruction be our lot we must ourselves be its author and finisher. As a nation of freemen we must live through all time or die by suicide."[157]

Washington and Lincoln were unique and very different in personality, but both were men of wisdom, vision, courage, and persistence. Both were humble, unselfish, and willing to sacrifice their lives for the greater good of establishing and preserving a nation that would be unique in providing its people the freedom and right to pursue life, liberty, and happiness, and to empower the nation to be the light and beacon of hope for the world.

Presidents' Day offers us the opportunity to think about the qualities of these two unique individual leaders—the greatest American presidents. To the extent we can internalize and build character around the virtues that each embodied, we, too, can achieve great things, find greater meaning as individuals, and gain deeper understanding and commitment to a more active citizenship to keep government accountable.

CHAPTER 9

Martin Luther King Day: The Fulfillment of the Ideas Conceived in the Declaration and Advanced by Lincoln

Martin Luther King Day is unique among American holidays in that it honors the one American who delivered the fulfillment of a core value expressed both in the country's founding Declaration of Independence in 1776 and in President Abraham Lincoln's Gettysburg Address in 1863.

The Declaration's self-evident truth "that all men are created equal, that they are endowed by their Creator with certain unalienable Rights, that among these are Life, Liberty, and the Pursuit of Happiness," wasn't realized when the US Constitution was ratified some fourteen years after the Declaration. Nor was Lincoln's Gettysburg proposition "that all men are created equal" fulfilled through the Civil War and the Emancipation Proclamation that abolished slavery.

While the Founding Fathers were the first in human history to pen such a revolutionary statement, they were really setting the trajectory of those ideals, the fulfillment of which would require time and effort. What we need to remember is that the time and dedicated efforts that it would take to achieve those goals does not diminish them.

Nearly half the fifty-five delegates who had come to the Philadelphia Convention in May 1787 to replace the Articles of Confederation by drafting a Constitution for the newly formed United States were from six Southern slave-holding states. Many of the delegates from these states and almost the entirety of delegates from the Northern states were morally opposed to slavery, but all were in a quandary—recognizing that tolerance and compromise would be required to create a new nation at that time out of diverse states with very different economies and social classes.

Ultimately, the Constitution's wording avoided any mention of slaves or slavery, but it established a legislative framework to enact new laws to correct injustice, such as inequality between racial classes. It also included the provision in section 9 of article 1 that ended the slave trade in 1808.

The Constitution had to be drafted in such a way as to assure ratification, and to provide the substance for a limited democratic government that could bring unity and provide essential resources, such as providing for the military defense of the nation. The compromise with slavery was seen as temporary, and it was generally believed that it would diminish and die of its own accord in the near future by moral conviction of the vast majority and then by the force of law in a Constitutional amendment of abolition.

As it turned out, the institution of slavery that had become woven into the economic fabric of the Southern states did not die out of its own accord or by the recognition of being morally repugnant and illegitimate. That evil would in the end be eradicated by a greater force, what turned out to be a Civil War.

The reelection of Lincoln for a second term in the face of an all but defeated Confederacy provided hope of more than just the end of slavery. While the nation was more divided than it had been at any previous time, Lincoln had a unique ability to see both sides, and he had a deep heart for national reconciliation, best described in his own words in his second inaugural address on March 5, 1865:

With malice toward none, with charity for all, with firmness in the right as God gives us to see the right, let us strive on to finish the work we are in, to bind up the nation's wounds, to care for him who shall have borne the battle and for his widow and his orphan, to do all which may achieve and cherish a just and lasting peace among ourselves and with all nations.

The .41-caliber bullet with which John Wilkes Booth would assassinate Lincoln in Ford's Theatre five weeks later, on the night of April 14, 1865, may have been the most lethal gunshot in American history, "bringing more distress, disaster and dishonor upon the South than all the bullets fired by the two million Union soldiers during the entire period of the Civil war."[158] Only five days earlier, Confederate General Robert E. Lee had surrendered to Union General Ulysses S. Grant at Appomattox Court House, Virginia—effectively ending the Civil War. But now, the compassionate man and president to whom so many Americans looked for guidance in reconstructing the war-ravaged South and bringing about national reconciliation was gone.

Lincoln's Gettysburg Address that closed with the vision "that this nation, under God, shall have a new birth of freedom" gives us some sense of how Lincoln would have administered reconstruction. Many forget that from 1862, Lincoln faced a political challenge from a sizeable radical wing of his Republican Party, who wanted to take a more punitive stance toward the Confederate States. In an effort to forestall vindictiveness from those radicals in Congress, in 1863, Lincoln took the initiative to start shaping Reconstruction in Confederate states under Union control—such as in Louisiana, Arkansas, and Tennessee—by installing military governors of his choosing.

Lincoln had a heart to lift blacks out of poverty and dependence, expressed as early as his 1860 campaign speech in which he said, "I want every man to have the chance—and I believe a black man is entitled to it—in which he can better his condition."[159] Lincoln expressed a commitment to extend voting rights in January 1864, noting that even if the Confederates resisted trading amnesty for voting rights, there was really no alternative. Lincoln believed it was only the voting power of the newly freed slaves that could offset the political dominance of whites in the South.

One of Lincoln's presidential campaign appeals was to save the new Western territories from the scourge of legitimizing slavery. Lincoln seems to have regarded the West as an attendant part of Reconstruction with homestead legislation and his Freedmen's Bureau being able to not only claim and redistribute land abandoned by plantation owners in Confederate states, but also to open up huge tracts of public land in the Western territories to private ownership to former slaves to farm as their own.

As successful as Lincoln was in his moral and eloquent speeches, he also faced the political challenges of reelection in 1864, when there was still some insecurity about the outcome of the Civil War. His calling to bring about healing and national reconciliation required a second term. But without military victory of the Union forces before November 1864, Lincoln felt somewhat uncertain about reelection. Many forget that this is why Lincoln decided to replace his first-term Republican vice president, Hannibal Hamlin, with Andrew Johnson—a Southern War Democrat who had opposed secession from the Union. Lincoln believed that having Johnson on the ticket would help deliver Southern votes and secure reelection.

While Lincoln's political calculation may have assured his reelection, his assassination meant that Vice President Johnson would take over as president in leading the nation just as the Civil War was ending. Johnson appeared to be aligned with much of Lincoln's vision favoring measured steps to bring the South back into the Union, but he lacked the vision, compassion, and leadership skills of Lincoln, and he didn't view blacks as equals.

In January 1865, General Sherman sought to carry out Lincoln's policy to extend land ownership to blacks, issuing Field Order No. 15, which reserved island and coastal land in Georgia and South Carolina for black settlement. Each family would get forty acres and a mule. Less than a year after Sherman's order, after forty thousand former slaves had settled on four hundred thousand acres of coastal land, Johnson intervened and ordered most of that land returned to its former owners—dispossessing tens of thousands of black landholders.

Johnson also accommodated the Southern states' prerogatives to establish their own racial policies, which came to be known as Black Codes. The Black Codes were established between 1865 and 1867 and were a series of restrictive laws on civil rights, property rights, crime and punishment, and, perhaps most importantly, on labor—to ensure the availability of blacks as a cheap labor force after slavery was abolished.

Increasingly, Johnson found himself at odds with opposition from the Republican-dominated Congress—especially after the Republican Party gained congressional seats and dominated both houses of Congress following the 1866 election. The new Congress favored more far-reaching changes "to revolutionize Southern institutions, habits, and manners"— goals that were vague, unsettling, and disrespectful—prompting resistance from many Southerners.[160]

Part of the failure of the Reconstruction period was also due to the backdrop of a Southern economy in ruins from war devastation. Other contributing factors for distrust, resentment, and failure were related to inconsistent policy implementation and the military occupation of Union troops in many urban areas in the South.

In spite of the legacy of failure associated with the Reconstruction era, there were three constitutional amendments, sometimes called the Reconstruction Amendments, adopted and added to the Constitution during this time. The Thirteenth Amendment abolishing slavery was ratified in 1865. The Fourteenth Amendment guaranteeing US citizenship and federal civil rights to all persons born in the United States was proposed in 1866 and ratified in 1868. The Fifteenth Amendment decreeing that the right to vote could not be denied because of "race, color, or previous condition of servitude," was passed in 1870.

Unfortunately, these Reconstruction Amendments established rights that were largely negated by the rise of Jim Crow laws in the late 1870s— to legalize racial segregation and marginalize blacks by denying them the right to vote, hold jobs, attend school, live and buy property anywhere for many decades. Many forget that the impetus for separating the races, which was the essence of Jim Crow Laws that legalized segregation, actually started in the North before the Civil War.[161] But it was the power of the Constitution and the legal foundation of those Reconstruction Amendments that led to Supreme Court rulings in the mid-twentieth century that would strike down school segregation and open the way for the civil rights movement and new laws ending segregation and guaranteeing the right to vote.

Because prejudice and racism are engrained attitudes—a condition of hardened hearts—they cannot be entirely removed or eradicated by laws, judicial rulings, and politics. Changing attitudes requires spiritual transformation and that is largely the work of the church and spiritual leaders. And it turns out that Martin Luther King, Jr. would be that leader within the black community with the heart, wisdom, courage, and patient temperament to succeed where others before him could not.

When Martin Luther King came of age in Atlanta in the 1940s, Jim Crow laws were entrenched, mandating racial segregation in public facilities and transportation, including the coaches of interstate trains and buses, public schools, public places, local buses, restaurants, parks, cemeteries, theatres, public bathrooms, and even drinking fountains. Jim Crow laws had been codified at local and state levels and justified with the famous "separate but equal" decision of the US Supreme Court in *Plessy v. Ferguson* in 1896.

King was clearly gifted, entering Morehouse College when he was fifteen and graduating with a BA in 1948 at age nineteen. He chose to follow in his father's footsteps in the ministry and earned a theology doctorate from Boston University. After marrying Coretta Scott on June 18, 1953, he began a search for a full-time pastoral position, not realizing that the stage was being set with perfect timing for his life's work by the Supreme Court's reversal of *Plessy* in its May 17, 1954 *Brown v. Board of Education of Topeka* decision, in which segregation in public schools was declared unconstitutional. And of course, by extension, that ruling applied to other public facilities.

It was probably providential that everything would come together for Dr. King with a pastorship job offering at the Dexter Avenue Baptist Church in Montgomery, Alabama—then one of America's most segregated cities and destined to be the epicenter of a dignity-and-civil-rights movement whose time had come. Reverend Martin King was installed as pastor there on October 31, 1954.

King's first sermon was delivered with the admonition of Paul from Romans 12:2 that says, "Do not conform to the pattern of this world, but be transformed by the renewing of your mind." The congregation and the wider world were in for a powerful awakening. King would quote from Thomas Jefferson: "I have sworn upon the alter of God eternal hostility against every form of tyranny over the mind of man."[162] And he went on to say that "in these days of worldwide confusion there is a dire need for men and women who will courageously do battle for truth."

Right from his first sermon, Martin Luther King had a gifted ability to frame social injustice with the roots of causality within man, and also explain solutions in a timeless way with broad future applications. His first sermon that "the hope of a secure and livable world lies with disciplined nonconformists…" made that point. And he concluded by saying, "The trailblazers in human, academic, scientific, and religious freedom have always been nonconformists. In any cause that concerns the progress of mankind, put your faith in the nonconformist!"[163]

From the very beginning of his Dexter Avenue church ministry, King would speak about and confront injustice by combining theology with social change utilizing words and sermons as given to him by God combined with nonviolent confrontation. King believed the best measure of truth in carrying out God's work was in discerning the fruit of action, noting that "the aftermath of nonviolence is the creation of the Beloved Community, while the aftermath of [conflict and] violence is tragic bitterness."[164]

When Rosa Parks, secretary of the Montgomery chapter of the NAACP, showed up at the Dexter Avenue Baptist Church to learn about nonviolent resistance, King may have doubted that she would be capable of using nonviolent skills in the challenging field that lay ahead in the civil rights movement. But four days later, he would get the answer when Parks stood firm against humiliation of discrimination—refusing to give up her public bus seat to a white passenger. That led to her arrest and triggered the Montgomery Bus Boycott, a nonviolent action that went on for more than a year. An attendant part of the plan by all the blacks to boycott the public bus system in Montgomery was their establishing a voluntary carpool in order to get people to and from their jobs. For nearly a full year, that carpool functioned exceedingly well. That was until Montgomery Mayor Gayle took legal action to stop the operation of the carpool.

On the very eve of the legal decision to order the shutdown, King gathered with the leaders of the carpool—discouraged as they all were—and reminded them that, "We have moved all these months in the daring faith that God is with us in our struggle…. Tonight we must believe that a way will be made out of no way."[165]

The next morning in court, just as it was becoming clear that the judge was moving ahead with ruling in the affirmative to enforce a city-wide carpool shutdown, a recess was called. There was an unusual commotion near the bench, with reporters coming and going. Moments later, it was disclosed that an official notice had been delivered, stating, "The United States Supreme Court today unanimously ruled bus segregation unconstitutional in Montgomery, Alabama." Someone in the back of the courtroom shouted, "God Almighty has spoken from Washington."[166] And so it appeared.

The success of the Montgomery Bus Boycott was a catalyst for a spiritual revival and restoration of dignity and minority rights throughout the South, and King was sought after to teach and give speeches and sermons. He was asked to give a sermon to commemorate the second anniversary of the Supreme Court's desegregation decision in *Brown v. Board of Education* at New York City's Cathedral of St. John the Divine before a full house of over twelve thousand on May 17, 1956. King took that occasion to tackle one of the most difficult questions of theology: Why does God permit evil to persist rather than eradicate it with his sovereign power. Phrased differently, why does God allow man to suffer—sometimes for long periods?

King framed the question of why slavery and inequality were permitted in America for as long as they were by pointing to the Hebrew people—the Israelites—who were held under the yoke of slavery for four hundred years. "Egypt symbolized evil in the form of humiliating oppression, ungodly exploitation, and crushing domination," said King, "and the Israelites symbolized goodness in the form of devotion and dedication to the God of Abraham, Isaac, and Jacob."[167] Yet it took four hundred years for God to find a man—Moses—who had the determination and character to persevere through ten plague trials and lead the Israelites out of Egypt and across the Red Sea on a journey to the promised land.

It took eighty-seven years from the nation's founding Declaration of Independence to Lincoln's Emancipation Proclamation, King noted, "thus bringing [the Negro] nearer to the Red Sea…" with political and social opportunities opening up during the Reconstruction. But with the 1896 "separate but equal" decision of the Supreme Court in *Plessy v. Ferguson*, and the rise of Jim Crow laws across the South, King lamented that "the Negro soon discovered that the pharaohs of the South were determined to keep him in slavery."[168]

While there was cause for celebration in King's sermon at the Cathedral of St. John the Divine, acknowledging the hand of God being at work with the Supreme Court's *Brown v. Board of Education* decision on desegregation, there was also an acknowledgment that much remained to be done to realize God's ideal of equality. "The Kingdom of God as a universal reality is not yet," said King, "because sin exists on every level of man's existence…[and] the death of one tyranny is followed by the emergence of another tyranny."[169]

The power and resonance of King's message and action thrust him into a leadership role, helping found, in January 1957, the Southern Christian Leadership Conference (SCLC), located in Atlanta, Georgia. He continued to develop the theory and practice of nonviolent resistance pioneered by Mahatma Gandhi with Christ's teaching that unconditional love for one's adversaries is the best and most moral response for the downtrodden to bring about positive social change. He stressed three interrelated elements.

First, King taught that nonviolent resistance does not seek to defeat or humiliate the opponent, but to win his friendship and understanding. The end is redemption and reconciliation and the creation of the beloved community, in contrast to violence, which only begets more hostility and violence.

A second key teaching in King's approach to nonviolent response is to recognize that the attack is directed against forces of evil rather than against persons, who are often caught up in forces they don't fully understand. On overcoming segregation, King said, "The tension in this city is not between white people and Negro people. The tension is at bottom between justice and injustice, between the forces of light and the forces of darkness. And if there is a victory it will be a victory not merely for 50,000 Negroes, but a victory for justice and the forces of light. We are out to defeat injustice and not white persons who may happen to be unjust."[170]

The third dimension of nonviolent resistance is that its center is Christ's standard of love, which is to love your enemy. Oppressed people must never allow themselves to become bitter or indulge in hate, for to respond in hate or vindictiveness would only invoke retaliation and intensify more hate. Keeping love in the center of our lives enables the projection of goodwill in both demeanor and in action, thus breaking the chain of hate.[171]

King championed minority rights, marching for labor and voting rights and conducting sit-ins and prayer vigils. On Good Friday, April 12, 1963, King defied a state court's injunction and led a nonviolent demonstration and protest against discriminatory treatment of blacks in Birmingham, Alabama. Peacefully marching from the 16th Avenue Baptist Church, he was arrested and jailed. In solitary confinement, King read a newspaper statement of eight local clergymen, who criticized his activities being the work of an opportunist and outside instigator that is "unwise and untimely."

From that jail cell, with no assistance or reference books, King penned a response to those clergymen that proved to be a timeless and truly inspired document that accurately drew on the work of St. Augustine and St. Thomas Aquinas. He wrote:

> An unjust law is a human law that is not rooted in eternal and natural law. Any law that uplifts human personality is just. Any law that degrades human personality is unjust. All segregation statutes are unjust because segregation distorts the soul and damages the personality. It gives the segregator a false sense of superiority and the segregated a false sense of inferiority. Thus it is that I can urge men to obey the 1954 decision of the Supreme Court, for it is morally right; and I can urge them to disobey segregation ordinances, for they are morally wrong.[172]

He concluded his letter by asserting, "We will reach the goal of freedom in Birmingham and all over the nation, because the goal of America is freedom...[and] our destiny is tied up with America's destiny." Furthermore, wrote King, "We will win our freedom because the sacred heritage of our nation and the eternal will of God are embodied in our echoing demands."

That letter, smuggled out of the jail by King's lawyer, was known as his "Letter from a Birmingham Jail," which was reprinted in prominent journals across America and came to be the most important statement that sustained and inspired the civil rights movement. Some historians even rate King's letter as one with the power, merit, and historical significance to be ranked among the most important American documents.

King was recognized as "Man of the Year" by *Time* magazine and received the Nobel Peace Prize in 1964. But the actions that got him accolades from some also brought him threats, beatings, stabbings, bombings, and assassination attempts from other people resisting change. King would go to jail twenty-nine times to advance the cause of freedom and human dignity, ultimately losing his life to an assassin's bullet in 1968.

The life of Martin Luther King, Jr. was not without controversy, such as charges of plagiarizing others' words and exercising poor judgment by allowing communists into his inner circle and leadership roles of the SCLC. Most recently, it has been alleged that King was a womanizer and had numerous affairs. In King's defense is Christ and his teaching that we are all sinners and so are in no position to judge other sinners, and Paul's admonition that we should extend grace, for "all have sinned and fall short of the glory of God." History reveals that God's work has often been carried out by very flawed people. There are countless examples—many covered in this book—when God has worked through flawed people. And it is so because God has only sinners through whom he can work.

In King's most famous "I Have a Dream" speech, delivered before the Lincoln Memorial in Washington on August 28, 1963, it was as if the Almighty was calling America to rise up and fulfill its spiritual destiny declared two hundred years earlier in the Declaration of Independence— that of a self-evident truth "that all men are created equal." To that he added an equally timeless truth, that people "should not be judged by the color of their skin but by the content of their character." It naturally follows that for King, there is no place for identity politics or critical race theory in a moral civil society.

What is particularly moving and powerful about Martin Luther King, Jr. was that he fulfilled the course of redemption in American history that extended over nearly two hundred years, starting with the Declaration of Independence, and continuing with Lincoln's emancipation of slavery. If King were resurrected today, he might be shocked by the regression that has taken place in America in the three generations since he led the civil rights movement of the 1950s and 1960s. He would find the rise of hatred in politics deplorable, just as he would find the wholesale desensitization of young people troubling. He would also find unacceptable the eclipse of group, gender, and ethnic identity paradigm over the merit and character of the individual as the primary criteria for evaluation for acceptance, hiring, and advancement in schools and in the workforce.

King's lesser-known speeches and sermons provide prescient insight for the times in which we live. In a sermon a year before his national recognition from the Birmingham protest and jail time, Rev. King quoted scripture about the need to be "wise as serpents, and harmless as doves," arguing that people need to have a tough mind and a tender heart. He expressed concern that the "prevalent tendency toward softmindedness is found in man's unbelievable gullibility,"[173] further asserting that "few people have the toughness of mind to judge critically and to discern the truth from the false, the fact from the fiction.... One of the great needs of mankind is to be lifted above the morass of false propaganda."[174] He concluded his theme, reminding us that "a nation or a civilization that continues to produce soft-minded men purchases its own spiritual death on the installment plan."[175] Such counsel is more pertinent today than ever with the last few generations of young people being weaker in discernment and character—and more gullible—than prior generations.

We cannot be sure what King's assessment of America today would be. But based on the clarity of his mind expressed in the voluminous record of his many sermons and speeches,[176] he would find the trends on many of the campuses of American universities and colleges today alarming. Witnessing the cancel culture enforcers of safe spaces and gender neutral language, who also want to ban language associated with trigger warnings and microaggressions, King might have a hard time believing his eyes and ears. He might well conclude that if the present generational indoctrination, moral confusion, and misguided pettiness continues unchecked, America's collapse and defeat could easily ensue from adversaries who might not even have to go to war to take power.

In Dr. King's life, death was never far away. He had told his wife, Coretta, after JFK was killed in 1963, "This is what's going to happen to me." He began facing mounting criticism from other black activists, like Malcolm X, who were rejecting King's beloved doctrine of Christian nonviolence, and favoring a more confrontational approach to bring about more and faster change.

In the long, hot summer of 1967, dozens of race riots erupted across the United States. In June, there were riots in Atlanta, Boston, Cincinnati, Buffalo, and Tampa. In July, there were riots in Birmingham, Chicago, New York City, Milwaukee, Minneapolis, New Britain, Rochester, and Plainfield. King had nothing to do with these uprisings except being a symbol of racial equality and social justice, but there were some who blamed him for being a catalyst for rising expectations that others fomented into violence.

At one point, King even doubted and asked, "Are we still relevant?" As a result of opposition and social unrest, King may have been influenced to widen his social justice ministry. He began to speak out against the Vietnam War and formed coalitions of poor Americans—black and white alike—to address issues of poverty and unemployment.

In the spring of 1968, while meeting to discuss and plan a march in Washington to lobby Congress on behalf of the poor, King and other SCLC members were called to Memphis, Tennessee, to support the sanitation workers' strike. On the night of April 3 at the Mason Temple Church in Memphis, King's appearance was billed to deliver a speech in support of the strike. But what King delivered was a prophetic vision about the struggle and his role in it. "We've got some difficult days ahead," said Dr. King. "Like anybody, I would like to live a long life—longevity has its place. But I'm not concerned about that now. I just want to do God's will. And He's allowed me to go up to the mountain. And I have looked over and I've seen the Promised Land. I may not get there with you. But I want you to know tonight, that we, as a people, will get to the Promised Land." King went on to say, "And so I'm happy tonight. I'm not worried about anything. I'm not fearing any man. Mine eyes have seen the glory of the coming of the Lord."[177]

No one can know for sure whether King discerned what was coming. But historic destiny tied the mission and work of Martin Luther King to what was begun with Abraham Lincoln a hundred years earlier. And both men seemed prescient in having similar deep feelings that their calling and central work would bring such wrath upon themselves that their lives would be cut short.

Fewer than twenty-four hours after Dr. King had told the Mason Temple Church audience in Memphis that he had "seen the glory of the coming of the Lord," he was killed by an assassin's bullet.

Martin Luther King Day, the newest of American holidays, has taken its place alongside the others as being the one that contributes immensely to helping us understand that progress on the most important national and human issues can be slow and arduous.

Indeed, the road to establishing Martin Luther King Day as a federal holiday was slow and fraught with difficulty. Legislation was introduced to create such a holiday in remembrance of King after his assassination on April 4, 1968, but it was not taken up. In the 1970s, support for a federal Martin Luther King holiday grew, with a number of states enacting statewide holidays. Coretta Scott King continued to fight for approval of the holiday and testified before Congress multiple times. In 1979, President Jimmy Carter called on Congress to vote on the King Holiday Bill, but the bill fell short by five votes in the House. Following that defeat, pop star Stevie Wonder released a song in memory of King called "Happy Birthday," and he teamed up with Coretta Scott for the cause—ultimately delivering a petition with over six million signatures in favor of the holiday to the Speaker of the House in 1982, which led to a successful vote in both houses of Congress. On November 3, 1983, President Ronald Reagan signed a bill marking the third Monday of January as Martin Luther King, Jr. Day.

Racial prejudice cannot be ultimately solved by political legislation and law. It is a condition of the heart that takes time and inner spiritual healing to change. The memory of Martin Luther King's recounting of Jesus Christ's admonition to his disciples when he sent them into the field to "be wise as serpents, and harmless as doves"—that is, to have a tough mind and a tender heart—calls us to live in truth and love. Truth will defeat falsehood every time, and when we live with love at the center, we are gradually transformed so that our truth is framed with tolerance and empathy, which leave no inner space for hatred and prejudice to remain.

CHAPTER 10

Memorial Day: The Holiday that
Connects the Past with the Present

The Civil War was America's most costly war with some 360,222 Union and 258,000 Confederate lives lost. Some analysts say the national toll reached 700,000, but the approximate number most often quoted is 620,000. This number of casualties would exceed the nation's loss in all its other wars combined—the two World Wars, the Korean and Vietnamese Wars, and subsequent wars right up through conflicts in Syria, Iraq, and Afghanistan.

In spite of the Civil War death toll being so staggering, Abraham Lincoln expressed no blame or bitterness toward the South in his second inaugural address. Rather, he held both sides—the North and the South—accountable for the causes that led to this most costly war. The country paid more in deaths to reunite this nation and correct the offense of slavery than it paid for all the other causes for which the nation fought in its ensuing history.

While Lincoln expressed that both sides shared blame for the Civil War, many in the Union brass and the Federal government considered the Confederates traitors. After battles that took place in the North like at Gettysburg, the dead of the Union army were taken care of with proper burials in individual grave sites, while bodies of the slain Confederates were often put in mass graves, some containing more than 150 bodies. General Robert E. Lee had expressed hope that eventually these Confederate dead would be brought home.[178]

Memorial Day had its origin as Decoration Day and was established to honor those lost while fighting in the Civil War. The holiday's origin dates back to April 25th, 1866, when a former chaplain in the Confederate Army accompanied a group of women from Columbus, Mississippi, to Friendship Cemetery—the burial ground for about sixteen hundred men who died in the Battle of Shiloh—for the purpose of honoring the dead with decorations of flowers. At that time, Columbus, like the rest of the South, was occupied by Union Army forces, and some townspeople were fearful of creating new animosity, assuming that the decorations would favor Confederate over Union graves.

The Columbus women had no such intention in spite of the Union's indiscriminate burial treatment of Confederate army fatalities on Northern battlefields. Their equal decoration of the graves of both sides became a catalyst for a national reconciliation movement. At the time, the *New York Herald* published a tribute, noting: "The women of Columbus, Mississippi, have shown themselves impartial in their offerings to the memory of the dead. They strewed flowers alike on the graves of the Confederate and of the Union soldiers."[179]

A second claimant for the first Decoration Day service is Belle Isle, which is adjacent to Richmond, Virginia in the James River—the capital of the Confederacy. On May 30, 1866, bouquets of flowers were placed on the graves of Union soldiers who were victims of the Confederate prisoner of war camp located there. That may have been the reason for May 30 being selected as the day for the holiday. But May 30 was also near the anniversary date of the surrender of the last Confederate Army regiment under the command of General Kirby Smith on May 26, 1865.

About a year after the war was over, in 1866, it came to be known that Congress had appropriated funds for the care of Union soldiers' graves without making similar consideration for Confederates. The ladies of Richmond again led the way, forming groups to care for the soldiers' graves and to bring home the remains of Southerners who fell at Gettysburg or were hastily buried elsewhere in battles on Northern territory. This led to the formation of other memorial associations throughout the South, often led by women, to oversee the caring for, disposition, and memorial of Confederate soldiers who had given their lives.[180]

* * *

With the conception of Memorial Day coming out of the Civil War—the most costly American war in terms of the sheer numbers of human lives sacrificed—it's appropriate to remember two Civil War leaders who came from each side of the conflict. The two figures to honor—Robert E. Lee and Joshua L. Chamberlain—were remarkable in their attitude, courage, and character that was reflected in the love and high esteem that their soldiers had for them.

First, a tribute to Robert E. Lee. More has been written about Lee than any other figure in the Civil War, and yet most people have missed the broad strokes across the canvas of his life and heritage, while also knowing so little about his character. Lee, a native of Virginia, had two relatives who signed the Declaration of Independence, was the son of Revolutionary War hero Henry "Light Horse Harry" Lee, and married the granddaughter of President George Washington. He attended West Point, graduating second in his class, and today he still has the distinction of being one of only two cadets in the 120-year history of the institution to graduate without a single demerit.

Lee's first combat was in the Mexican-American War, when he served under General Winfield Scott in 1847. Over the course of various battles from Veracruz to Mexico City, Lee distinguished himself three times—receiving promotions on each occasion to major, lieutenant colonel, and colonel—for his unconventional tactical genius in daring reconnaissance, finding routes of attack, and employing battlefield tactics that resulted in swift victories. General Scott would subsequently comment that "Lee was one of the best soldiers he had ever seen in battle."[181]

In 1857, after the passing of the father of Lee's wife Mary Custis, they inherited the plantation estates of the Arlington House and Romancock and the 189 enslaved blacks working those properties. The will, designating Robert E. Lee as executor, included a directive to emancipate all those enslaved at Arlington House and any of the other properties after the estate debts and the bequests were taken care of, to be accomplished no later than five years hence.

Mary had been following the tradition of her mother—tutoring the plantation's enslaved people to sew, read, and write over many prior years.[182] Both Robert and Mary Lee recognized the need to help the slaves prepare for the transition from being dependent and bonded to becoming free and independent. Robert would later execute a deed of manumission in the midst of his wartime duties, freeing all the Custis slaves at the end of December 1862, before Lincoln's Emancipation Proclamation.[183]

Following the inauguration of Abraham Lincoln as president in March 1861, General Scott, then serving as the top general in the US Army, but aging and in declining health, recommended to Lincoln that Robert E. Lee not only be promoted to full colonel but also be offered command of Federal forces to protect the capital and defend the nation.[184] Lee was thought to be the most competent and energetic candidate to fill the need for national military leadership to deal with near and longer term challenges—of which the secession of the Southern slave states was most pressing.

Lee was steeped in West Point education and opposed to secession, as well as disagreeing in principle with slavery, ruminating four years earlier to his wife about the issue that "slavery as an institution is a moral and political evil in any country."[185] But he was also opposed to taking a position that would require taking up arms against his family and his people who had been in Virginia for two hundred years.

It was the second week in April 1861 that General Scott told Lee of his promotion to full colonel and then approached him with Lincoln's desire to give him command of the Federal Army. Because Lee was a man defined by commitment to duty and honor, he was then faced with the most momentous struggle of his life: the choice of either answering the call to serve the president and preserve the Union, or answering the call of honoring the Constitution's provision for states' rights, the redressing of legitimate grievances with the North, and loyalty to his fellow Virginians. While the Constitution made no mention of secession, Lee was well aware of the beliefs and arguments made by many of the Southern states that they had only agreed to sign and ratify the Constitution because of the addition of the Bill of Rights, the 10th Amendment of which they interpreted as granting states the right to leave the Union for cause associated with abuse of federal government power, just as the original thirteen colonies had organized to leave Great Britain.

Lee had a deep love for Virginia, recognizing that Virginians were key actors in giving birth to the United States republic, and making the largest contribution in terms of "Founding Fathers"—who included a more formidable aggregation of the greatest minds, statesmen, and leaders than those from any other state. Virginians played dominant roles in drafting the Declaration of Independence, the Constitution, and the Bill of Rights. One might even say that these key founding documents were primarily the product of Virginia. Four out of the first five US presidents were Virginians.

Unwilling to betray the people of his heritage or betray states' rights established by the Constitution, Lee chose the South. He stayed a few days with his wife Mary at their home, Arlington House, with its eleven-hundred-acre plantation outside Washington. On April 17, the Virginia legislature voted to follow suit with the other seven Southern states who had already seceded from the Union. On April 20, Lee tendered his resignation from the US Army, and went to Richmond. Three days later, Lee accepted command of Virginia's forces on April 23, 1861.

Meanwhile, Lee began pleading with his wife Mary to evacuate Arlington House, as Union Forces were certain to seize the property. She struggled to leave her beloved family home, the slaves whose welfare she worried about without her presence, and the George Washington family relics that were on display like a museum in one of Arlington House's wings.[186] She finally did leave Arlington House in mid-May with her daughters, staying with various relatives in the area before moving to Richmond, where she would live for most of the war years.

Lee's military leadership of the Confederate forces was punctuated in the first two years with a number of victories against larger Union troop numbers, accomplished by his tactical genius of taking initiative in such daring actions as dividing his troops, followed by aggressive offensive moves which he mastered as a means to force retreat of larger enemy forces. If the Virginia regulars were unsure about their new leader when the conflict started, by the end of 1862, Lee achieved a matchless reputation as a field commander, with reports of soldiers being fanatically devoted to him.

What went largely unreported in the popular press were Lee's many acts of service that transformed so many soldiers' lives. In 1862—his first full year of war command—Lee issued a general order that all military duties be suspended on Sundays to afford troops rest, prayer, and time for Bible reading and religious service attendance. There are many accounts of Lee riding his horse, "Traveller," among his troops with spontaneous dismounting to join in with groups of soldiers in prayer. Lee had an unrelenting faith in the sovereignty of God that deeply affected his personal and public military life. Rev. J. William Jones, who later served as chaplain under Lee, described him as a man "who humbly tried to walk the path of duty, 'looking unto Jesus' as the author and finisher of his faith, and whose piety constantly exhibited itself in his daily life."[187] It has been said by various chroniclers of those challenging war years that Robert E. Lee brought more people to having faith in Christ—numbering in the thousands—than any other military leader in American history.

John Esten Cooke, the esteemed biographer of Robert E. Lee, wrote in 1883 that "his military genius will always be conceded…but this does not account for the fact that his very enemies love the man…. The soldier was great, but the man himself was even greater." Cooke also wrote: "The crowning grace of this man…was the humility and trust in God, which lay at the foundation of his character."[188]

Lee had mounted a remarkable effort on the many battlefields of the four-year Civil War, but in the end, he lost to the more powerful

Union forces that were also able to enlist European financial support and mercenary soldiers. But defeat revealed yet another side of Lee's unusual character, for he accepted that crushing disaster, which ended his military career, with calmness and equanimity because he trusted in a merciful and overruling Providence. Lee was honored after the war with an invitation to become president of Washington College (which became Washington and Lee University), a post he kept until his death in 1870.

Today, if Robert E. Lee looked down from heaven, he might marvel at the irony of history that provided him the honor of giving up the Arlington House plantation that was seized from him and his wife because they sided with Virginia and the South. The eleven hundred acres of that plantation would become the Arlington Cemetery—the most hallowed ground in America—providing a final resting place for future patriots who gave their lives for the cause of freedom and the American republic.[189]

The second Civil War figure to whom tribute is due is the Union soldier, Joshua L. Chamberlain, who entered the war as an unknown of low rank with no prior military experience, but who ended his service as major general presiding over the Confederate surrender of arms at Appomattox Courthouse, Virginia on April 12, 1865.

Joshua Chamberlain was born in 1828 and raised in Maine, graduated with distinction from Bowdoin College in 1852, and then pursued graduate studies at the Bangor Theological Seminary. In 1855, he accepted the invitation to return to Bowdoin to teach languages and rhetoric. A patriot and a strong believer in the American Republic, Chamberlain was five years into his professorship when the talk of secession that turned into action by multiple Southern states weighed heavily upon him with a concern that it meant the dissolution of the United States.

Chamberlain felt compelled to serve his country, but Bowdoin administrators and colleagues were against his enlisting in the military. He was, however, granted a two-year leave of absence, supposedly to study languages in Europe, whereupon he offered his services to the governor of Maine. The governor's staff was apparently impressed with Chamberlain's academic credentials, and offered him the position of colonel, even though he had no military experience. Chamberlain declined, preferring to "start a little lower and learn the business first," and agreed to enlist with the rank of lieutenant colonel for the Twentieth Maine Infantry Regiment.[190]

The regiment left Maine for Washington, DC, where it was incorporated into a brigade of the Fifth Corps, Army of the Potomac. Chamberlain's first battle experience was in the Maryland Campaign in the fall of 1862, although the Twentieth Maine Infantry was held in reserve during the bloody Battle of Antietam. As events unfolded, Chamberlain and the Twentieth Maine were put in the forefront of the conflict in freezing weather at Fredericksburg on December 13—a battle involving two hundred thousand combatants, which some historians believed to be the largest concentration of troops in the Civil War. Despite Union forces numbering some 120,000 versus the Confederate force of 80,000, Robert E. Lee's brilliant battlefield tactics and his nimbleness delivered a resounding defeat to the larger Union forces, which sent Union morale plummeting.

By this time, Chamberlain was respected and well-liked by his men, often treating them like they were members of his family. He carried a pocket Bible in his left front chest pocket and was known to be fair and unbiased even with the enemy—viewing all men as equal, having a "divine spark." While most soldiers never quite got used to the discomforts, inconveniences, and dangers of army life, Chamberlain loved it. The battlefield made him feel more alive and connected to others than he had ever experienced in his scholarly endeavors in the stuffiness of Bowdoin. For him, the sight of hundreds of soldiers marching in formation to attack with flags waving had a certain thrill unparalleled by anything he had experienced in his prior life.

By June of 1863, Chamberlain had been promoted to colonel, and under the command of Colonel Strong Vincent, he was ordered to march the Twentieth Maine northward in pursuit of Robert E. Lee's forces that were making their second run into Pennsylvania. Days later, 120 men from the Second Maine Regiment had been combined with

Chamberlain's Twentieth Maine, so he had 386 infantrymen under his immediate command.

Approaching Gettysburg, Chamberlain was told to take his men to a position on Little Round Top to fill a gap in the Union line. And no sooner were they all positioned on the left flank of the Union line, than some 820 seasoned soldiers of Fourth and Fifth Texas regiments under Confederate general John B. Hood began attacking the middle section of the line to their right. Then the Fifteenth and Forty-Seventh Alabama under Colonel William C. Oates began hammering up the slope right at them, firing in waves. After nearly an hour, Chamberlain's ranks were being shredded and they were running out of ammunition.

Being the calm and keen observer that he was, Chamberlain sized up the Confederate forces, and recognized they were exhausted in fighting uphill and that they, too, were probably at the end of their ammunition. He called an impromptu meeting among his line leaders, yelling out, "Bayonet." The message traveled like electricity down both sides of the line, and with the brave color guard leading the charge and the distinct metal-on-metal clank of bayonets being snapped into place, Chamberlain's men charged in unison in a counter-clockwise curve down the slope so as to flank the enemy.

The action was so swift and uniform that the Confederates thought that a new regiment of fresh reinforcements had miraculously appeared and was charging to finish them off. The psychology of the battle suddenly changed, and Chamberlain would later recount two ensuing incidents of taking prisoners. One Alabama soldier twice failed to pull the trigger of his rifle because he had second thoughts about killing the brave Colonel Chamberlain. In another confrontation, the commanding Confederate officer tried to shoot his pistol in Chamberlain's face, but misfired. Chamberlain immediately had his saber at the Confederate officer's throat, who immediately gave up sword and pistol into Chamberlain's hands. Describing his attitude toward the surrendering Confederates, Chamberlain said at that time, "And these were manly men, whom we could befriend and by no means kill, if they came our way in peace and good will."[191]

The charge of the Twentieth Maine Infantry brought victory to the Union forces at Little Round Top. Many attribute that to the overall Union victory at Gettysburg, which many also believe was the battle that turned the tide in the Civil War. Chamberlain was awarded the Presidential Medal of Honor by Congress for his "daring heroism and great tenacity…"

Through the course of the Civil War, Chamberlain had six horses shot out from under him and was wounded six times. In the last full year of the war, he suffered potentially mortal wounds on two occasions, but had the will to survive. At the siege of Petersburg in April 1864, he was shot through his two hips, and in March 1865, during Grant's final advance along Quaker Road that would be one of the last skirmishes in the war, Chamberlain was severely wounded in his left upper arm and a bullet entered his chest from an angle, then banked around the rib cage and exited his backside. Yet through it all, he continued to encourage his men to fight. In the last year of the war, Chamberlain became a legend of bravery and was promoted twice, first to brigadier general and then to major general.

Robert E. Lee agreed to terms of surrender but chose not to be present at the official ceremony. Nor was Ulysses S. Grant going to be present, having chosen Joshua Chamberlain to preside over the parade of the Confederate infantry in their formal surrender at Appomattox Courthouse on April 12, 1865. General John B. Gordon was the presiding Confederate officer, and his soldiers came marching down the road as in a funeral procession to surrender their arms and colors. Chamberlain ordered his men to come to attention and "carry arms" as a show of respect. Years later, Gordon would recount in his memoirs that Chamberlain was "one of the knightliest soldiers of the Federal Army."[192] And to that, Lee might have added that "it takes one to know one."

* * *

Memorial Day, as Decoration Day gradually came to be known, originally honored those lost while fighting in the Civil War. When the United States became embroiled in World War I and World War II, the holiday evolved to commemorate American military personnel who died in subsequent wars. However, the observance of Memorial Day was not at all consistent in the first hundred years after the Civil War.

Finally, in 1968, Congress declared Memorial Day a federal holiday in passing the Uniform Monday Holiday Act. That Act also established the date of annual celebration as the last Monday in May, in order to create a three-day weekend for federal employees. That change to Monday holiday recognition went into effect in 1971, and also applied to Washington's and Lincoln's Birthday—that facilitated the combination of celebrating the two greatest presidents in a new holiday, Presidents' Day; Columbus Day; and Martin Luther King Day, which became a holiday on January 20, 1986.

* * *

Memorial Day is also an occasion to associate those who died with the just causes for which the United States was willing to go to war. World War I, World War II, Korea, and Vietnam were conflicts where freedom was clearly at stake. The post 9/11 engagements in Afghanistan, Iraq, and Syria remain a bit more complicated, being responses to horrific abuse of power and to transnational radical Islamist terrorism.

A discussion of Memorial Day would just not be complete without appreciating the significance of the Tomb of the Unknown Soldier, formally established on what was then known as Armistice Day, three years after the end of World War I. The US Congress had approved the burial of an unidentified American soldier who had fallen somewhere on a battlefield in France at Arlington National Cemetery in Virginia. The Tomb of the Unknown Solider would come to be considered the most hallowed grave at Arlington Cemetery—the most sacred military cemetery in the United States.

And so it was on November 11, 1921, what was then Armistice Day, the Tomb of the Unknown Soldier was consecrated in the presence of President Harding and other government, military, and international dignitaries. That Unknown Soldier from World War I was buried with highest honors, lowered to his final resting place on top of a two-inch layer of soil brought from France—that he might rest forever atop the earth on which he died.

The selection process for the World War II Unknown proved more difficult than that of World War I, since American soldiers had fought on three continents. Then the process was interrupted by the Korean War, which resulted in numerous deaths of soldiers who could not be identified. Finally, on May 28, 1958, caskets bearing the Unknowns of World War II and the Korean War arrived in Washington. The caskets were rotated such that each unknown serviceman rested on the "Lincoln catafalque," a raised platform that held President Lincoln's casket in April 1865. Two days later, on May 30, then the official date of Memorial Day, those Unknowns were transported to Arlington, where they were interred in the plaza beside their World War I comrade.

Due to the advances in DNA identification technology, most every Vietnam War casualty recovered could be identified. Yet with so many "missing in action," it was decided that the crypt designated for the Vietnam Unknown should remain empty. It was rededicated to honor all missing US service members from the Vietnam War on September 17, 1999, with the inscription on the crypt reading, "Honoring and Keeping the Faith with America's Missing Servicemen, 1958-1975."

The inscribed words on the Tomb of the Unknown Soldier of "Here Rests in Honored Glory an American Soldier Known but to God" are an uplifting reminder that all those who died for the American cause should have a special place in our hearts as they do in God's. Anyone who visits the Tomb of the Unknown Soldier, which is guarded twenty-four hours a day, 365 days a year regardless of weather by special armed Tomb Guard sentinels, cannot but be humbled and reminded of what Lincoln said at Gettysburg, "...that from these honored dead we take increased devotion to that cause for which they gave the last full measure of devotion—that we here highly resolve that these dead shall not have died in vain—that this nation, under God, shall have a new birth of freedom—and that government of the people, by the people, for the people, shall not perish from the earth."

Some US military engagements were ill-advised, and history shows that the instances of injustice were probably greater from actions taken by Washington politicians and bureaucrats than by the military in the field. For instance, the government's willingness to authorize and deploy military force in Vietnam without clear objectives and a strategy for victory—which put American lives in harm's way and cost 58,220 lives—was the great injustice of the Vietnam War. In other cases, such as in Iraq, President Obama's political decision to withdraw US military forces by the end of 2011 directly led to the injustice of reversal of hard-fought gains made by the military in the prior eight years, which resulted in a power vacuum that was filled by the rise of ISIS and growing Iranian influence.

More recently, after America's longest military engagement—some twenty years—to prevent Afghanistan from regaining its status as a terror-sponsoring state, a policy costing 2,352 American lives and over $2 trillion, the Biden administration hastily and inexplicably withdrew all remaining American forces without following established military evacuation protocols. The blunder effectively surrendered military bases, forts, and $85 billion of sophisticated military equipment to the ruling Afghan Taliban, the very tribal faction that gave safe haven to the training of the 9/11 terrorists.

* * *

Over a million Americans have given their lives in defending US interests in conflicts large and small. And while remembering those people is a central purpose of this holiday, Memorial Day takes on its deepest meaning when we connect it with our roots.

Americans were unique in sacrificing their treasure and giving their lives to found the first country in history that established that all people have natural rights that come from God rather than from rulers or government. The Declaration of Independence affirmed the equality of all people, who were endowed with unalienable rights to life, liberty, and the pursuit of happiness. And just because it took nearly two hundred years for those to be fully realized, it does not diminish the founding based on those ideals. Thus, when Americans sacrifice their lives in military service, we should remember that it was not just to defend the United States, but it was also to uphold the natural rights and spiritual values associated with the nation's founding that provide inspiration for others worldwide.

There were times and places in human history when there were nation-states of cultural achievement, virtue, and efflorescence, such as in Periclean Athens, in the Florence of the Medicis, and in England of Elizabeth I and Shakespeare. But none were founded the way America was—that is, by a collection of the nation's most learned statesmen, well-versed in classics of law, political philosophy, and Biblical understanding, who prayerfully approached drafting the Declaration of Independence in 1776 and then the US Constitution in 1787. The Constitution provided a charter for an unprecedented arrangement of governmental institutions that would mitigate corruption and abuse of power while also protecting the citizens' unalienable God-given rights. The Bill of Rights, an integral part of the Constitution, enabled people living in America to rise to levels closer to the divine image in which all were created than they would have under any government previously conceived.

When the Puritans departed England in 1630 for the New World, they had the Charter of the Massachusetts Bay Company and sponsorship from the British Crown, but they couldn't have known what independence and the future of American government would look like a century and a half later. Their leader and future governor, John Winthrop, had a vision taken from Scripture, Matthew 5:14–16, asserting that they were to be an example for the rest of the world in rightful living. Upon leaving England and again before arriving in Massachusetts aboard the *Arabella*—a name of Latin origin meaning "yielding to prayer"— Winthrop declared to his people their purpose quite clearly: "We shall be as a 'City upon a Hill,' the eyes of all people are upon us."

The governing guidelines for that "City" would in part turn out to be the US Constitution, which arguably became one of America's most important exports to the world. Writing about the benefits of the Constitution, Thomas Jefferson stated, "We feel that we are acting under obligations not confined to the limits of our own society. It is impossible not to be sensible that we are acting for all mankind."[193] In only two centuries since that time, almost every nation has come to accept the need and value of having a constitution, regardless of differences of culture, history, and legal heritage. Most of the world's constitutions have been written in the last seventy-five years, and the Constitution of the United States continues to be the guiding template, as well as a source of inspiration and fundamental principles.[194]

* * *

Yet another aspect of celebrating Memorial Day is recognizing the example set by Americans in how they have treated their vanquished foes.

The respect displayed by General MacArthur, Supreme Commander for the Allied Powers (SCAP), and the occupying American forces after Japan's surrender surprised and won over many of the Japanese people. They had assumed the victorious Americans would execute their beloved emperor and plunder and treat them in ways similar to what Japanese soldiers did to those they had conquered in China, Korea, and Southeast Asia. It was not easy for the proud Japanese people to be subject to a seven-year (1945–1952) American-dominated Allied occupation. However, the courtesy and respect shown by the Americans helped mollify resistance to the occupation's policies that forced demilitarization and fundamental change on the country.

One of the big changes that General MacArthur oversaw required the postwar Japanese government to initiate the drafting of a new constitution, with five governing principles: democratic rule that ensured the sovereignty of the people through voting rights and universal suffrage; school reform that separated the educational system from government control; the renunciation of war and the use of military force; the protection of human rights; and judicial review of the constitutionality of legislation and governmental actions. After a number of revisions, the new constitution that was accepted actually created a government closer to the British style of parliamentary government than the American system.

In addition to overseeing the rewriting of the Japanese constitution, MacArthur also required that new laws and mandates be enacted to bring about land reform—so as to break up large land holdings and broaden private property ownership, and to break up and restructure business conglomerates, known as the zaibatsu—to broaden ownership and ensure more competition, fairness, and opportunity.

What was remarkable about the US defeat and reorganization of Japan was that American actions were conducted in such a way that helped the Japanese to become a more formidable economic competitor at America's own expense, but that also brought about respect and friendship between the two countries that has remained ever since.

After armistice, the war-indebted United States launched the Marshall Plan that gave some $146 billion of grant aid in current dollar value that helped reconstruct war-devastated regions in Western Europe. Eighteen countries received aid and initiatives that largely targeted the rebuilding of the industrial base. And similar to the aid given to Japan, US generosity gave Europeans a leg up on the US with the building of state-of-the-art factories and facilities that were in many cases more efficient than what then existed in the US.

In sum, Memorial Day means more than remembering and honoring those who died in military service to the country. It means connecting with a heritage that began with a courageous and faithful group of founders, who risked their lives for the birth of freedom and the establishment of America as a "city on a hill." It also means remembering all who subsequently died for their nation, and especially those who collectively paid the highest price, such as those who died in the Civil War, and "the greatest generation" sacrificed in World War II, who—after experiencing the loss of so many lives to assure victory for the Allied nations—then went on to sacrifice and support the effort to rebuild and preserve the independence of its former enemies.

There is no other nation in history like the United States.

CHAPTER 11

Veterans Day: A Celebration of the Greatest Love

Veterans Day had its origin at the end of World War I in 1918, a conflict so horrendous that it was dubbed "the Great War," or "the war to end all wars," with the United States playing the decisive role in the Allied powers' final victory.

It was first known as Armistice Day, celebrated on November 11 because that was the day agreed upon by the Allied nations and Germany to begin a total cessation of hostilities. It went into effect on the eleventh hour of the eleventh day of the eleventh month in 1918, after some twenty million people from both sides had given their lives in the war effort.

Although the Treaty of Versailles was signed seven months later, on June 28, 1919, marking the official end of World War I, the armistice date of November 11, 1918—when the guns and mortars went silent—remained in the public mind as the date that marked the end of the Great War. President Woodrow Wilson expressed support for commemorating Armistice Day on November 11, proclaiming: "To us in America, the reflections of Armistice Day will be filled with solemn pride in the heroism of those who died in the country's service and with gratitude for the victory, both because of the thing from which it has freed us and because of the opportunity it has given America to show her sympathy with peace and justice in the councils of the nations…"[195]

On November 11, 1920, unidentified soldiers from Great Britain and France respectively were laid to rest at Westminster Abbey in London and at the Arc de Triomphe in Paris.

A year later, on November 11, 1921, an unknown American soldier killed in the war on the European theater was buried at Arlington National Cemetery with highest honors, consecrated in the presence of President Harding and other government, military, and international dignitaries. Thereafter, for many years, Armistice Day was widely recognized, with some twenty-seven state legislatures making November 11 a legal holiday.

Finally, on May 13, 1938, the US Congress passed an act to establish Armistice Day as a legal federal holiday—"a day to be dedicated to the cause of world peace." The politicians were apparently in denial and behind the curve, for two months prior, a rearmed Germany under Hitler had already annexed all of Austria and had submitted a war plan to take over Czechoslovakia. So, the holiday dedicated to honoring World War I veterans became official at the very time World War II was unfolding.

As it turned out, World War II was almost four times more costly, with some seventy to eighty-five million war-related deaths, than World War I. As for the United States, the statistics were similar, with 405,400 lives lost in World II, as compared with 116,516 lives lost in World War I.

Not surprisingly, the focus on the 1918 Armistice was overshadowed, and eventually, after World War II and the Korean War, veterans service organizations lobbied Congress to amend the 1938 Act by striking out the word "Armistice" and inserting the word "Veterans." President Eisenhower supported and signed off on the name change on June 1, 1954, making November 11 a federal holiday "to honor American veterans of all wars."

As the holiday evolved, Veterans Day became one of America's most patriotic holidays, with profuse display of the red, white, and blue, and Main Street parades of veterans in towns across the country. But Veterans Day distinguished itself in another way from a number of other holidays after the US Congress passed the Uniform Holiday Bill in 1968 for the purpose of spurring both family activities and the economy by establishing three-day weekends. The Uniform Holiday Bill was intended to permanently move to a Monday five Federal holidays in the US—Presidents' Day, Memorial Day, Labor Day, Columbus Day, and Veterans Day. That meant these holidays would "float" and come up on different calendar days each year. No one seems to know the reasons why, but the recognition of Veterans Day was moved out of November and designated to the fourth Monday of every October.

The arbitrary month and date change of recognizing Veterans Day not only was confusing, but many people—veterans and veterans' groups in particular—were distraught by politicians' arbitrary change of the sacred date of Veterans Day, when the guns originally fell silent on the eleventh hour of the eleventh day of the eleventh month in 1918. There was such strong support for keeping the original date because of its historic and patriotic significance that Congress and President Gerald Ford decided to make an exception for Veterans Day, passing Public Law 94-97, which returned the annual observance to its original date of November 11.

In some way, this exception made for Veterans Day, particularly in contrast to its patriotic archrival Memorial Day, might suggest it is a more special holiday. But the two holidays are distinctly different. Memorial Day specifically commemorates the men and women who died while in service of their country and made the ultimate sacrifice for their country. Veterans Day is the day set aside to thank and honor all who have served, living or deceased, but particularly the living veterans among us.

Perhaps more than anyone, distinguished military leaders who have witnessed the tragedy and horror of war on the front lines, understand what Veterans Day really means. We know that we owe our veterans so much, for they were willing to make the ultimate sacrifice—to fight to their deaths, if need be—in the defense of freedom for homeland as well as for other countries.

General George S. Patton, one of America's greatest battlefield generals, was a front-line combat leader in both World War I and II in the

North African and European theaters. He was born on November 11, 1885, the very day that later would become Veterans Day, and died in a tragic car accident nearly eight months after the war ended. Patton developed a military leadership philosophy to explain how to assure more veterans would return home than would be left in the field as casualties. Many of his theories are equally applicable to civilian life and business, and can be readily appreciated by a few of his one-liners, such as:

> "Always do everything you ask of those you command."

> "Never tell people how to do things. Tell them what to do, and they will surprise you with their ingenuity."

> "Don't fight a battle if you don't gain anything by winning."

> "There are three ways that men get what they want; by planning, by working, and by praying…"

> "A good solution applied with vigor now is better than a perfect solution applied ten minutes later."[196]

General Douglas MacArthur was distinguished in serving in the front lines of three wars: World War I, World War II, and the Korean War. He was credited with military genius that was decisive in bringing victory in the Pacific in World War II and in the Korean War. He shared a lifetime of wisdom in his military retirement speech on the occasion of receiving the Sylvanus Thayer Award at West Point on May 12, 1962:

> "Duty, Honor, Country" – those three hallowed words reverently dictate what you ought to be, what you can be, what you will be. They are your rallying point to build courage when courage seems to fail, to regain faith when there seems to be little cause for faith, to create hope when hope becomes forlorn.

Youth is not entirely a time of life; it is a state of mind. Nobody grows old by merely living a number of years. People grow old by deserting their ideals. You are as young as your faith, as old as your doubts; as young as your self-confidence, as old as your fear; as young as your hope, as old as your despair.

A true leader has the confidence to stand alone, the courage to make tough decisions, and the compassion to listen to the needs of others. He does not set out to be a leader, but becomes one by the equality of his actions and the integrity of his intent.

The soldier, above all other men, is required to perform the highest act of religious offering—sacrifice. In battle and in the face of danger and death he discloses those divine attributes which his maker gave when he created man in his own image. No physical courage and no brute instincts can take the place of the Divine help which will alone sustain him.[197]

As a child, Leigh Ann Hester had a patriotic calling from the time her father took her to see a military parade. Watching the men and women march in uniform, she longed to be one of them and serve her country. And so, at nineteen, after graduating from high school, she enlisted to become a military police officer in the Army National Guard, knowing then, in 2001, that it was the only sure path for a woman to get out into the field. Of course, she had no idea that that single step in her life would lead to her becoming a national hero, a media celebrity, and even making it into the history books.

After completing basic training and Army Military Police School, in 2004, Leigh received her deployment orders to Iraq in support of Operation Iraqi Freedom with the 617th Military Police Company in Baghdad. Joining that police company virtually guaranteed exposure to combat, something the Pentagon was not even allowing women to officially engage in at that time. Their primary mission was to protect critical routes and supply convoys, which involved clearing the roads of improvised explosive devices (IEDs) and insurgents.

On March 20, 2005, Sergeant Hester and her unit within the 617th Military Police, known as the Raven 42, were providing protection by identifying and destroying IEDs for a thirty-truck supply convoy of semi-tractor trailers, when they were ambushed by waves of AK-47 and heavy machine gun fire and rocket-propelled grenades firing from both irrigation ditches and an adjacent orchard field. The insurgents immobilized the lead supply truck, which halted the whole convoy in the kill zone.

Without hesitation, Hester directed her team away from enemy fire into a flanking position that exposed multiple irrigation ditches and the orchard from which enemy fire was coming. She then directed her gunner to send Mk 19 grenade rounds to the insurgents firing from the orchard and down the irrigation trench lined with a dozen or so heavily armed insurgents. She then grabbed her M203 grenade launcher, attaching it to her M4 rifle as she jumped out of her Humvee. Getting her sights lined up on target a ways down the trench, she fired off grenades to neutralize them, and then stormed the area in pursuit of remaining insurgents.

Sergeant Hester was joined by her squad leader, Timothy Nein, and together they cut through two additional trenches and proceeded to charge the remaining enemy insurgents in close combat with their M4s. Sergeant Hester bravely killed three insurgents at close range. Finally, with the orchard and the irrigation ditches cleared, they called a ceasefire. In spite of being outnumbered five to one, twenty-seven enemy combatants lay dead, six were wounded, and one was taken prisoner. Sergeant Hester was unharmed, and only three of her comrades suffered non-life-threatening wounds.

Before the attack, without knowing what it really meant, soldiers in the Raven 42 unit of the 617th Military Police Company and the convoy truck drivers put their trust in a twenty-three-year-old woman, Leigh Ann Hester. They had much for which to be grateful. For her brave actions that day, she was awarded the Silver Star, specifically cited for conspicuous gallantry—making her the first woman in the Army to receive the award since World War II, and the very first woman ever to receive the Silver Star for combat valor. In addition to serving in Iraq, she would also serve in Afghanistan and later receive the Combat Action Badge, Army Commendation Medal, Afghanistan Campaign Medal, and Iraq Campaign Medal. Through it all, Sergeant Hester never sought credit or recognition, commenting on more than one occasion that, "I was trained to do what I did, and I did it."

Military service generally inculcates veterans with patriotic traits that keep them engaged in political participation later in life. If one wonders why America has become more divided than it has been probably since the Civil War, perhaps it is in part due to the fact that far fewer members of Congress today have sacrificed and served their country in armed forces than previously. In 1967 and in 1975, respectively, 75 percent of House members and 81 percent of US Senators were veterans. Today, only 17 percent of lawmakers in both houses have had any military experience.

Among voters, veterans tend to be more patriotic than non-veterans. As a result, with the exception of Vietnam War veterans, the number of veterans who turn out to vote has been consistently higher than nonveterans by 16 percent to 30 percent. The political importance of veterans has also advanced with the passage of time, particularly under Republican administrations.

In March 1989, President Reagan elevated the Veterans Administration (VA) to a Cabinet-level department, with the creation of the secretary of Veterans Affairs. Shortly after taking his oath of office upon becoming the forty-fifth President, Donald Trump acknowledged his intentions to keep his campaign promise of making VA reform a top priority. Within months of becoming president, he signed into law a new kind of assistance for veterans, passing the most sweeping reforms of the VA in more than fifty years. Part of the reform, called the VA Accountability and Whistleblower Protection Act, ensures veterans receive the highest quality of care in the VA system. And when urgency is needed and wait times are too long, the Veterans Choice program authorizes veterans to receive care outside the VA medical system.

The US military never initiated major hostilities and was often more of a reluctant responder. That was true for World Wars I and II and subsequent wars in Korea, Vietnam, Iraq, and Afghanistan.

The United States has always stood for freedom and against aggression and tyranny.

Surely, many Americans who enlisted to serve in wartime knew neither the forsaken places they were going nor what they would encounter, but they all had a distinct conviction that they were fighting not only to set overseas captives free, but to protect freedom at home.

Of all the foreign wars in which Americans were engaged, World War II was by far the largest, with over sixteen million soldiers serving or deployed overseas. But less than 2 percent of World War II veterans—the remnants of the "Greatest Generation"—are still alive. When we think about these heroes on Veterans Day, almost all of whom will have passed away by 2025, Jesus Christ's words, "Greater love hath no man than this, that a man lay down his life for his friends," takes on new meaning in light of Christ's sacrifice on the cross to provide salvation for all who believe.

The nation was reminded of this greatest love at the Department of Veterans Affairs' National Veterans Day Observance ceremony at Arlington Cemetery on November 11, 2019. There, Vice President Mike Pence told the story of twenty-one-year-old Marine hero Corporal Kyle Carpenter, who was serving in the dangerous Helmand Province of Afghanistan some nine years earlier. He was on a surveillance mission with a fellow Marine positioned on a rooftop, when suddenly an insurgent threw a grenade up into their midst. Without a moment's hesitation, Corporal Carpenter threw himself on the grenade, absorbing the impact of the blast to protect his comrade. Although every unprotected part of his body suffered injury—his face, neck, thigh, foot, and lung—he somehow survived. His subsequent treatment required seventy procedures and forty separate surgeries over three years, and several times during the arduous process, he was at death's doorstep with cardiac arrest.

For his sacrifice to save his comrade, Carpenter received the Medal of Honor, the highest military honor any soldier can achieve. The Medal of

Honor is only given to soldiers who have distinguished themselves "conspicuously by gallantry and intrepidity at the risk of his life above and beyond the call of duty while engaged in an action against an enemy of the United States."

Vice President Pence continued by saying, "I promise you, and him, that the American people will never forget or fail to honor the service of the youngest living recipient of the Medal of Honor, Corporate Kyle Carpenter." He finished by telling the veterans in attendance, "You counted our lives more important than your own. You stood for a cause greater than yourselves."[198]

The world remains as unsettled with bad actors as in previous times.

Let us hope that present and future generations never forget the importance of courage and sacrifice. This was the conviction of former president John F. Kennedy, a World War II hero, who later gave his life while serving in office. "The cost of freedom is always high," said Kennedy, "but Americans have always paid it. And [there is] one path we shall never choose and that is the path of surrender or submission."[199]

CHAPTER 12

Labor Day: A More Complete
Understanding of the People's Holiday

Among American holidays, Labor Day is certainly one that few really understand. Coming at the end of summer on a Monday, it's usually appreciated as the last hurrah—a three-day weekend—to party and close out the summer before getting serious about work and school in the fall season.

The idea of a "labor day holiday" was conceived in the 1880s by union labor leaders who sought recognition for the social and economic achievements of American workers. Finally, in 1894, Congress voted to establish Labor Day as a national holiday to celebrate workers and their contributions to the strength, prosperity, and well-being of the country.

Labor has certainly played a vital part in the American story, just as it has for prior civilizations over the last six thousand years—from the Mesopotamians and the Asian civilizations that sprang up around the Indus and Yellow River valleys, to the Egyptians, Greeks, and Romans. While the labor factor in each of these civilizations contributed to progress during their respective periods of many hundreds of years in which they flourished, none of these civilizations unleashed the kind of productivity and economic development witnessed in the first two hundred years of the American civilization.

What is hard to understand is that the tools brought by the first colonists that arrived in the New World, who settled in Virginia, New England, and elsewhere in the early seventeenth century, were mostly the same basic primitive and rudimentary tools of sustenance—such as shovels, axes, hoes, and ploughs—that the ancient civilizations had also used. So, what was different about the American experiment?

Something clearly happened in America that sped up economic development and transformed labor output beyond what had ever happened previously in human history. There were both material and non-material factors present in the colonial period that extended well into the twentieth century that drove economic growth.

One of the key material factors that was conducive to economic development in the New World was the assurance that colonists could easily obtain and own property. Their views were shaped by the English constitutional tradition that dated back to the Magna Carta of 1215, which was the source of the phrase, "law of the land," still in use today. The Magna Carta acknowledged the principle that government could not take away peoples' property without due process and without compensation. Later, John Locke would establish that liberty and property rights were inextricably linked. William Blackstone, who was more widely read than Locke by the founders at the time of their drafting the Constitution, established that property ownership was an absolute right, "...which consists in the free use, enjoyment and disposal of all his acquisitions, without any control or diminution, save only by the laws of the land."[200]

The basis for the pricing of all assets—that is properties and goods—can only be reliably established by free exchange, which sets prices based on what buyers are willing to pay. Prices are determined by ongoing voluntary trade and exchange, and work in such a way that the price of a particular good rises when it's scarce and in high demand and it falls when it's plentiful and in low demand. And it is the prices of assets that are the most important driver in the allocation of resources. In a free market, resources are automatically allocated to where they are most needed. So, liberty, property, and prices are inextricably linked in the efficient allocation of resources.

To produce and deliver any particular good, the farmer, hunter, or manufacturer must make a profit. The profit margin can be thought of as the primary means to compensate the party producing and delivering the goods for his or her time in producing a particular product. Profit is also essential for measuring the relative success of deploying capital into different products. Improvement and excellence are achieved by trial and error, creativity, and innovation. There is no measure of excellence, success, or failure in business without a measure of profitability.

Because the price and profit margin of a product generally rises when its quality is improved or enhanced with more features, and falls when a product becomes common and commoditized, there is an ongoing natural incentive to innovate, enhance, and improve products. Conversely, when products fail to be profitable, they are often discontinued. It is this interplay of trial and error—success and failure—that is the source of learning and the advancement of knowledge, which is the key driver of progress.

It's also essential to understand how the price mechanism and price discovery is the key to efficient allocation of resources. For instance, a location that has a shortage of a product or resource would see the demand and price rise for that product, to which suppliers will quickly respond by selling goods and capturing those higher prices, volume and profits, rather than selling to markets where there is a surplus and lower prices and profits for the same good. All this happens freely and quickly without any need for the state to be involved. In contrast, statist and socialist systems that suppress and prevent accurate and timely price signals will invariably have slow response time and fail to supply what is needed.

Socialist economies will inevitably misallocate resources for the simple reason that they lack incentives of free exchange, market prices, property rights, and the profit motive. Because government subsidized and socialist economies distort prices and thus provide no meaningful measurement of profit and therefore no measurement of success or failure, they waste resources and hobble economic growth, while at the same time providing little in the way of learning. This is why most technological advancements and new products are developed in market economies, not socialist economies.

Private property is essential in creating incentives that foster economic growth and development. In contrast, in socialized economies when property is publicly owned, there are no incentives to nurture stewardship and manage resources wisely. Private ownership encourages conservation and the responsible use of property, while public property fosters irresponsibility and waste. When everyone owns a property, people act as if no one owns it. And when no one feels they own the property, no one really takes care of it. Thus, with public ownership, which is the core of socialism, neglect and mismanagement invariably follow. The economic stagnation that is characteristic of socialism is a function of the combination of the lack of private property, the misallocation of resources, and the demoralization of labor.

Why would anyone want to work hard if there is no measurement of success? Socialism fails not only because it misallocates recourses, but also because it discourages and destroys the human spirit.

The non-material factors that were present in America's colonial period were many. In addition to property, capital, and physical attributes of labor, one has to acknowledge that the character and spirit of the early Americans were driving forces that enabled upward mobility and prosperity and propelled the American economy to take off. And the recognition that Americans achieved such rapid economic success starting out from almost nothing or a low base made the United States a model that benefited other countries around the world who adopted similar ways.

America's beginning certainly benefited from the fact that early settlers tended to be tough, willing to make enormous sacrifice and take on considerable risk, for they left the familiarity of their European homes to cross a dangerous ocean in what were often rather unseaworthy boats. These settlers not only prospered, but within a few generations, many of their descendants achieved surprising wealth that in many cases was created from nothing. In addition, in contrast to today, what stands out about towns and cities in colonial America was the absence of poverty.

What is underappreciated about the founders—a total group of about 250 people—is that they understood human nature. More than 95 percent were Christian believers who accepted that all humans are sinners and flawed. The founders had no illusion—they believed government had a propensity to abuse power and even do more harm than good. So, establishing a system of checks and balances and separation of powers was essential. Equally important was the Bill of Rights, guaranteeing individual freedom and initiative, that was amended to the Constitution to ensure ratification in all the states. The founders believed that if society was to progress and prosper, it would come from the moral character, initiative, and productivity of the private sector—the common man—rather than from government institutions and programs.

The idea that work is good for the soul and necessary to a fulfilling life is generally understood by Christians and Jews. In fact, the Bible makes some 450 references to the value and importance of work—more references than many of the biblical attributes commonly associated with living a good life. The Bible specifically refers to work as a virtue more often than it refers to other virtues such as faith, hope, joy, forgiveness, grace, or peace. Thus, work is an essential part of self-dignity and living a meaningful and fulfilling life.

In contrast, condescending views toward labor have long and deep roots elsewhere. Ancient Greek mythology promoted natural fatalism, suggesting that some people are born to rule, some to labor and be ruled. Aristotle argued that nature builds some human bodies to being servants and doing nothing else but physical labor, while others are born to perform "intelligent" tasks. Other cultures have denigrated common laborers and handymen for centuries, entrenching a deep-seated prejudice against manual labor. Hinduism has created a complex mythological framework to delegate physical work to lower castes. While Brahmins do the intellectual work, lower castes must clean and do the "dirty jobs"—with castes even being identified by the type of manual labor they perform.

Early European societies may have been subliminally shaped by the influence of the ancient Greeks, but it's still the case that many in modern Europe still view leisure as being more honorable than work. The fact that South American countries have been more influenced by aristocratic European immigration than North America probably accounts for attitudes throughout Latin America, wherein the educated class generally look down on those in the laboring class.

In contrast, in America, attitudes toward labor have always been more progressive and respectful. It was the Frenchman Alexis de Tocqueville, whose ever-relevant classic *Democracy in America* pointed out that Americans regard work "as positively honorable." This observation by Tocqueville in the late 1830s became better understood and explained in Max Weber's classic *The Protestant Ethic and the Spirit of Capitalism*, written after the turn of the twentieth century.

In Weber's analysis, prior to the Protestant Reformation, the Roman Catholic Church assured salvation to individuals who accepted the church's sacraments and submitted to the clerical authority of the Pope and his representatives. The Reformation had effectively removed such assurances and replaced it with a "priesthood of all believers." Many who adopted the Protestant faith had some difficulty adjusting to this Christian worldview. Being left with some uncertainty about their salvation, Protestants were inclined to overcome that lingering self-doubt by developing self-confidence through economic success and the work ethic of a job well done. If lack of self-confidence was synonymous with insufficient faith, self-confidence from being successful seemed to take the place of priestly assurance of God's grace. And for many Protestants, worldly success became a measure of both self-confidence and God's blessing. There can be little doubt that America's early economic growth was in large part driven by the fact that almost all the early American settlers were Protestants.

An additional contributing factor for America's economic success was that there were no feudal traditions and social hierarchies in the United States, in contrast to the class stratification and class consciousness that was characteristic of Europe and Asia. As a result, Americans were a highly mobile people—both socially and economically. They could enter the workforce as laborers, and then become business owners and entrepreneurs and build their own wealth without much to constrain them. In addition, Americans were geographically mobile, often moving westward from place to place in search of improving their fortunes.

Labor union membership peaked as a percentage of the entire American labor force at 26 percent in 1953. In 2020, the share of workers belonging to unions dropped to a new post-World War II low of 10.3 percent.[201] But what's most striking in the face of general decline in private sector union membership has been the growth of union membership in government agencies. Some 35 percent of the public sector is unionized, while only about 6.3 percent of private sector business employees now belong to unions.[202] It has often been noted that government produces nothing while the private sector produces almost all the goods and services that people want. The fact that public sector union membership is more than five times higher than the rate in private sector employers suggests that non-unionized workplaces are more highly correlated to productivity than unionized entities. Little wonder that many Americans no longer see a need for unions, except in the trades where certain worker training and skill are required.

What is distinct about the US economy is the strong and widespread entrepreneurial tradition, wherein there is frequent crossover from being a laborer to becoming a business owner who creates jobs that employ other people. Many wage earners decide at some point to take the risk of starting a new business, which—if successful—generally provides upward mobility for the owner and employment opportunities for new wage earners.

Labor Day is the only holiday of the year that provides the opportunity to give thanks to labor, but also to appreciate and celebrate the free market economy that utilizes labor and capital to lift the fortunes of the poor far better than any other economic system.

It is an interesting fact of history that 1776 was not only the year of the Declaration of Independence, but it was also the year that Adam Smith published *The Wealth of Nations*, which was the first major work providing a comprehensive understanding of the essential elements of the free market system—capital, labor, and private property—and why entrepreneurs, scientists, inventors, laborers, and consumers freely work together for the economic benefit of society more proficiently than in any other system, notably the socialist system. Smith described the free market system of private enterprise as "the obvious and simple system of natural liberty."

It's logical and axiomatic that the free market system was the natural system and means of exchange and barter dating back to primitive times, wherein two different parties—perhaps two Neanderthals—freely chose to trade and make an exchange because each side saw it in his or her interest to do so. The introduction of money facilitated exchange and made the price system universal, which is the key driver of efficient allocation of resources.

Years before Marx wrote the *Communist Manifesto* and *Das Kapital*, Tocqueville asserted, "Democracy and socialism have nothing in common but one word, equality. But notice the difference: while democracy seeks equality in liberty, socialism seeks equality in restraint and servitude." He continued, "You can't have it both ways. Socialism is a new form of slavery."[203] It has been Tocqueville's arguments rather than those of Marx which have been vindicated by results produced by the competing systems over the last 150 years. Anyone can see across nations and cultures worldwide that socialism has been associated with diminished prosperity and abuse of power by political hirelings who waste and steal, while free enterprise has been associated with the pursuit of happiness, cultivating virtue, and accruing physical and intellectual property under God and secured by limited government.

Labor Day is perhaps what might be called the holiday in need of a broader perspective. It is certainly important to commemorate those who labor. But we should also celebrate the people and the economic institutions who are most prolific in creating new jobs. It is entrepreneurs operating in market economies who are the ones most willing to take risks in developing new products, services, and market opportunities. It is these visionaries who have been the primary drivers of progress and wealth creation that took the country from colonial poverty to world economic superpower in a little more than two hundred years—making the United States the envy of the world.

Four of the eight largest employers in the United States—Walmart, Amazon, Home Depot, and Starbucks—were founded within the last fifty years while unionized labor was declining. Each of these companies was formed by visionary entrepreneurs who transformed different sectors of the consumer products retailing industry—to deliver a wider variety of products with greater efficiency and usually at lower prices.

As the US economy has become more oriented around service and information than manufacturing, it should come as no surprise that the four largest public stockholder companies in terms of market capitalization—Apple, Amazon, Google, and Microsoft—are all in the business of information technology. Each has greatly increased efficiencies for individuals and businesses, while also catalyzing a multiplier effect spawning the formation of a vast number of new companies and new jobs. Unfortunately, as these big tech information companies have become an oligopoly, they are exerting control over information, news, commerce, and even politics through censorship and "cancel culture" practices.

If competitive free markets in information can be restored and the patterns of past economic history prevail, the development and application of automation and artificial intelligence should not be feared as they are likely to create as many new jobs as those make obsolete. Remember, there was the same fear of job loss when the assembly line was introduced at the turn of the twentieth century.

Many assume that it was invention that came out of the Scientific Revolution that was the most important factor in economic development and the elimination of poverty. But it turns out that it was actually the discovery and implementation of the assembly line that was far more important for advancing economic well-being. Assembly line production drove down prices and made it possible for luxuries of the upper class—such as sewing machines, washing machines, refrigerators, and automobiles—to become affordable to common people. Mass production and the innovation of installment financing made it possible for people of the lower middle class to afford and acquire essential products, which were previously the exclusive domain of the rich.

This same pattern of the market economy has continued time and again with new technologies and new products—from a full range of smart home appliances to computers, cellular smartphones, large flat screen TVs, and digital cameras—being driven down in price while including continuous improvements in quality and features. In summary, it is private enterprise that has primarily led the way to the efficient use of capital and labor in developing new products that people want, and it is competitive, free markets that have driven prices down, making these products more and more affordable. Adam Smith was prescient when he wrote *The Wealth of Nations* in 1776, in which he stated that private enterprise and free markets would enable a standard of living of "universal opulence which extends itself to the lowest ranks of the people."[204]

The rapidity of change in our present high-tech economy can be unsettling. Even more unsettling is the rise of censorship and political corruption manifest in a new form of fascism within the United States wherein the big tech information oligopoly has aligned itself with Democratic Party policies and positions while censoring and canceling many of the views and news stories that favor or originate with Republican Party sources. No one and no party has a monopoly on truth, and such practices continuing unchecked pose an imminent danger to both our economic and political future.

Many of our problems could be greatly reduced by enforcement of existing laws under the Constitution. And while there are limitations to what new laws and regulation can achieve, the goals and framework of new legal and regulatory initiatives should be directed at increasing transparency and competition, improving the protection of real and intellectual property rights, promoting individual responsibility and accountability, and enforcing equal justice and equal opportunity under the law.

Maintaining a fair and level playing field is the proper role of government, and it helps provide people with confidence to achieve success through their labor. This is particularly important in today's economy, which is characterized by dynamism, change, and mobility—an environment requiring a labor force willing to constantly learn and adapt.

So, when we celebrate the Labor Day holiday on the first Monday in September, preferably at that last beach party or barbecue, let us not just commemorate the dignity and value of those who labor, but let us also remember and celebrate the free market institutions and entrepreneurs who drive renewal and progress—creating the new labor and employment opportunities of tomorrow.

CHAPTER 13

Constitution Day: Our Most Important (but Forgotten) National Observance Holiday

Constitution Day, which falls on September 17, is a national observance holiday rather than a federal holiday. As such, because there is no day off work, most Americans don't even realize that there is a Constitution Day. Yet it's probably our most important national charter holiday, which makes it fitting as the concluding chapter in this "history through the holidays."

July 4th is considered one of America's biggest holidays because it commemorates the nation's birth. But writing the Declaration of Independence was relatively easy, compared to the laboriously hard work of drafting a constitution that would protect individual and state liberties while also unifying states with very different interests, cultures, traditions, and economic institutions for carrying out national purposes. Without the Constitution providing the means to keep governmental order and protect liberty, surely the Declaration would have come to naught. As Supreme Court Justice Joseph Story put it, the establishment of the Constitution was a "more glorious triumph, in the case of liberty, than even that [Revolutionary War victory], by which we were separated from the parent country."[205]

America's founders were, on average, better read and more learned about history and political philosophy than today's politicians.[206] They were familiar with the fate of earlier republics, whose rise, progress, and decline invariably ended in failure—with the primary cause of ruination coming from their own people within the country.[207] A good number of the delegates to the Constitutional Convention believed that even if they could come up with a blueprint for a democratic republican government, it wouldn't last. Even the optimist Ben Franklin observed that "with luck and wisdom, they would produce a government that could forestall, for a decade perhaps, the inevitable decline of the Republic into a tyranny of a few, or a tyranny of the majority."[208]

Still, while many were skeptical and history suggested the odds of success in establishing a democratic republic with longevity were low, there were also a good number of the founders who felt that America was a chosen land with a different destiny. When they looked back at America's roots in the early New England colonies, the message of John Winthrop—who established the Massachusetts Bay Colony in 1630— stood out and encapsulated their aspirations.

Winthrop, who became the first governor of Massachusetts, was well-known for repeatedly saying that people who answered the call to come to America "consider that we shall be as a city upon a hill, the eyes of all people are upon us."[209] By the time of the American Revolution and founding nearly 150 years later, the ideal that Winthrop had expressed, which originally pertained to the New England Puritan church setting the example for the reform of the Church of England, had evolved into the ideal of an American nation being a beacon of liberty setting the example for the world. But that could only happen if the founders could find a way to come up with the right balance of power and mix of in-stitutions in a new "revolutionary" constitution to enshrine liberty in a successful and lasting democratic republic.

Some might point out that the birth pains of constitutional self-government started earlier with the Pilgrims and the Mayflower

Compact in 1620. Others might say that self-government really gained substance with each of the thirteen colonies drafting their own state constitutions. But without a doubt, the greatest birth pains were experienced after the founders created the first constitution, known as the Articles of Confederation, which was drafted shortly after the Declaration of Independence established the new nation of the United States. Because the Articles of Confederation precipitated such disastrous results, the framers of the Constitution meeting in Philadelphia had a heightened awareness of what was needed and what to avoid in crafting a new replacement constitution. It's also noteworthy that it took some twelve years from the Declaration in 1776 for the final Constitution amended with the Bill of Rights to become legally binding with ratification by a two-thirds majority of nine out of thirteen states.

Suffice it to say that arriving at the point where the United States Constitution became the law of the land, establishing the institutions and arrangements of the American democratic republic, was a long and arduous process, punctuated by misstep, failure, and delay along the way. But once properly established, the US Constitution has proven to be more vital than military power in enabling the United States to not only survive and weather storms, but also to thrive as a democratic republic longer than any other democracy in human history.

In spite of that remarkable achievement, the Constitution is threatened more now than at any time since seven Southern states seceded from the Union and Civil War broke out on April 12, 1861. To understand how to address these twenty-first century threats, we need to go back in time and understand what gave rise to our Constitution and what makes it unique in protecting liberty for its large and diverse body of citizens, while also providing the right arrangement and balance of government institutions to protect and promote American national interests.

The Boston Tea Party's rebellious action in December 1773 was a symbolic marker for many across the colonies that it was time to coordinate resistance efforts against British oppression. Early the following year, with the helpful prodding of John Adams of Massachusetts, leaders from all the colonies but Georgia decided to send delegates to a meeting in Philadelphia of the Continental Congress to deliberate on the common good and develop a consensus on how to deal with British abuse. However, that First Continental Congress, which met from September 5 to October 26, 1774, was consumed with procedural matters and managed only to agree on boycotting British goods. They decided to adjourn with much unfinished business, although firmly committed to meeting again after the winter season the following May.

The Second Continental Congress was intended to be a reconvening of that first congress, and all the colonies were represented. But by the time of meeting, the winds of war against the British were already blowing, with the "shot heard round the world" in the Battle of Lexington and Concord having occurred just a few weeks before on April 19, 1775. Circumstances now required that the Congress act as a de facto governing body of the United Colonies and create an army—the Continental Army—to which they unanimously appointed George Washington as general and commander in chief on June 15, 1775. Given the circumstances, the delegates decided that the Continental Congress should stay in session during time of war.

By spring of 1776, with Washington having driven the British from Boston, the Continental Congress was moving toward declaring independence from the British Empire, a necessary step to facilitate European countries' financial support for and alliance with the American colonies. Congress decided on three objectives: 1) drafting and issuing a resolution of independence; 2) drafting a model treaty; and 3) drafting a constitution in the form of governing Articles of Confederation. A committee of five, consisting of John Adams, Benjamin Franklin, Thomas Jefferson, Robert R. Livingston, and Roger Sherman, was given responsibility to come up with a document establishing separation and independence.

The committee of five quickly decided that Jefferson and Adams were best suited to the task of drafting that document. Jefferson deferred to the senior statesman Adams, but Adams insisted that Jefferson was better suited, having a "happy talent for composition," and "peculiar felicity of expression."[210] In short, Adams explained, "I had a great opinion of the elegance of his pen and none at all of my own."[211]

Jefferson is attributed with primary authorship of that document, which of course came to be known as the Declaration of Independence. Jefferson's preamble, which drew extensively from John Locke's *Second Treatise* on government and from his recent prior work drafting the preamble to the Virginia Constitution, was eloquent and powerful. But Adams and Franklin had to come to the rescue in salvaging some of the other mangled language that followed.

Finally, the edited Declaration was presented to the full Congress on July 1, which set off a titanic debate between the two oratorical giants, John Dickinson and John Adams. Dickinson, a Quaker delegate from Delaware who had written the "Olive Branch Petition" to secure a non-violent solution with King George the prior year, argued against a hasty separation, while Adams was passionate about independence already being overdue.[212] The heated debate drew in many of the other delegates and went on for some nine hours. After taking a preliminary vote, which revealed four states siding with Dickinson, it was decided to adjourn the meeting and move the discussion to the City Tavern and the boarding-houses of Philadelphia where delegates were staying.[213]

There are scant records of the discussions that ensued late into that night, but we do know that the next morning, on July 2, there was a vote in favor of issuing the Declaration that now included justification by "appealing to the Supreme Judge of the world for the rectitude of our intentions."[214] And it was made unanimous because opponents like John Dickinson and Robert Morris of Pennsylvania had the good sense to absent themselves from the vote, assuring the affirmative support of a majority of the delegates from their respective states.

Members of the Congress then insisted on further revisions to the document, and to the chagrin of Jefferson, they proceeded to rework the language on about a quarter of the text, with the end result being as close to a masterpiece of political and inspirational prose as anyone could hope for. On July 4, 1776, Congress then issued the Declaration of Independence, even as the British fleet sailed through the Narrows and anchored off Staten Island with more than thirty-four thousand troops, positioned to invade New York.

In addition to overseeing the funding and foreign diplomacy to support the war, one of the next major accomplishments of the Continental Congress was the passage of the Articles of Confederation on November 15, 1777, which served as the founding constitution of the United States. The Articles facilitated the colonial states' banding together during a time of war, creating the semblance of a centralized government for the nation. But there were serious deficiencies that came out of the delegates' fear that centralized power would corrupt and jeopardize the respective states' rights that each enjoyed. Because the Articles only provided for a unicameral legislature, but no executive branch or full-fledged judicial system, it was a defective and badly crippled governmental structure. One has to remember that the colonists' firsthand experience with the tyrannical abuse of power under King George III prompted them to err on the side of creating a flimsy government that could not easily abuse power. They preferred a weak rather than a corrupt and abusive government.

With the War of Independence ending in victory at Yorktown, the deficiencies of the Articles became increasingly obvious and painful in the peacetime that followed. With limited authority to regulate commerce, and no agreed-on national currency, states issued their own money, which complicated interstate trade. Additionally, the Articles had no provision for levying taxes to raise necessary funds. Thus, Congress found itself in the embarrassing position of being unable to pay back its wartime debt to Holland and France. Nor could the new nation maintain an army or a navy to quell violence on the frontier, protect its borders and territory from incursions by France, Spain, and Britain, and defend American maritime trade against piracy. This weakness encouraged foreign governments to push their advantage, causing commerce and trade to fall into a tailspin. The inability of the federal government to quell violence that erupted in rural Massachusetts in what came to be known as Shays' Rebellion was a final wakeup call that something needed to be done.

Morale and attendance at congressional sessions had been declining, and by the first half of 1786, quorums could rarely be met and the business of Congress was grinding to a halt. John Adams captured just how bad things were in saying, "The United States was doing more harm to itself than the British army had ever done."[215] To George Washington, the floundering government under the Articles of Confederation was condemning America to appear as a "humiliating and contemptible figure… in the annals of mankind."[216]

Sharing those sentiments, James Madison and Virginia governor Patrick Henry decided to take action and write letters to all the states' governors asking them to send delegates to meet in Annapolis, Maryland, on September 11, 1786, to discuss steps to improve commerce and to amend the weak Articles. But when only twelve delegates from five states showed up—New York, New Jersey, Pennsylvania, Delaware, and Virginia—hopes of achieving anything of substance were dashed. After just a few days' discussion, Alexander Hamilton did everyone a great favor in cutting the meeting short, preparing a summary report and a resolution to reconvene a proper meeting in Philadelphia the second week in May the next year on the grounds that delegates from all the states needed to be present on such a weighty matter as changing the constitution of the nation's government.

Madison looked forward with great anticipation to the reconvening of that Constitutional Convention involving all thirteen states (except Rhode Island, as it turned out). Madison arrived more than a week ahead of the anticipated commencement schedule, while most of the other delegates were nearly a week late. So, Madison unexpectedly had more than two extra weeks to continue his study and reflections on constitutions for republican and democratic government and otherwise prepare for what he anticipated would be "a second American revolution."[217]

Finally, after a quorum of seven states was accounted for, the delegates agreed it was time to get down to business. They met the following morning, the 25th of May 1787, at Independence Hall. That first day was preoccupied with delegate introductions, establishing procedural protocols, and nominating and confirming the unanimous choice of George Washington to serve as the Constitutional Convention's president.

The delegates who ended up attending the Constitutional Convention were highly educated and well read. Most all were public-minded and extremely accomplished, having had experience in one or more roles in either the Continental Army, or national and state politics: eight had signed the Declaration of Independence, fifteen had helped draft state constitutions, twenty-one had fought in the Revolutionary War, and three-quarters of them had been members of the Continental Congress.

Unknown at that time, attendees to the Convention included two future presidents of the nation they were founding, a future vice president, and five future members of the Supreme Court—two of whom would become chief justices. Ironically, they had not officially come together to draft a new Constitution, but rather had been sent by their states to make changes to the flimsy and ineffective Articles of Confederation.[218]

A colorful group they were, varying in temperament and personality—ranging from the gregarious, the self-assured, and the unbending to the self-confident introverts and brilliant, but socially awkward. The youngest was twenty-six and the oldest, at eighty-one, was Ben Franklin, who had to be brought into the daily proceedings in a "sedan chair," carried by two local prisoners with shoulder poles.

In the decade or two leading up to the Declaration, the Englishman John Locke was the most read and studied political philosopher in America. He influenced the founders in two important ways: First was his doctrine of natural law and natural rights—life, liberty, and property—rights which he argued came from God and were unalienable. Second was his doctrine of the social compact, a theory about the benefits of forming a government, established to protect man's natural rights and whose legitimacy came only from God and/or the people who accepted such authority.

In the 1780s, Montesquieu and Blackstone became more widely read. In fact, Blackstone was probably the most read political and legal thinker in the colonies, with more copies of his book, *Commentaries on the Laws of England*, sold in America than in the more populous England.[219]

The founders drew three major points from Blackstone: First, his conviction that all law has its source in God. A second significant point was the importance of the judiciary and judges, who were to interpret the law, but not make it. A third contribution from Blackstone was his systemization of the common law of England, which was founded on biblical principles. The common law of England reinforced the Christian foundation of law in America, in large part because of the power and logic of Blackstone's writing. As a side note, Charles Pinckney, a convention delegate from South Carolina, studied at Oxford University, and was considered one of Blackstone's first disciples, having studied law under his tutelage.[220]

Like Blackstone, Montesquieu believed that all law has its source in God. Men make their own laws, but these laws must conform to the eternal laws of God. In his primary text, *The Spirit of the Laws*, Montesquieu recognized the value of Christianity in fostering good laws and good government. But because of the sinful and self-centered nature of man, he advocated the separation of powers in government, in which one power would check another. Montesquieu's main contribution to the thinking of the founders was the doctrine of the separation of powers between the legislative, executive, and judicial branches of government.

Although Madison was short in stature at five feet four, he was an intellectual giant—having completed a four-year degree program at Princeton in only two years and being well read in classical political philosophy. Anxious for the fate of the country, Madison had used the extra time awaiting the arrival of convention delegates to prepare a plan to introduce his ideas about an entirely new Constitution, an approach that came to be known as the "Virginia Plan." But first, he had to be sure the delegates were ready to abandon any attempt at salvaging the Articles. He enlisted his fellow Virginia delegate and colleague, Governor Edmund Randolph, to lead the charge with the key points he had been working on.

On the third day of the convention, Randolph took the floor and recited the familiar litany of the Confederation's main flaws and failures. With that sinking in, he went on to offer fifteen resolutions to rectify those problems and transform the Confederation through changes that would result in a completely different and superior government.

Well aware of the glaring deficiencies of the Articles, the delegates were all ears to hear more of what Edmunds had to say. And so, he continued and introduced a key article in Madison's Virginia Plan focusing on the need for a constitution to provide a national government consisting of three branches—a legislative branch with two houses, an executive branch, and a judicial branch.

Madison took to the floor and made the case that a strong national government based on Montesquieu's theory of a separation of powers would actually mitigate government corruption and abuse of power because each of the three branches would provide "checks and balances" to the other branches. The Virginia Plan would reduce the states to a subordinate position to the federal government and the legislature—composed of two branches or houses—with the number of representatives from each state based on their population. The Virginia Plan also called for the election of the executive by the legislature, rather than a popular election.

This evoked a strong response from delegates representing small states, who did not want to play second fiddle to either the larger states or a new national government. The Virginia Plan would clearly favor large states whose proportional representation would be larger in the legislature.

Roger Sherman of Connecticut was one who argued that a strong central government would not protect citizens' liberties as well as the state governments could. Sherman, the second oldest delegate who had been deeply affected by the Great Awakening, was also highly respected as a statesman, being the only delegate to have signed all three prior foundational documents of American government: 1) the 1774 Articles of Association; 2) the 1776 Declaration of Independence; and 3) the 1777 Articles of Confederation.

While tripartite government made sense to almost everyone, it wasn't at all clear what powers and what form the legislature should have, and what its power in relationship to the states' legislatures should be—which raised general questions about the boundaries between state and federal jurisdiction, how the representation in each of the branches should be determined, and how long terms of office should be.

William Paterson, the leading delegate from New Jersey, introduced an alternative to Madison's Virginia Plan, which came to be known as the Small State Plan or the "New Jersey Plan." This plan also provided for three branches of government, but would give Congress expanded powers, with each state having one vote in Congress. Like the Virginia Plan, the New Jersey Plan called for the executive to be elected by the legislature. But to mitigate the corruption of power in the executive, the New Jersey Plan initially called for a plural executive in the form of a council rather than a single figure like a president.

By the end of the second week, there were wide divisions and a heightened awareness of the variety of issues, as well as a diversity of opinions on solutions. Some delegates were defenders of popular will on one issue, but then would be guardians of the elite class on others. Many felt that no matter what design they came up with, the republican form of government faced two nearly insurmountable challenges: First was the fear of greater corruption from a stronger and larger federal government. And second was the question of representation—whether states should have an equal vote or whether states' legislative representatives should be based on population to best serve the different variety of interests and different populations living in each state.

Despite the best efforts of the Pennsylvania delegate duo— Gouverneur Morris, a man blessed with the gift of humor, and James Wilson, an eloquent theologian turned lawyer—who each took to the floor more frequently than any of the other delegates, felicity and trust between convention members was slow to develop in the first month. The primary cause of division was the conflict between delegates from large states and those from small states over the issue of representation and voting in the national legislature. Delegates from the larger states argued that voting should be proportional to population; otherwise, the citizens of smaller states would have a greater voice than citizens of larger states. The smaller states argued the converse—that is, the smaller states should have the same number of votes as the larger states; otherwise, the larger states would dominate the smaller. This seemingly insurmountable conflict, and the apparent refusal of the large states to give an inch, so offended the two delegates from New York, John Lansing and Robert Yates, that they packed their bags and permanently left the Constitutional Convention.[221] Since the other New York delegate, Alexander Hamilton, was frequently away tending to pressing matters of his law practice, the state of New York was unrepresented for much of the convention's daily sessions in that fateful summer. Senior statesman Ben Franklin felt the fate of America hung in the balance and worried that all might be lost if the convention collapsed.[222]

On June 28, Franklin took the initiative to urge the members to recognize their own limitations and humbly seek divine guidance. Making a plea to save the faltering convention, he reminded them that the challenges and difficulties they were facing then were similar to what they had faced in the revolutionary war struggle. And just as members of the Continental Congress had daily prayer in the very same room for divine protection during the war, so Franklin argued, convention delegates needed to beseech "the Father of lights to illuminate their path and understanding to solve current problems." Franklin then closed his exhortation, showing deference to George Washington, who as president of the convention presided over its schedule, by offering a prayer, which included a reference to Psalm 117:1, which says, "Except the Lord build the House, they labor in vain that build it." Franklin continued his prayer before the delegates that he firmly believed this and "without His concurring aid, we shall succeed in this political building no better than the Builders of Babel."[223]

What is most noteworthy about Franklin's passionate prayer in hindsight—in addition to the fact that historians have labeled him a Deist and one of the least religious among the founders—is that it served to break the impasse that was crippling the convention. The delegates were dismissed for a three-day break, and some, moved by Franklin's prayer, attended the Old First Reformed Church, where Rev. William Rogers held a special time of daily prayer for the Constitutional Convention proceedings.[224]

The youngest convention delegate at twenty-six, Jonathan Dayton—a largely unsung hero of the Revolutionary War[225]—observed that when the delegates met again on July 2, much of the animosity was gone, noting, "We assembled again; and…every unfriendly feeling had been expelled, and a spirit of conciliation had been cultivated."[226]

Within days, Roger Sherman of Connecticut, one of the more devout Christians in the group, saw the solution, which he deemed as obvious. That was to give each state an equal vote in the Senate, and apportion the House of Representatives according to population. After some days of further discussion, it was voted on and passed in mid-July by a five-to-four margin, even in the absence of the New York delegates. Thus, Sherman is credited with what came to be known as the "Great Compromise" or the "Connecticut Compromise," which not only saved the convention, but also reinforced a more conciliatory atmosphere, providing more confidence to solve other problems going forward.[227]

The Great Compromise solved the problem of representation and voting in the two houses of Congress, but apportioning representatives based on population in the Southern states with many slaves was unresolved. All the delegates knew that the business of creating a constitution that would include the Southern states was never going to happen by making an issue of slavery at that time, although most looked forward to the day when the states themselves would end slavery. For the time being, the delegates agreed to count the slave population by the "three-fifths rule," obviously limiting the Southern states' representation in the House, which had been established by the prior Confederation Congress of 1783, and also creating language in the Constitution that would effectively ban the trading and importation of slaves after 1808.

The next challenge taken up by the convention concerned the election and authority of the executive. Under the prior system of the Articles of Confederation, there was no executive branch, and thus no real ability to execute policy. This obviously needed to be corrected, but Convention delegates had different ideas of what that should look like. The office and title of president was simply unknown at that time. Many delegates, including Hamilton, believed a monarchy a viable model for an efficient executive office. After all, there were plenty of kings and queens in Europe, but no presidents.

Convention delegates got used to the idea of a chief executive being called a president, perhaps in part because they had already made George Washington the president of the Constitutional Convention, and they recognized that he was the natural choice for first president of the United States.

There were questions of how long he should serve and who or what body should choose or elect the executive. Few of the delegates advocated for direct election of the president on the grounds that common people would be insufficiently informed regarding national candidates who lived far from their states. Madison found himself in a minority of advocating for a "president of the people," and a preliminary motion to have the executive chosen by the national legislature passed almost unanimously.[228]

Madison reminded the delegates that "the preservation of liberty depended upon the separation of the legislature, executive and judiciary powers."[229] With this came more debate and a recognition that putting the decision of electing the president in the hands of one of the three branches—the legislature—was fundamentally problematic. As the leading Pennsylvania delegate Gouverneur Morris put it, "If the legislature elect [the executive] it will be the work of intrigue, of cabal, and of faction; it will be like the election of a pope by a conclave of cardinals; real merit will rarely be the title to the appointment."[230] Morris then made a motion to reconsider the constitution of the executive, which easily passed.

So, with the debate on the executive coming full circle to where they had started a week before, Madison took the floor and painstakingly reviewed and eliminated the various methods of selecting the executive. He also explained why he thought four years was optimal for the president's term. By the time he finished, delegates were in basic agreement with Madison's conclusion that "the option before us then lay between an appointment by electors chosen by the people—and an immediate appointment by the people." [231] With this narrowed down but unresolved, along with uncertainty about the length and number of terms for the executive, and what would constitute grounds for impeachment, on August 18, the convention referred the executive matters to a Committee of Eleven to come up with recommendations for a vote in early September.

Madison's role in educating delegates about the simplicity and essential role of checks and balances in the Constitution at every stage of the convention cannot be underestimated. It was probably best expressed later, during the ratification stage in *Federalist* no. 51, in which he wrote:

Ambition must be made to counteract ambition...It may be a reflection on human nature, that such devices should be necessary to control the abuses of government. But what is government itself, but the greatest of all reflections on human nature? If men were angels, no government would be necessary. If angels were to govern men, neither external nor internal controls on government would be necessary. In framing a government which is to be administered by men over men, the great difficulty lies in this: you must first enable the government to control the governed; and in the next place oblige it to control itself.

It turns out that the convention's negotiations on structuring the third branch of government—the judiciary—went far more smoothly and quickly than the prior arduous proceedings. The convention delegates had truly wrestled over the provisions for a national legislature and the executive and the balance of federal and state authority.

With those challenges behind them, there was a sense that agreement on forming the judiciary would be far easier. After all, the delegates, like most Americans, accepted and even appreciated the values associated with the British judicial system. All the delegates had some familiarity with and appreciation of Sir William Blackstone's *Commentaries on the Laws of England*, which was universally rated as the most comprehensive treatise on common law, and about which there was wide agreement.

Madison's ideas about the necessity and the structuring of the judiciary came out of the Virginia constitution, which was the first state to establish the judiciary as one of the three independent branches of government. There was a general meeting of the minds that the Virginia Plan's recommendation of establishing a supreme tribunal and subordinate federal court system with judges chosen for life, patterned on the British system, was not only a good idea, but a necessary third leg for a complete tripartite government of checks and balances.

Hamilton for his part, felt that "there can be but few men in society, who will have sufficient skill in the laws to qualify them for the stations of judges...and the number must be still smaller of those who unite the requisite integrity with the requisite knowledge."[232] While he agreed that lifetime appointment of judges was one of the best ways to assure an independent judiciary, Hamilton also believed that the tenure of judges should be conditional on their "good behavior."

Madison's Virginia Plan recommendation of judges being chosen by the legislature was met with resistance for the same reasons the prior idea of the legislature choosing the president was rejected. Nathaniel Gorham, a delegate from Massachusetts and an ardent patriot who had managed military logistics and manpower during the War of Independence, proposed a solution on judicial appointment that his state had used since the British colonial court system had been dismantled in 1776. In Massachusetts, superior court judges had a lifetime tenure, and they were chosen by the state's governor, the executive, with advice and consent of the smaller branch of the state legislature. Madison took to the floor in favor of that idea and it didn't take much debate for convention delegates to embrace that framework—that federal judges would be appointed by the president with advice and consent of the Senate.

Now that things were taking final shape, early concerns about the new constitution creating a federal government with excessive power resurfaced. In a nutshell, that concern was that state and individual rights proclaimed by the Declaration of Independence and enjoyed previously under the Articles of Confederation would be encroached upon and lost by federal government overreach and abuse. At about this time, a proposal was made to ensure the sovereignty of the union and allow the federal government to prohibit future secession of states. James Madison rejected it, saying, "A union of the states containing such an ingredient seemed to provide for its own destruction. The use of force against a state would look more like a declaration of war [and] would probably be considered by the party attacked as a dissolution of all previous compacts by which it might be bound."[233]

At this stage, there was a vocalized, heightened concern about protecting state's rights against federal government abuse and providing a remedy along the lines of the right to secede. Virginia's George Mason remarked that he "wished the plan had been prefaced by a Bill of Rights."

Elbridge Gerry of Massachusetts, who would later become vice president in the Madison administration, had previously moved for the appointment of a committee to prepare such a bill, but the delegates defeated the motion. While not actually opposing the principle of a bill of rights, delegates generally felt that taking that up would delay the completion of their work, and also that state constitutions provided protection for those rights and that it would be unnecessary and redundant to include in a federal constitution that was basically focused on enumerated powers.

Madison, however, had the foresight to recognize that even if the US Constitution were ratified by two-thirds of the states but failed in one or more of the large states, the Constitution could be adopted but be stillborn. Thus, a commitment was made to add amendments in the form of a Bill of Rights to the Constitution after its ratification. Only by making such a pledge were the Constitution's supporters sure they could succeed both to get unanimous approval at the close of the convention and also achieve ratification by the people in such closely divided states as New York, Massachusetts, Rhode Island, and Virginia.

It was now the end of August, with only details on the Constitution yet to be worked out by the appropriately named "Committee on Postponed Matters." When the delegates looked back to their arrival in Philadelphia in May and June at the beginning of the Constitutional Convention, few other than Madison could have imagined that their votes and compromises would create a government of checks and balances based on a separation of powers concept that would establish the foundation for a republic that would survive for hundreds of years.

After the Committee on Postponed Matters had completed their work of reconciliation at the end of August, the delegates appointed the "Committee of Style and Arrangement" to enumerate the Articles and prepare a final Constitution from the textual provisions that came out of other committees and were approved by the convention. With handwriting that approached the elegance of John Hancock, loquacious Pennsylvania delegate Gouverneur Morris was assigned the task of drafting the final document. And with only a few revisions—such as reducing the number needed to override a presidential veto from three-quarters to two-thirds—the final copy was completed for the convention's final review, and voice vote on September 15.

That vote was nearly unanimous.

On September 17, sixteen weeks after the convention had been originally scheduled to begin, the delegates gathered to hear convention secretary, Major William Jackson, read the text of the Constitution document aloud. Immediately following, Ben Franklin arose, speech in hand. Too frail to project his voice, Franklin turned to his fellow Pennsylvania delegate, James Wilson, to read his words for him. Reminding everyone that while perfection by a group is impossible, and that there were parts of the document with which he did not agree (but that over a long life he had learned he was not always right), he commended the delegates' work as being both admirable and remarkable in that it delivered as flawless a system of government as had ever existed. "It would astonish our enemies," Franklin wrote, "who are waiting with confidence to hear that our councils are confounded like those of the Builders of Babel."[234] With that, he implored convention members to unanimously sign their names to the Constitution document. In the end, signatures by the states were unanimous, although because a bill of rights had yet to be drafted and formally amended, Virginia delegates Edmund Randolph and George Mason, and Massachusetts delegate Elbridge Gerry chose not to sign the Constitution as a matter of conscience that day.

With the work of the convention completed, on the eve of departing Philadelphia, the delegates enjoyed a farewell dinner at the City Tavern. It was quite a gathering to behold, with some delegates expressing relief and a bit of exhaustion, but most were in a well-deserved exuberant and celebratory mood. Many marveled at how the hand of Providence had been at work throughout the proceedings. How else could delegates from twelve disparate states have mustered the forbearance and magnanimity to agree on the terms of a new Constitution after only four months of deliberation? Other dinner conversations that evening broached the subject, with some trepidation about the uncertainty of the next stage, about the battle to win ratification by two-thirds of the states.

As it turned out, the ratification process moved along quickly in five states. Delaware, Pennsylvania, New Jersey, Georgia, and Connecticut ratified the Constitution by December. But in other states, notably Massachusetts, New York, and Virginia, it was clear that delivering on the Bill of Rights Amendments was critical to win ratification. Over the next months, Patrick Henry, George Mason, James Madison, Alexander Hamilton, John Jay, Samuel Adams, and John Hancock were among those who played various key roles in influencing each of the three states to ratify the Constitution—on the condition that amending it with a Bill of Rights provided legal protections on all the critical rights of civil liberties and states' rights.

The debate in New York was particularly fierce between the "Federalists," who favored ratification of the Constitution as written, and "Antifederalists," who opposed the Constitution and resisted giving stronger powers to the national government. Within days of the Philadelphia convention's approval of the Constitution, Antifederalists began publishing articles in the press criticizing it, arguing that the document gave Congress excessive powers, and that it could lead to the American people losing the liberties they had fought for and won in the Revolution.

This prompted Alexander Hamilton to undertake writing a comprehensive series of essays defending the Constitution, which came to be known as *The Federalist Papers*. To assist in these efforts, Hamilton recruited James Madison, who was then in New York serving in the Confederation Congress, and his fellow New Yorker, John Jay, who had helped negotiate the treaty ending the war with Britain and served as secretary of foreign affairs under the Articles of Confederation.

To avoid any appearance of betraying the convention's confidentiality, they chose to write under the pen name "Publius," after a general who had helped found the Roman Republic. Hamilton's first essay, appearing in the *Independent Journal* on October 27, 1787, argued that the debate facing the nation was not just about ratification of the proposed Constitution. More importantly, it was about the question of "whether societies of men are really capable or not of establishing good government from reflection and choice, or whether they are forever destined to depend for their political constitutions on accident and force."

Over the next seven months, the three authors behind Publius would write a total of eighty-five articles, which eventually were published in one volume known as *The Federalist Papers*. Together, the *Federalist* essays tried to assure the public of two key points: First, they explained that a strong government was needed for a variety of reasons, and particularly because the United States needed to act effectively in foreign affairs. Second, they explained how the separation of powers in the federal government would mitigate corruption and prevent the national government from evolving into a tyrannical power.

In subsequent years, *The Federalist Papers* would become one of the most important political documents in US history. Unmatched in the political discourse of the American political tradition, it provides touchstones for understanding the Constitution—a concise and comprehensive explanation of the philosophy and operation of the Constitution in action.

Originally, each state was given six months to meet and vote on ratifying the Constitution, but only six states had voted in favor in that time frame. Two of the most important large states, Virginia and New York, were holdouts. The contest in Virginia was close and bitterly fought for months and wasn't resolved in the affirmative until after the Constitution had become legal, with New Hampshire fulfilling the two-thirds requirement—becoming the ninth state to ratify the Constitution on June 21, 1788.

In New York, the last undecided large state, Hamilton managed a brilliant campaign combining both threat and accommodation. First, he argued that if New York did not ratify, the commercial downstate interests would likely separate from upstate agricultural interests. Second, he embraced the conciliatory path that had worked in Massachusetts, which was that amendments of a Bill of Rights were a necessary condition of an affirmative vote. The New York state convention voted 30–27 in favor of ratification on July 26, 1788. It took the thirteenth state, Rhode Island—which did not send delegates to the Constitutional Convention—nearly a year longer to ratify the Constitution.[235]

Because the Bill of Rights—also known as the Ten Amendments—is an integral part of the Constitution in delineating citizens' and states' rights, it's worth summarizing their key points:

- The First Amendment protects citizens' rights of freedom in speech, press, religion, peaceful assembly, and petition of government.
- The Second guarantees the right to keep and bear arms, which the government cannot infringe.
- The Fourth provides for people to be secure in their homes, property, and papers by prohibiting unreasonable searches and seizure by government.
- The Fifth and Sixth provide for due process and expedient and fair trials, and just compensation in the event of government seizure of property.
- The Ninth and Tenth Amendments reserve all powers and rights to the states and the people that are not specifically delegated to the federal government by the Constitution.

The US government established by the amended Constitution was the most dramatic departure from all prior governmental arrangements in human history. Taken together with the Declaration of Independence, the Constitution was the first political doctrine to contain a clear delineation of citizens' rights and establish that these rights came from God and not the state. Thus, these rights were sovereign and unalienable. In short, the US Constitution put the people in charge, requiring government to answer to and serve them, and not the other way around.

The genius of the Constitution was that it limited government abuse by creating checks and balances of power between three separate but equal branches of government—the executive, the legislative, and the judicial. The Constitution also separated power between the federal and state governing authorities.

Frequent elections established by the Constitution provided yet another important mechanism to limit the extent and duration of government incompetence and corruption. This also meant that the most sacred responsibility of citizenship established by the Constitution was and is the right of the people to vote and decide who shall govern. And those sacred votes must be protected by the integrity of honest elections.

This combination of limiting governmental power and maximizing people's rights makes the US Constitution uniquely revolutionary in all of human history. Compared with European and Asian powers, the United States is a young country, but it turns out that it's also the longest-running constitutional democratic republic in history. For most people, that should be the true measure of success.

The unique and specific limits put on government by the Constitution are what empowered Americans to exercise their freedom and ingenuity to create and build—driving the United States from colonial poverty to world economic superpower in just two hundred years. Another true measure of extraordinary success.

The Constitution makes it clear that everyone—whether in the public or private sector—is equal under the law. Additionally, every elected federal government officeholder, judicial appointee, and executive branch Cabinet secretary is required to pledge an oath before assuming office to "support and defend the Constitution of the United States against all enemies, foreign and domestic." And carved in stone in the façade over the entry to the Supreme Court are the words, "Equal Justice under the Law." And outside that court is a statue of a blindfolded Lady Justice holding scales, suggesting that fairness in America is a paramount virtue.

So, it comes as an unprecedented surprise to many Americans that a significant number of high-ranking US government officials appear to have stepped over legal lines and violated their oaths of office. There is overwhelming evidence that there were a variety of seditious activities undertaken against candidate Donald Trump, who was successful in the 2016 election—efforts that then continued for four years to overturn the results of that election. With little or no penalties adjudicated, seditious activities not only continued, but were amped up to carry out the greatest crime against the people—massive election irregularities and vote fraud in the November 2020 election—bringing about results that fundamentally compromised the legitimacy of the US government.

A new civil war has begun, but it is very different from the one that divided the country some 160 years ago between the Union and the Confederacy. In the crosshairs of today's civil war is the United States Constitution. Failing to win that battle and maintain the integrity and checks and balances in the US Constitution would likely be the end of freedom and independence of the United States. And if the torch of freedom is extinguished in the United States, so goes the rest of the world.

In conclusion, more than any other holiday and now more than ever, Constitution Day provides us with both the reasons and the prompting to reaffirm that equal justice under the law is the standard, that we the people are in charge, and that our federal government should answer to us first before we answer to it. As Thomas Jefferson said at the time of the founding, "*When governments fear the people, there is liberty. When the people fear the government, there is tyranny.*"

CHAPTER 14

America at the Crossroads: Still the Best Hope for a City on a Hill

Now that you are at the five-yard line—the last chapter—having completed our adventure and journey that spanned 'more than five centuries in the historical holiday chapters, what are we to make of the sweep of American history? How shall we now think about America?

First, the United States should be thought about in the context of other nations that existed at the time it was founded. What made America unique and different from all other nations? Second, it's important to understand and evaluate the United States today in the context of other nations in the contemporary world. For those inclined to be more critical than praiseworthy, America's shortcomings should be framed with comparative reality of alternatives found in other nations. And last, what is in America's cultural and governing makeup that can bring about correctives to whatever problems we face?

The first five holiday chapters of the book covered the people and developments that predated the formation of the United States. We could call these foundational holidays because they have had an enormous impact on our country from the founding to the present times—both in beliefs and attitudes that have shaped the culture and our identity as individuals, as well as in the dynamic between the people and the government. Specifically, these foundational holidays not only speak to us about a vision for an ideal type in societal relationships, but they also provide an understanding about the basis of peoples' natural rights, the limitations and responsibilities of government, and the source of course correction when corruption causes the actions of people and government to go awry.

The following seven holidays that take us up to the present time provide a broad understanding about the values that most people associate with America, such as the meaning of equality, liberty, patriotism, valor, the need for sacrifice, morality and religion, the melting pot of racial integration and the benefits of diversity, the dignity and importance of work, independence and creativity, federalism and states' rights and the importance of rule of law, and even the nation's unique status as a microcosm of an multi-ethnic ideal world—an identity also known as a "city on a hill."

With Columbus, we learned that there were two compelling reasons that drove him to be the first to cross the Atlantic Ocean from Europe by sailing south from Spain and then west. First, Columbus's maritime training, geographic worldview, and his love for the seafaring life instilled a conviction to find a westward passage to India and the Spice Islands when European trade was cut off by Islamic forces. Second, Columbus was also prompted to answer a "divine call" because of his genuine zeal about the opportunity for Christian evangelism to share the gospel with people unaware of that good news whom he would likely encounter along the way.

While Spain's sponsorship of Columbus's voyages created problems and unjustly tainted his legacy in the minds of some, we rightfully remember and celebrate him for his vision and his persistence of character that led to the discovery of the New World. Coming at the end of fifteenth century, it was a monumental event, and was clearly one of the markers of the beginning of the Modern Age. While Columbus never saw or set foot on any land that would become part of the continental US, his discovery of the New World opened the door and inspired subsequent adventurers, conquerors, traders, settlers, and missionaries pursuing opportunity and exercising their vital interests.

Columbus made his discovery only twenty-five-odd years before Martin Luther posted his famous *Ninety-five Theses* on the Wittenberg Castle bulletin board, the purpose of which was to enlighten people about corruption that had become part of the theology and the practices of the Catholic Church in hope that the church could be realigned with the true teachings of Christ and the Bible. Luther's positions challenging papal authority were not received well and he was branded a heretic and an outlaw to be hunted down. Fortunately, Luther's supporters and friends protected him and gave him refuge and a hiding place at the Wartburg Castle. He and his theses survived and succeeded in launching a spiritual revolution. Luther would go down in history as the founder of the Protestant Reformation, which would reshape the Western world, providing another marker and significant leap forward into the Modern Age.

Luther's reformed understanding of Jesus Christ and the Bible was also shared by other towering figures such as John Calvin and John Knox, who brought about major reformation movements in Europe: in the case of Calvin to Switzerland, France, and the Netherlands,[236] and in the case of Knox to Scotland and the British Isles.[237] Another small reformation group who faced persecution from the Church of England became pilgrims taking refuge in Holland in 1608. A little more than a decade later, they went from obscurity to becoming known as the historic Pilgrims who courageously chose in 1620 to embark on the *Mayflower*, leave the old European world behind, and risk their lives to get to the New World.

The Pilgrims who settled in Plymouth, Massachusetts in 1620 and the Puritans who followed them in 1630, coming to what is now the Boston area, thought in Hebraic terms. Both the Pilgrims and the Puritans likened their voyage across the ocean to the New World to the ancient Israelites who broke free from persecution and slavery in Egypt and sacrificed everything to get to "the Promised Land." They believed that life was not a succession of random events, but rather that history had a providential purpose. And under the leadership of William Bradford and John Winthrop, they likened their respective groups to being participants in furthering God's plan for the world, just as God's elect accomplished three thousand years previously under the leadership of Moses. Winthrop reminded his followers who accompanied him on the ship *Arabella*, bound for New England, that they would avoid failure and provide for their posterity by following the counsel of the Old Testament prophet Micah in being "knit together and maintaining affection in community." In so doing, Winthrop specifically looked to Micah and the covenant between God and the Israelites as a model of political community, and invoked his followers to think that *"we shall be as a city upon a hill—the eyes of all people are upon us."*[238]

So, it should be of little wonder that with these foundational early settlers in Massachusetts seeing themselves in the same spiritual terms as the ancient Israelites seeking the Promised Land, the largely Christian America became a safe haven for Jewish people, who came in large numbers centuries later, contributing much to the nation's family culture and economic growth.

The Mayflower Compact was a covenant that predated the Lockean social contract that powerfully influenced the founders and the writing of the Constitution. The difference between a "contract" and "covenant" is subtle, yet profound. The former is an arrangement in which people agree to give up some of their freedom to gain something for themselves. The latter—a covenant—was a Hebraic concept that represented a stronger commitment than a contract because it was a sacred promise between two or more parties who came together under God's watchful eye to achieve something noble that could not be achieved separately.

We might think of covenants as being too restrictive and the Pilgrims being a rather stoic and cheerless group. Yet, the Pilgrims were uniquely successful in establishing an inclusive community, made up of both Christian believers referred to as "Saints" and nonbelievers referred to as "Strangers." The Strangers made up slightly less than half the passengers on the *Mayflower*, yet they all went along with the Pilgrims in signing the Mayflower Compact, an agreement on the rules for self-government, which was a forerunner to the US Constitution. It turns out that the Plymouth Colony was far more peaceful, tolerant, inclusive, and less repressive than the semi-theocracy that developed in the Puritans' Massachusetts Bay Colony centered in Boston, who took up arms against the Indians in the Pequot War and later became famous for the "Salem witch trials"—a dark legacy of judgmental intolerance that took place within their jurisdiction.

The Pilgrims were close to being model colonizers, being respectful of the native Indian population, working alongside them, and even going to their aid voluntarily when there was need. The Indians in turn helped the Pilgrims, and they both celebrated the first harvest with a three-day thanksgiving party. Perhaps more substantially, the Pilgrims signed a peace treaty with that tribe, the Wampanoags, which lasted more than fifty years. These acts of tolerance, generosity, and trust are really quite remarkable and worth reflecting on today, four hundred years later, given our contemporary state of intolerance, low trust, seditious activity, and division in twenty-first century America.

The next three chapters on the Christmas, New Year, and Easter holidays are in many ways the most foundational of all because they explain the beliefs and attitudes that shaped early American culture in all thirteen colonies and provided the key motivational forces for the colonists to risk their lives in declaring war on Great Britain to achieve independence. And once independence was achieved militarily and diplomatically, it was again Christian beliefs and attitudes that were dominant in shaping the thinking and the debates of the fifty-five delegates at the Constitutional Convention, resulting in the final drafting of the Articles and language in the Constitution in 1787.[239]

In contemporary times, Americans tend to take for granted their rights of life, liberty, and the pursuit of happiness. But the fact is that there was little appreciation or understanding of those rights anywhere else in the world at the time of America's founding. In fact, just the opposite was true most everywhere. The common understanding that was fairly universal was that rights came from an earthly authority, which was typically the state, the king, the emperor, the military ruler, or the feudal baron.

While the concept and the term "democracy" and "constitution" as a form of government originated with the Greeks in the fourth century BC, its implementation was limited to a few city-states and had no staying power. In the first century BC, Marcus Cicero, A Roman lawyer, political philosopher, and statesman, rediscovered those Greek political ideas and argued that Rome's political turmoil could be resolved and virtuous government restored by adopting a republican form of government. While he was widely considered one of Rome's greatest orators and prosaic writers and rose to the position of Consul in the Roman government, Cicero was also a political rival and seen as a threat. And so, in 43 BC, on the order of Mark Antony, he was assassinated. And with his death, so went the ideas about the virtues of republican and constitutional government and democratic participation.

It would be some fourteen hundred years later that those ideas came back into the public mind in Europe, partially by way of the Renaissance, which originated in the fourteenth century with Petrarch's discovery of Cicero's letters and a rebirth of interest in classical Greek and Roman civilization. The Renaissance, which extended over the next two and a half centuries, was also characterized by a rebirth of learning and development of fine arts, literature, science, and architecture.

But it was Christianity, and specifically the Protestant Reformation movement of the sixteenth century, that led more directly to the ideas about equality, liberty, rule of law, and unalienable natural rights becoming incorporated into the Declaration of Independence. It was a truly revolutionary understanding that these rights did not come from the sanction and authority of the state or a church institution, but from God himself—thus being unalienable. The Reformation established that there was an equality in "the priesthood of all believers" who could have a direct relationship with God, without any Catholic Church hierarchy or mediating authority. It was and is a truly liberating understanding of how life is meant to be lived.

When the US Constitution built on these ideas and prescribed a representative and limited government with the checks and balances of three branches, and at the same time embraced a federalist system of state laws and authority which pushed back against the federal government, America's formal founding accomplished something truly revolutionary that existed nowhere else in the world. For the first time in human history, a government was established by the people and for the people. It was these ideas at that time in history that made the founding of the United States absolutely unique and exemplary—the most profound single event in shaping the modern world.

It would take some fifty-eight years after the US Constitution was ratified for the next nation in the world, Switzerland, to adopt a democratic representative government.[240] And it took another thirty-five years for New Zealand, Canada, and the United Kingdom to follow suit and establish democratic constitutional parliamentary governments.[241] Meanwhile, Asian countries almost all continued to live under authoritarian and military dictatorships, as they had to greater and lesser degrees for thousands of years. It is amazing to think that the most populated part of the world had almost no experience with democracy and people's rights until well into the twentieth century.

It wasn't until after World War II that constitutional democracy arrived in Asia. And that was a direct result of the United States and its victory in World War II, which led to the occupation of Japan under the direction of General Douglas MacArthur. MacArthur undertook reforms that broadened economic participation in Japan by breaking up large landholdings and zaibatsu corporate conglomerates. He asked the Japanese authorities to sever the relationship between the Shinto religion and the state, and he reformed and separated the Japanese educational system from government control. In the end, MacArthur encouraged the Japanese to take responsibility to rewrite their constitution and create a new democratic government. And he applauded the end result: the Japanese authorities chose a parliamentary system of representative democratic government, which was closer to the British than the American system of government.

Focusing primarily on MacArthur's political and economic democratization policies, historians have given almost no attention to the other part of rebuilding Japan to which MacArthur was attentive. MacArthur understood the Japanese had believed prior to World War II that they were a superior race and invincible because, according to the national religion of Shintoism, the emperor was a descendant of the sun goddess Amaterasu. But with defeat in 1945, all of Japan's gods—its supreme military, its divine emperor, its thousand-year belief that the Land of the Rising Sun would rule the world—had all failed. This shocking military defeat left the Japanese people utterly despondent and demoralized, with suicide rates escalating sharply. Recognizing that this total collapse of faith among the Japanese had resulted in a spiritual vacuum, MacArthur took action with pleas for spiritual help from America and abroad. He recounts in his memoir:

> Whenever possible, I told visiting Christian ministers of the need for their work in Japan. "The more missionaries we can bring out here, and the more occupation troops we can send home, the better." The Pocket Testament League, at my request, distributed 10,000,000 Bibles translated into Japanese. Gradually, a spiritual regeneration in Japan began to grow.[242]

After leading the American and UN forces in the Korean War and returning home in 1955, MacArthur recounted his experience in Japan in an interview published in *U.S. News and World Report*, noting that, "No phase of the occupation has left me with a greater sense of personal satisfaction than my spiritual stewardship."[243]

But that was not the end of the story. Remarkably, these Western reforms to the political and economic institutions imposed by a foreign army and the spiritual goodwill that was established took root, and friendship and respect between Japan and the United States has remained strong ever since. Today, there are intense debates regarding provisions of the constitution, but the essential decision that Japan will remain a democracy is unquestioned. And Japan's commitment to its military alliance with the United States is stronger today than at any prior time.

The Philippines became a territory of the United States after Spanish rule ended in 1898 with Spain's defeat in the Spanish-American War. The Filipino people came to admire and love Americans so much that, in 1935, they decided to draft a new constitution—copied entirely from the US Constitution. It would take another ten years to become operational after World War II, when the Japanese were driven out of the Philippines.

Something analogous happened in India in 1947 when British colonial rule ended, but left behind democratic institutions, which were adopted and treasured by Indians. In the late 1980s, two equally remarkable events occurred. In South Korea and Taiwan, powerful military dictatorships voluntarily initiated a transition to constitutional democracy. In both countries, the changes took root and have remained vibrant ever since.[244] The fruit of that democratic reform was also seen in explosive economic growth—frequently called "the East Asian miracle."[245]

Returning to what happened in America from its founding until today, there is a story that has eluded most people, including many historians. And that is what I call the arc of progress and redemption in America. Of late, critics of the United States have largely converged on 1619, when slavery was allegedly introduced to the Jamestown, Virginia, colony, arguing that that was the beginning of what is said to be America's systemic racism. By our standards today, slavery in America was reprehensible. However, understanding how that injustice began and how it was resolved takes a bit of time.

At the time of the founding of the Jamestown colony, slavery existed all over the world, but it was not planned or predetermined by the Jamestown settlers. The Africans introduced to Jamestown were in fact former slaves captured by an English privateer ship from Portuguese slave ships at sea, and they were traded for food and water. In that trade, the Africans were accepted by the Jamestown colonists as indentured servants, with a status equal to the English, Scottish, and Irish-born indentured servants who also came to America in this time frame. The status of indentured servants meant that freedom was granted after their indenture or bond was completed—generally a term of four to seven years.[246]

The slave trade did later come to Virginia around 1650, but not in the time and way of the common narrative surrounding Jamestown, which does not in any way diminish the problem or excuse the institution of slavery in early America.[247]

While slavery came into America in both the Northern and Southern states—but proliferating more in the southern agricultural states—it became a crisis in the making for Americans whose morality was grounded in Christianity. Because slavery played a big role in shaping the economy and social order of the Southern states, it would later threaten the continuity of the nation by the mid-nineteenth century.

In the next century, after independence was achieved and representatives from the thirteen states gathered in Philadelphia to draft a new constitution for governing the United States, it was understood that the issue of slavery could not be taken up in a substantive way, as it was likely to prevent the union of the states under a new constitution. However, there were nearly as many voices from the South as there were from the North who were morally opposed to slavery. And so, the Convention did agree to put a clause in the Constitution which would end the slave trade by 1808.[248] Since many believed the Southern states were more culturally infused with Christianity than were the Northern states, there was considerable confidence that moral attitudes about slavery would advance, and that the South would abolish slavery by successive state initiatives.

While the slave trade did legally end in 1808, slavery in the Southern states did not end, and at the time Abraham Lincoln got into politics, there was increasing concern and debate about whether slavery would be allowed in the new states being formed with western expansion of the United States. Lincoln was strongly opposed to any expansion of slavery in new states, and there was growing division in the country. When Lincoln ran for president in 1860, most informed people from both the Northern and Southern states knew where he stood. But while they knew Lincoln was against slavery on principle, he also let Americans know that each of the states needed to take the action they deemed right, with an implied philosophic warning for the nation that "a house divided against itself cannot stand."

For their part, the Southern states had experienced a long train of abuse from the Northern states beyond the slavery issue, and they understood that such an abuse of power was justification for separation from the Union, just as it had been in the colonies' declaring independence from Great Britain. In fact, the US Constitution ratification documents of Virginia, New York, and Rhode Island explicitly said that states had the right to resume an independent status should the federal government abuse its powers.[249] Additionally, many were aware from records of the discussions at the Constitutional Convention, and then the drafting and inclusion of the Bill of Rights, that they had the prerogative to secede from the Union.

As it turned out, the catalyst for the Civil War was the secession of the Southern States, which started shortly after Lincoln's election as president in November 1860. South Carolina was the first to secede on December 20, 1860, followed by six other Southern states prior to Lincoln's inauguration in March 1861. Lincoln was decidedly against the dissolution of the Union.

The winds of war began with Lincoln sending what was assumed to be a hostile fleet to resupply the federal army who continued to occupy Fort Sumter located in the territory of the then independent state of South Carolina. The South Carolina state militia decided to preemptively fire on Fort Sumter, when the federal resupply ships were near—perhaps in a calculated move to prevent a two-front battle of being fired on from the fort in front and from the resupply ships soon to arrive in the harbor in position to fire from the rear.[250]

The die was cast for Lincoln's Civil War to commence, undertaken first to preserve the Union, and later to end slavery. And Lincoln believed that the answer to his reference that "a house divided against itself cannot stand" would in the end be answered by God. The Civil War, which raged on for four more years before Robert E. Lee was forced to surrender to Ulysses S. Grant, would be so costly in the loss of American lives that the 620,000 deaths would outnumber all those lost in the combined wars in which the US would subsequently fight, including two World Wars, the Korean War, the Vietnam War, and all the wars in the Middle East.

Of that number, about forty thousand or 6.5 percent were black soldiers, who primarily fought on Union side.

So, with the emancipation of slavery being consummated by this huge sacrifice of white Americans, it seems inappropriate for people today, six generations later, to even talk about reparations. A huge and immeasurable price has already been paid. The Civil War was followed by the Reconstruction of the South, which while protecting black people from any recidivism of the chains of slavery, did not accomplish the ideals of freedom and equality expressed in the Declaration of Independence.

That would have to wait for almost another century and the arrival of Martin Luther King, Jr., whose single-minded calling was to free America of the injustice of racial discrimination and segregation. In his famous "Letter from a Birmingham Jail"—a message that comes close in eloquence to Thomas Paine's *Common Sense* or John Adams's *Thoughts on Government*—King reminded everyone that, "All segregation statutes are unjust because segregation distorts the soul and damages the personality. It gives the segregator a false sense of superiority and the segregated a false sense of inferiority."[251]

The civil rights crusade became an unstoppable movement of people, both black and white, Christian and Jew, who sought to realize the Promised Land in race relations in America, with true freedom and equality. In King's most famous "I Have a Dream" speech, delivered before the Lincoln Memorial in Washington on August 28, 1963, it was as if the Almighty was calling America to rise up and fulfill its spiritual destiny declared nearly two hundred years earlier in the Declaration of Independence—that of a self-evident truth "that all men are created equal." To that he added an equally timeless truth, that people should not "be judged by the color of their skin but by the content of their character." It naturally follows that for King, there would be no place for either identity politics or critical race theory in a moral civil society.

No one can know for sure whether King was certain of what was coming. But historic destiny tied the mission and work of Martin Luther King, who completed what started with Jefferson and the Declaration of Independence and continued with Abraham Lincoln a hundred years prior. Martin Luther King and Abraham Lincoln seemed prescient in having similar deep feelings that their calling and central work would bring such wrath upon themselves that their lives would be cut short. It turns out that martyrdom, which history shows has been a part of the Jewish and Christian legacy, has brought about moral progress that may have been otherwise impossible.[252]

The fact is that all people, with the exception of Christ, are flawed. And we tend to be impatient with progress that often proceeds slowly and imperceptibly—a disposition that is additionally heightened by our conditioned consciousness shaped by the fast pace of the digital modern age. What is particularly moving and powerful about the story linking these middle three holidays is recognizing the upward, if intermittently plateauing, arc of progress and redemption in American history that extended over nearly two hundred years, to which we should be grateful heirs.

The work of Martin Luther King and the civil rights movement provided a catalyst for twelve major civil rights acts that were passed in the US Congress and signed into law between 1957 and 2006.[253] And it's worth noting how things have changed from what came out of Martin Luther King, Jr. and the civil rights movement.

By most measures, equal opportunity in the public sector for American citizens of all races has now been fully if imperfectly realized. There has been a long-running trend toward higher numbers of non-White lawmakers on Capitol Hill. Overall, 124 lawmakers today identify as Black, Hispanic, Asian/Pacific Islander, or Native American. This represents a 97 percent increase over the 107th Congress of twenty years ago.[254] Nearly a quarter of voting members (23 percent) of the US House of Representatives and Senate are racial or ethnic minorities, making the 117th Congress that convened in 2021 the most racially and ethnically diverse in history. In the House, the representation of some racial and ethnic groups is now on par with their share of the total population—fifty-eight, or 13 percent, of House members are black.[255]

In the private sector, there is a black-white employment gap in some industries, particularly in the science and technology fields and also in the executive suites in large companies. But significant progress is being made. At Walmart, which is the largest private or public company employer in the United States, among its nearly 1.5 million employees, 54 percent are white and 45.7 percent are people of color, and among the management ranks at Walmart, about 12 percent are black.[256]

In the sports and entertainment sector, blacks are overrepresented relative to the population. In virtually every sport in which they compete, people of African descent dominate. Blacks comprise approximately 75 percent of the athletes in the National Basketball Association, over 50 percent of professional football players, and close to 25 percent of professional baseball players.[257]

In entertainment, blacks are on balance equally or overrepresented relative to whites. American pop music has its roots in African-American culture in many genres. Ragtime, blues, jazz, spiritual, gospel, soul, funk, rap, and hip-hop all have African-American roots. Much of the popular music of the twentieth century owes its existence to African-Americans. As for Hollywood, in recent years (data limited to 2018 and 2019), researchers have found that films having the highest gross ticket sales had slightly more than 25 percent of lead roles going to minorities, and among acting roles in those films, over 30 percent went to people of color.[258]

The two chapters on Memorial Day and Veterans Day provide insight on the meaning of patriotism by way of recounting the stories of sacrifice and courage, the traditions and the unique accomplishments carried out by the US military in the course of defending US and international interests and defeating tyrannical regimes and transnational terrorist forces. Just as remarkable was what America did in the aftermath of war, rebuilding its defeated former enemies, then assisting in the establishment of institutions safeguarding their people's freedom and helping those nations reestablish their own independent sovereignty.

In taking these magnanimous actions, Americans were extending the arc of national redemption beyond the equal opportunity accomplishments at home that started with the Declaration and were consummated in Martin Luther King and the civil rights movement. Indeed, we find a bigger arc that extends all the way from the Pilgrim and Puritan founding in the New England colony to the present—from John Winthrop's call to the early settlers to be an exemplary city on a hill to modern America becoming an example and key protector to other nations of the world.

In spite of America's remarkable heritage, there is a dearth of patriotism among the younger generations and growing cynicism among the older generations. Patriotism, rightly understood, does not mean to stand by the party or the leader in power or any other public official, but rather to stand by the Constitution and the institutions and principles behind its creation.

The United States is history's oldest democratic constitutional republic, but its survival is perhaps more precarious now than ever before. John Adams put the stakes this way, "But a constitution of a government once changed from freedom can never be restored. Liberty, once lost, is lost forever."[259]

The fact is that every other nation came into being from an evolution of tribes or clans, from royalty and blood lineage, inevitabilities of language, tradition, geography, or from the results of war where the victors carve up the vanquished. America is the only nation in human history that was completely born of noble ideas: that all men are created equal, that they have been given by God certain rights that cannot be taken away by any man or earthly authority, and that those rights combine to create and protect a thing called freedom in life. And that has meant that Americans were free to pursue happiness, free to worship God, free to speak publicly of their views, and, of course, free to choose their leaders.

There can be little doubt that America's founders and its greatest leaders, like Washington and Lincoln, had a more profound understanding of patriotism as a group than most political leaders of today. So, it's appropriate to bring our journey to a close by drawing on the wisdom of those earlier times. In 1780, before the Constitution had been drafted, Samuel Adams said, "If ever the time should come, when vain and aspiring men shall possess the highest seats in government, our country will stand in need of its experienced patriots to prevent its ruin."[260] That time is now.

Because America is an open society, we have more vulnerability than other nations, and our enemies, both external and internal, know that.

Our external enemies see no need to go to war with us now because their active measure campaigns of internal subversion and demoralization—rooted in Marxism, neo-Marxism, cultural Marxism, and the latest iteration, known as critical race theory—have proven effective in dividing and dispiriting Americans. Our internal enemies may even believe they have achieved the impossible in what they think is an unassailable moral high ground of surmounting Christianity and Judaism with a new secular religion of being "woke."

It's noteworthy that the two presidents we celebrate on Presidents' Day every February, Washington and Lincoln, both forewarned that if the decline and fall of the United States would ever happen, it would be the result of internal causes rather than external military invasion.

Washington's final gift to his country was his Farewell Address, calling it "a warning from a departing friend." Prophetic in nature, it was a penetrating articulation of the three key threats to freedom and the republican form of American democracy: 1) the failure of institutions to keep people informed and enlightened; 2) the problems of factions and hyper-partisanship; and 3) the decline of religious obligation and national morality. Expressing concerns similar to those of Washington, Lincoln said in a public speech in 1838 in Springfield, Illinois: "If [danger] ever reach us it must spring up amongst us; it cannot come from abroad. If destruction be our lot we must ourselves be its author and finisher. As a nation of freemen we must live through all time or die by suicide."[261]

Many of us long for the place we remember in our childhoods, but we have to face the fact that neither we nor our progeny will get that back unless we can win the ideological and spiritual battle against the new woke culture. And make no mistake, the United States is now in a fight for its life. We can all see the woke agenda, which includes destroying the American people's connection to their heritage by anti-American indoctrination in schools and tearing down and defacing our historical monuments and statues; destroying the First Amendment through blacklists, pushing the cancel culture, and mass censorship; politicizing the judiciary; and destroying the separation of powers. This is utterly antithetical to how we should be governed and live under the American Constitution.

In closing, the best way to frame what we need to do in order to win is to really understand how intolerable it is to live in darkness, which is characterized by ignorance, anxiety, and unhappiness that comes from disconnectedness, division, and intolerance. In the political realm, darkness seeks to impose and maintain one-party dictatorial rule—the essence of fascism and communism—that results in corruption and arbitrary government control in more areas of our personal lives.

Being woke is, in reality, its opposite. Wokeness is synonymous with being indoctrinated in darkness. Additional manifestations of darkness that we can all now see include condoning an unequal two-tiered justice system; open borders and the preferential treatment of illegal aliens over American citizens; the nullification of the First Amendment by the censorship of free expression, and fake news; the negation of the Second Amendment and the unalienable right to keep and bear arms to assure self-defense; the rewriting of history as in the 1619 Project; persecution and assaults on Christians and Jews; and the corruption of youth and the eradication of family values while celebrating and elevating relationships counterproductive to procreation—an imperative for any civilization that wants to survive.

However, in spite of cancel culture and mass and social media censorship, the dark forces cannot prevent the truth from getting out and becoming widely known. Americans have become increasingly aware of the seriousness of what has been allowed to grow in the American cultural and political petri dish over the last two generations—a mixture whose contagious influence is as riddled with absurdities and hypocrisies as it is impaling and life threatening.

Parents were already aware that union control of teachers and influence on public school educational curricula have dumbed down teaching, robbed their children of innocence, and given them a jaded view of America as the great villain. Now with the coronavirus epidemic having run its course, citizens can see the governors and mayors who violated the Constitution and abused their people with arbitrary dictatorial order.

Similarly, parents can see the governing authorities and public school boards and administrators who unnecessarily resisted the normal resumption of traditional classroom teaching. In institutions of higher education, universities and colleges have ill prepared students for succeeding in real world careers by instituting coddling campus policies of safe spaces, banning "microaggressions" and certain types of speech and alleged trigger words, and censorship and barring of patriotic and controversial speakers.

In 2016, Americans witnessed an attempted presidential coup that would have nullified the Constitution and the people's sovereignty; then, when that failed, there was a two-year investigation of the elected president that turned up nothing, followed by a baseless and wasteful impeachment in 2019; and then, there was disgraceful character assassination of nominees to the Supreme Court. But we reached the limit—a bridge too far—in 2020, when many states allowed political operatives from outside to dismantle electoral process safeguards and failed in due diligence in the operation of computer-based vote counting machines, allowing political operatives to put in the fix with industrial-scale election fraud. For all intents and purposes, America has for the time being taken on the same status as other lawless banana republics.

The good news from all this is that Americans understand better than ever before what it means to live in darkness. Any one of the above developments is troubling. But when we digest the entirety of the list, which is punctuated at the end with election fraud that disenfranchises the people and delegitimizes the unique American constitutional republic, we know it is time to put on the armor of God and fight with more conviction and determination than ever to defeat darkness and bring back the light.[262] The American system of government and rule of law is unique in human history, being born of noble ideas with its legitimacy coming from God and the participation of the people. It naturally follows that it's absolutely imperative to restore and maintain trust in our voting systems to protect the integrity of US elections in which only legitimate votes are counted.

The prophet Isaiah tells us, "I will lead the blind in a way that they do not know, in paths that they have not known I will guide them. I will turn the darkness before them into light, the rough places into level ground."[263] In Ephesians, Paul reminds us: "For at one time you were darkness, but now you are light...[So] walk as children of light."[264]

We will close where we began, with the arrival of the first Puritan settlers under the leadership of John Winthrop, whose inspirational homily given just before boarding the ship for the New World expressed his vision that the New England colony would be "like a City on a Hill, [with] the eyes of all people...upon us." Winthrop's discourse was taken from Christ's famous teachings on the Beatitudes delivered to the multitudes, in which he proclaimed to believers that, "You are the light of the world. A city that is set on a hill cannot be hidden.... Let your light so shine before men, that they may see your good works..."[265]

It's time for modern-day American patriots committed to the defense of freedom and the pursuit of truth and equal justice under the law to work together with the same conviction and courage that our forebears had—being willing to sacrifice everything in the defense of God-given unalienable rights of life, liberty, and happiness. It's time for the American people to be the light that drives out the darkness.

ENDNOTES

1   Herbert Schlossberg, *Idols for Destruction* (Nashville: Thomas Nelson Publishers, 1983).

2   Wilfred M. McClay, *A Student's Guide to U.S. History* (Wilmington: ISI Books, 2000), 22–31.

3   John Dyson, *Columbus: For Gold, God and Glory* (New York: Simon and Schuster, 1991), 38.

4   Samuel Eliot Morison, *Admiral of the Ocean Sea* (New York: Little Brown, 1942), 47.

5   Quote from Christopher Columbus, *Book of Prophecies*, as cited in William J. Federer, *America's God and Country: Encyclopedia of Quotations* (Fame Publishing: 1996), 113.

6   Federer, *America's God and Country*, 113.

7   Federer, *America's God and Country*, 113.

8   Dyson, *Columbus*, 119–120.

9   Dyson, *Columbus*, 120.

10   Dyson, *Columbus*, 118.

11   Neil L. Whitehead, "Carib cannibalism. The historical evidence," *Journal de la Société des Américanistes* 70 (1984): 69–87.

12   Charlotte Yue and David Yue, *Christopher Columbus: How He Did It* (Boston: Houghton Mifflin Harcourt, 1992), 121.

13   Roy Porter and Mikulas Teich, eds., *The Scientific Revolution in National Context* (Cambridge and New York: Cambridge University Press, 1992).

14   Andrew Johnston, *The Protestant Reformation in Europe* (New York: Routledge, 2014). See also https://en.wikipedia.org/wiki/Reformation_in_Den-

mark–Norway_and_Holstein and https://en.wikipedia.org/wiki/Reformation_in_Sweden.

[15] Larry Schweikart and Michael Allen, *A Patriot's History of the United States* (New York: Sentinel/Penguin Books, 2007), 13–16.

[16] "The First General Assembly: The Oldest Continuous Law-Making Body in the Western Hemisphere," The Historic Jamestowne Visitor Center, https://historicjamestowne.org/history/the-first-general-assembly/.

[17] "African Americans at Jamestown," Historic Jamestowne, updated August 24, 2020, https://www.nps.gov/jame/learn/historyculture/african-americans-at-jamestown.htm.

[18] Diarmaid MacCulloch, *The Reformation: A History* (New York: Penguin, 2004), 34–36, 368–380.

[19] William Bradford, *Of Plymouth Plantation*, ed. Samuel Eliot Morison (New York: Knopf, 1970). Also see Harold Paget, *Bradford's History of the Plymouth Settlement 1608–1650* (New York: E.P. Dutton & Co., 1920).

[20] Nathaniel Philbrick, *Mayflower* (New York: Penguin Books, 2006), 13.

[21] Z. A. Mudge, *Views from Plymouth Rock: Early History of the Plymouth Colony* (New York: Carlton and Lanahan, 1869), 36.

[22] "Pilgrims, Bible, Persecution and Thanksgiving," http://www.crossroad.to/heaven/Excerpts/chronologies/pilgrims.htm.

[23] Mudge, *Views from Plymouth Rock*, 39.

[24] Harold Paget, *Bradford's History of the Plymouth Settlement 1608–1650* (New York: E.P. Dutton & Co., 1920), 11–12.

[25] Jerry Newcombe, *The Book that Made America: How the Bible Formed Our Nation* (Ventura: Nordskog Publishing, 2009), 80.

[26] Martyn Whittock, *Mayflower Lives* (New York & London: Pegasus Books, 2019), 5.

[27] The Treaty of Antwerp, which initiated the Twelve Years' Truce, was an armistice signed in Antwerp on April 9, 1609, between Spain and the Netherlands, creating the major break in hostilities during the Eighty Years' War for independence conducted by the Seventeen Provinces in the Low Countries.

[28] Whittock, *Mayflower Lives*, 19.

[29] Philbrick, *Mayflower*, 18–21.

[30] Rebecca Fraser, *The Mayflower: The Families, the Voyage, and the Founding of America* (New York: St. Martin's Press, 2017), 50.

[31] Fraser, 50.

[32] Meir Y. Soloveichik, Matthew Holbreich, Jonathan Silver, and Stewart W. Halpern, *Proclaim Liberty Throughout the Land: The Hebrew Bible in the United States: A sourcebook* (London and New Milford: The Toby Press LLC, 2019), 8.

33   *Publications of the American Jewish Historical Society* 38, no. 4 (June 1949), 289–303.

34   Schweikart and Allen, *A Patriot's History of the United States*, 27–28. See also Philbrick, *Mayflower*, 40–43.

35   Philbrick, 42.

36   Whittock, 94-95.

37   Whittock, 95-96. See also Joseph Bruchac, *Squanto's Journey: The Story of the First Thanksgiving* (New York: Silver Whistle, Harcourt Inc., 2000), 3–4.

38   Whittock, 99-101. See also "Squanto Facts," Native American Indian Facts, https://native-american-indian-facts.com/Famous-Native-American-Facts/Squanto-Facts.shtml.

39   Philbrick, *Mayflower*, 98–103.

40   Priscilla Frank, "Christie's Tried [sic] to Sell The Proclamation That Established Thanksgiving, Signed by George Washington," *HuffPost*, updated December 6, 2017, https://www.huffpost.com/entry/thanksgiving-proclamation_n_4078958.

41   "Proclamation of Thanksgiving (October 3, 1863)." Abraham Lincoln Online, http://www.abrahamlincolnonline.org/lincoln/speeches/thanks.htm.

42   Federal Holidays: Evolution and Current Practices, May 9, 2014, https://www.everycrsreport.com/reports/R41990.html.

43   Lee Strobel, *The Case for Christ* (Grand Rapids: Zondervan Publishing House, 1998), 21–172.

44   Herbert Lockyer, *All the Messianic Prophecies of the Bible* (Grand Rapids: Zondervan Publishing House, 1973).

45   Hebrews 7:14–16; John 10:17–18, 23–33.

46   Roy G. Pittman, *60 Days that Shook the World: The Last Days of Jesus Christ* (Mustang: Tate Publishing and Enterprises, 2007), 335–347.

47   John 20:30.

48   There are occasional years when the Christian Easter Holy Week and Passover week do not overlap. For a time, early Christians used the Jewish calendar as a reference, celebrating Easter on the first Sunday after Nisan 15. But at the First Council of Nicaea in 325 AD, the Church decided to set its own date for Easter, independent of the Jewish reckoning. Today most Christian communities celebrate Easter on the first Sunday after the first full moon after March 21. But sometimes this full moon isn't the same as the Jewish one.

49   Robert J. Myers, *Celebrations: The Complete Book of American Holidays* (Garden City: Doubleday and Company, 1972), 309–310.

50   It is likely that the Wise Men or Magi that came from Persia knew of the writings of the prophet Daniel, who in times past had been the chief of the court

seers in Persia. Daniel 9: 24–27 includes a prophecy that gives a timeline for the birth of the Messiah.

51 Ace Collins, *Stories behind the Great Traditions of Christmas* (Grand Rapids: Zondervan, 2003), 227–228.

52 Brian Handwerk, "From St. Nicholas to Santa Claus: the surprising origins of Kris Kringle," *National Geographic*, December 25, 2018, https://www.nationalgeographic.com/history/article/131219-santa-claus-origin-history-christmas-facts-st-nicholas.

53 *Britannica*, s.v. "St. Nicholas," https://www.britannica.com/biography/Saint-Nicholas.

54 Charlotte Riggle, "St. Nicholas takes the executioner's sword," December 5, 2020, https://charlotteriggle.com/st-nicholas-takes-executioners-sword/.

55 "Bishop Nicholas Loses His Cool," St. Nicholas Center, https://www.st-nicholascenter.org/who-is-st-nicholas/stories-legends/traditional-stories/life-of-nicholas/bishop-nicholas-loses-his-cool.

56 "Three Impoverished Maidens," St. Nicholas Center, https://www.st-nicholascenter.org/who-is-st-nicholas/stories-legends/traditional-stories/life-of-nicholas/three-impoverished-maidens.

57 Mary Fairchild, "Overview of the Nicene Creed," Learn Religions, February 26, 2019, https://www.learnreligions.com/the-nicene-creed-700366.

58 "How did St. Nicholas become a saint?" Answers.com, https://www.answers.com/Q/How_did_St._Nicholas_become_a_saint.

59 Annemarie van de Wouw, "Santa Claus was first introduced to the U.S. by Dutch immigrants," Dutch Alien Lands in the U.S., December 25, 2016, www.chicagonow.com/dutch-alien-lands-in-us/2016/12/santa-claus-was-first-introduced-to-the-u-s-by-dutch-immigrants.

60 Collins, *Stories behind the Great Traditions of Christmas*, 227.

61 George Grant, *Third Time Around* (Brentwood: Wolgemuth and Hyatt, Publishers, Inc., 1991), 1–50.

62 Kenneth Scott Latourette, *A History of Christianity, Volume I* (New York: Harper and Row, 1953, 1975), 244–246.

63 Michael Breen, "Daughters Unwanted: Asian Quest for Boys Backed by Sex Tests, Abortions," *Washington Times*, February 13, 1993.

64 Will Durant, *Caesar and Christ: A History of Roman Civilization and of Christianity from their Beginnings to A.D. 325* (New York: Simon and Schuster, 1944, renewed 1972), 71.

65 Durant, 667.

66 Thomas Cahill, *How the Irish Saved Civilization* (New York: Anchor Books, 1995).

67 D. James Kennedy, *What if Jesus Had Never Been Born* (Nashville: Thomas Nelson Publishers, 1994), 42–46.

68 Leland Ryken, *Worldly Saints: The Puritans as They Really Were* (Grand Rapids: Zondervan, 1986), 177.

69 Paul Lee Tan, *Encyclopedia of 7700 Illustrations: Signs of the Times* (Rockville: Assurance Publishers, 1984), 157.

70 Halpern, *Proclaim Liberty Throughout the Land*, 131.

71 Halpern, *Proclaim Liberty Throughout the Land*, 179.

72 Philemon 1:16.

73 Barry Hankins, *The Second Great Awakening and the Transcendentalists* (Westport: Greenwood Press, 2004), 137.

74 Frances FitzGerald, *The Evangelicals: The Struggle to Shape America* (New York: Simon and Schuster, 2017), 40.

75 David T. Maloof, *Christianity Matters* (New York: 70x7 Publishing, 2016), 51–60.

76 Maloof.

77 Amber Stelmaschuk, "The School at Salerno: Origin of the European Medical University," Medievalists.net, https://www.medievalists.net/2012/01/the-school-at-salerno-origin-of-the-european-medical-university/.

78 "Most Valuable Paintings in private hands," The Art Wolf, http://www.theart-wolf.com/articles/most-valuable-private-art.htm. Calculating the aggregate value of Christian Renaissance art is impossible because almost all of the great works are in museums and have not been subject to a market sale. It is very conceivable that DaVinci's *Last Supper* or Michelangelo's *David* would fetch ten times more than the highest price paid for any work of art previously sold anywhere in the world.

79 Calvin Coolidge, as quoted in Goodreads, https://www.goodreads.com/quotes/118968.

80 John 18:36.

81 Mircea Eliade, *The Myth of the Eternal Return: Cosmos and History* (New York: Harper and Row, 1954).

82 Eliade, *The Myth of the Eternal Return*. See also Mircea Eliade, *Patterns in Comparative Religion* (Cleveland: Meridian Books, 1958).

83 Fergus, "Christmas Mistletoe: The Underlying Celtic Traditions," The Irish Place, https://www.theirishplace.com/heritage/underlying-traditions-behind-use-mistletoe-christmas/.

84 Walter Tittle, *Colonial Holidays* (Garden City: Doubleday, Page & Co., 1910).

85 Robert J. Myers, *Celebrations: The Complete Book of American Holidays* (Garden City: Doubleday & Co., 1972), 11.

86 Dianne M. MacMillan, *Easter* (Aldershot Hillside: Enslow Publishers, 1993), 7.

87 Pamela Kennedy, *An Easter Celebration* (Nashville: Hambleton-Hill Publishing, 1990), 8.

88 Vexen Crabtree, "The True Meaning of Easter," The Human Truth Foundation, April 11, 2017, www.humanreligions.info/easter.html.

89 Myers, *Celebrations*, 109. See also Eliza Castile, "Why Do We Have Easter Egg Hunts?" Bustle, March 27, 2016.

90 See Eliade, *The Myth of the Eternal Return*, entry "Egg." See also Jack Tresidder, *1001 Symbols* (London: Duncan Baird Publishers, 2003), 47. See also MacMillan (1993), 21.

91 Pamela Kennedy, *An Easter Celebration* (Nashville, TN: Hambleton-Hill Publishing, 1990), 9.

92 Eliza Castile, "Why Do We Have Easter Egg Hunts?" Bustle, March 27, 2016, https://www.bustle.com/articles/150327-why-do-we-have-easter-egg-hunts-the-tradition-has-been-around-longer-than-youd-think.

93 Myers, *Celebrations*, 110.

94 Kennedy, *An Easter Celebration*, 31.

95 Stephen J. Vicchio, *Abraham Lincoln's Religion* (Eugene: Wipf and Stock, 2018), 148.

96 Luke 5:31–31; Mark 2:17; Matthew 9:13.

97 Mark 2:1–12; Matthew 9:1–8; Luke 5:17–26.

98 Gillian Brockell, "Doctors demanded male nurses during the Civil War. Clara Barton defied them," *Washington Post*, May 6, 2019.

99 Romans 5:8.

100 Dr. Jeannie Constantinou, "The Crucifixion of Christ, Part I," Orthodox Christianity, April 12, 2017, https://orthochristian.com/102611.html.

101 Mark 2:17 from the Christian Standard Bible.

102 Pittman, *60 Days that Shook the World*, 335–347.

103 Strobel, *The Case for Christ*, 60. See also Josh McDowell and Sean McDowell, PhD, *Evidence that Demands a Verdict* (New York: HarperCollins, 2017), 41–123, 232–312.

104 "There's No Other Book Like The Bible ! [sic]" http://soul-net.freeservers.com/NOOTHERBOOK.html. See section on Manuscript Evidence. See also McDowell and McDowell, 41–123 and 232–312.

105 Matt Slick, "Manuscript evidence for superior New Testament reliability," CARM, December 6, 2008, https://carm.org/manuscript-evidence.

106 Gary Amos and Richard Gardiner, *Never Before in History* (Seattle: Discovery Institute, 2016), 25–26.

107 R. T. Kendall, *The Influence of Calvin and Calvinism upon the American Heritage* (Rushden: Stanley L. Hunt, 1976). See also David W. Hall, *The Genevan Reformation and the American Founding* (New York: Lexington Books, 2003).

108 John Knox, *The Works of John Knox, ed. David Laing* (Edinburgh: James Thin, 1895), 4:415–416.

109 John Ponet, *A Short Treatise of Politike Power, and of the True Obedience which Subjects owe to Kyngs and other Civil Governours*, reprint (New York: De Capo Press, 1972).

110 Charles Francis Adams, editor, *Works of John Adams* (Boston: Little Brown & Co., 1856), 6:3–4.

111 "Session 1: The Great Awakening, by Dr. Steve Lawson," sermon by Steven J. Lawson, uploaded to YouTube October 25, 2018 (https://www.youtube.com/watch?v=2FbFec1h4MU) See also: "The Great Awakening: Spiritual Revival in Colonial America | Full Movie | Brenda Schoolfield Phd." video uploaded to YouTube on December 9, 2020, https://www.youtube.com/watch?v=vELS8e8hATk&ab_channel=VisionVideo.

112 Daniel N. Gullotta, "The Great Awakening and the American Revolution," *Journal of the American Revolution*, August 10, 2016, https://allthingsliberty.com/2016/08/great-awakening-american-revolution/.

113 John Adams letter to Hezekiah Niles, February 13, 1818, *The Works of John Adams*, ed. Charles Francis Adams, vol. 10 (Boston: Little Brown, and Company, 1850-6), 282.

114 National Humanities Center Resource Toolbox, Becoming American: The British Atlantic Colonies, 1690-1763, "Benjamin Franklin on Rev. George Whitefield 1739," http://nationalhumanitiescenter.org/pds/becomingamer/ideas/text2/franklinwhitefield.pdf.

115 Kent Tollakson, Biographical sermon on George Whitefield, July 8, 2018, East Lincoln Alliance Church, https://eastlincolnalliance.com/sermons/george-whitfield/.

116 Susan Juster, "The Evangelical Ascendency in Revolutionary America," in the *Oxford Handbook of the American Revolution*, eds. Edward G. Gray and Jane Kamensky (Oxford: Oxford University Press, 2013), 407.

117 Carl Van Doren, *Benjamin Franklin* (New York: The Viking Press, 1938), 136–138.

118 Tamera Lynn Kraft, "The Great Awakening Influences the American Revolution," *Colonial Quills* (blog), April 18, 2014, https://colonialquills.blogspot.com/2014/04/the-great-awakening-influences-american.html.

119   Varnum Lansing Collins, *President Witherspoon* (Princeton: Princeton University Press, 1976), 218–220.

120   Wallis W. Wood, "The Signers of the Declaration of Independence: Would You Be So Brave?" *The New American*, posted Friday July 1, 2011, https://www.the-newamerican.com/reviews/opinion/item/5217-the-signers-of-the-declaration-of-independence-would-you-be-so-brave.

121   The clash between the colonial minutemen at Lexington and Concord has been characterized as "the shot heard 'round the world" that marked the beginning of the American Revolution.

122   David McCullough, *1776* (New York: Simon and Schuster, 2005), 118. On the subject of the strategic value of New York, see: 80, 118–119, 132–133.

123   Bill Federer, "The Fog which Saved George Washington," American Minute, *WND*, August 26, 2018, https://www.wnd.com/2018/08/the-fog-which-saved-george-washington/.

124   Peter A. Lillback and Jerry Newcombe, *George Washington's Sacred Fire* (King of Prussia: Providence Forum Press, 2006), 161–162.

125   Lillback and Newcombe, 164–165.

126   Lillback and Newcombe, 165.

127   William J. Federer, *America's God and Country: Encyclopedia of Quotations* (Fame Publishing, 1996), 639.

128   Addressing the impact of the Declaration of Independence, Pauline Maier, an MIT professor, is credited with having said: "It changed the whole character of the war."

129   McCullough, *1776*, 137.

130   McCullough, *1776*, 182-191. See also Richard Brookhiser, *Founding Father* (New York: The Free Press, 1996), 18–19.

131   Because of insufficient records on enlistees and deserters, accounting for numbers of soldiers in the Continental Army at any given time is difficult and imprecise. It should be remembered that Washington's greatly reduced troop count upon leaving New York was also a result of placing some four thousand of the American troops active in the New York campaigns with two other generals—Lee and Gates—who had separate assignments from Washington's march south through New Jersey.

132   McCullough, *1776*, 284.

133   McCullough, 289.

134   Paul Johnson, *A History of the American People* (New York: HarperCollins, 1997), 204.

135   Natasha Frost, "Two Presidents Died on the Same July 4: Coincidence or Something More?" History Channel, July 3, 2018, updated September 4,

2018, https://www.history.com/news/july-4-two-presidents-died-same-day-coincidence.

[136] Lillback and Newcombe, *George Washington's Sacred Fire*, 399.

[137] Lillback and Newcombe, *George Washington's Sacred Fire*, 397.

[138] General George Washington's correspondence to William Gordon, March 1781, as cited by Susie Federer, *Miracles in American History* (Virginia Beach: Amerisearch, 2012), 69.

[139] Madison Clinton Peters, *Haym Salomon: The Financier of the Revolution* (New York: Andesite Press, 2017), 1–3.

[140] Peters, *Haym Salomon*.

[141] Peter Wiernik, *History of Jews in America* (New York: The Jewish Press Publishing Company, 1912), 96.

[142] Wiernik, *History of Jews in America*.

[143] Donald N. Moran, "Haym Salomon—The Revolution's Indispensable Financial Genius," https://www.plaintruth.com/the_plain_truth/2014/07/haym-salomon-the-revolutions-indispensable-financial-genius.html.

[144] Olivia B. Waxman, "George Washington and the Real History Behind a Yom Kippur Legend," *Time Magazine*, September 29, 2017. https://time.com/4958652/yom-kippur-george-washington-history/.

[145] Paul Cornish, "Northwest Ordinance of 1787," The First Amendment Encyclopedia, Middle Tennessee State University, https://www.mtsu.edu/first-amendment/article/871/northwest-ordinance-of-1787.

[146] "Washington's farewell address. Declaration of independence," Library of Congress, https://www.loc.gov/resource/dcmsiabooks.washingtonsfarew00wash_3/?st=gallery.

[147] William M. Thayer, *From Pioneer Home to the White House: Life of Abraham Lincoln: Boyhood, Youth, Manhood, Assassination, Death* (New York: John B. Alden Publisher, 1885), 76.

[148] Joe Wheeler, *Abraham Lincoln: A Man of Faith and Courage* (New York: Howard Books/Simon and Schuster, 2008), 78.

[149] Eric Foner, *The Fiery Trial: Abraham Lincoln and American Slavery* (New York: W. W. Norton & Company, 2010), 26.

[150] James Smith, *The Christian's Defense* (London: Forgotten Books, 2012).

[151] Probably the most comprehensive philosophical and historical analysis of Lincoln's House Divided speech and the Lincoln-Douglas debates is written by Harry V. Jaffa, *Crisis of the House Divided: An Interpretation of the Issues in the Lincoln-Douglas Debates* (Chicago: University of Chicago, 1959, 1982, 2009).

[152] Albert J. Beveridge, *Abraham Lincoln* (Boston: Houghton Mifflin, 1928), 268.

[153] Wheeler, *Abraham Lincoln: A Man of Faith and Courage*, 19.

154 Tulane University, "Lincoln Provoked the War," Reflections, https://www.tulane.edu/~sumter/Reflections/LinWar.html.

155 Major Jones, *Four Years in the Army of the Potomac: A Soldier's Recollections* (London: Forgotten Books, 1888, reprinted 2012), 94.

156 Central Intelligence Library, "Lost Order, Lost Cause," CIA Historical Review Program release dated September 22, 1993.

157 Lincoln's Address to the Young Men's Lyceum of Springfield Illinois, January 27, 1838.

158 John W. Frazier, "If Lincoln Had Lived," address delivered by John W. Frazier, of the California Regiment, the 71st of the Pennsylvania Line, before Col. W. L. Curry Post, no. 18, Department of the Penn., Grand Army of the Republic, Thursday evening, February 11, 1909.

159 Abraham Lincoln, "Speech at New Haven," The History Place, March 6, 1860.

160 James M. McPherson, *Battle Cry of Freedom: The Civil War Era* (Oxford: Oxford University Press, 1988), 701.

161 Steve Luxenberg, "The Forgotten Northern Origins of Jim Crow," *Time*, February 12, 2019.

162 Martin Luther King, Jr., *Strength to Love* (Minneapolis: Fortress Press, 2010), 15.

163 King, 16.

164 King, X.

165 King, *Strength to Love*, 63.

166 King, 64.

167 King, 77.

168 King, *Strength to Love*, 81.

169 King, 83.

170 Martin Luther King, "Nonviolence and Racial Justice," *Christian Century*, February 6, 1957. See also: https://kinginstitute.stanford.edu/king-papers/documents/nonviolence-and-racial-justice.

171 King.

172 Martin Luther King, Jr., "Letter from a Birmingham Jail," April 16, 1963.

173 King, "Letter from a Birmingham Jail," 2.

174 King, 3.

175 King, 5.

176 In addition to "Letter from a Birmingham Jail," the most concise and accessible source on the range of Martin Luther King, Jr.'s insights and beliefs is probably the collection of his works in *Strength to Love* (Minneapolis: Fortress Press, 2010).

177 Owen Amos, BBC News, Washington, DC, March 27, 2018.

178 Ann Hunter McLean, *Unveiling the Lost Cause; A study of Monuments to the Civil War Memory in Richmond, Virginia and Vicinity* (The University of Virginia, PhD Dissertation, Department of Art History, May, 1998), 31–33.

179 Frances Miles Finch, "The Blue and the Gray," *Atlantic Monthly* 20, no. 119 (September 1867): 369–370.

180 Finch, "The Blue and the Gray."

181 Richard G. Weingardt, "Robert E. Lee: Larger-than-Life Icon," American Society of Civil Engineers Library, June 14, 2013, https://doi.org/10.1061/ (ASCE)LM.1943-5630.0000236.

182 "Mary Anna Randolph Custis Lee," National Park Service, June 8, 2021, https://www.nps.gov/arho/learn/historyculture/mary-lee.htm.

183 Robert E. Lee, personal correspondence dated December 29, 1862, obtained through the Eleanor S. Brockenbrough Library Museum of the Confederacy.

184 R. E. Lee correspondence to Agnes [Lee], Fort Mason, Texas, 29 January 1861, Lee Family Papers, Virginia Historical Society.

185 Elizabeth Brown Pryor, "Robert E. Lee and Slavery," HistoryNet.com, https:// www.historynet.com/robert-e-lee-slavery.htm.

186 "Mary Anna Randolph Custis Lee," National Park Service, https://www.nps. gov/arho/learn/historyculture/mary-lee.htm. See also Larry Fox, "The House that Custis Built," *Washington Post*, May 26, 1989.

187 Pastor David Martin, "The Christian Character of Robert E. Lee," 2006, http://www.solidrockbaptist.net/the-christian-character-of-general-robert- e-lee.html.

188 John Esten Cooke, *A Life of General Robert Edward Lee* (New York: D. Appleton and Company, 1883; reprinted in Bedford: Applewood Military History Series, 2017), 1–2.

189 An 1882 Supreme Court decision declared the federal government had con- fiscated Arlington House from the Lees without due compensation, and the property was returned. George Washington Custis Lee sold the house and 1,100-acre estate back to the government for $150,000.

190 John J. Pullen, *Joshua Chamberlain: A Hero's Life and Legacy* (Mechanicsburg: Stackpole Books, 1999).

191 "Colonel Joushua L. Chamberlain & the 20th Maine at Gettysburg," Parks and Places, ScienceViews.com, https://scienceviews.com/parks/chamberlain.html.

192 William Marvel, *A Place Called Appomattox* (Chapel Hill: University of North Carolina Press, 2000), 261.

193 From Thomas Jefferson to Joseph Priestley, June 19, 1802, Founders Online, National Archives, https://founders.archives.gov/documents/ Jefferson/01-37-02-0515.

194 Albert P. Blaustein, "Influence of the Constitution Abroad," 1986, Encyclopedia.com, https://www.encyclopedia.com/politics/encyclopedias-almanacs-transcripts-and-maps/influence-american-constitution-abroad.

195 "History of Veterans Day," Office of Public and Intergovernmental Affairs, U.S. Department of Veterans Affairs, updated July 20, 2015, https://www.va.gov/opa/vetsday/vetdayhistory.asp.

196 Rex Hammock, "Veterans Day Small Business Motivation From General Patton," SmallBusiness.com, November 9, 2015, https://smallbusiness.com/monday-morning-motivation/motivational-quotes-veterans-day-from-general-patton/.

197 General Douglas MacArthur, Sylvanus Thayer Award Acceptance Address at West Point, May 12, 1962.

198 Remarks by Vice President Pence at the Department of Veterans Affairs' National Veterans Day Observance, Arlington National Cemetery, November 11, 2019.

199 John F. Kennedy, Cuban Missile Crisis Address to the Nation, delivered October 22, 1962.

200 William Blackstone, *Commentaries on the Laws of England*, vol. 1 (1765, reprint 1979), 135.

201 Jeffry Bartash, "Share of union workers in the U.S. falls to a record low in 2019," Economic Report, *MarketWatch*, January 31, 2020, https://www.marketwatch.com/story/share-of-union-workers-in-the-us-falls-to-a-record-low-in-2019-2020-01-22.

202 "Union Members Summary," Economic News Release, U.S. Bureau of Labor Statistics, January 22, 2021, https://www.bls.gov/news.release/union2.nr0.htm.

203 Ken Abramowitz, "Time to Commemorate Alexis de Tocqueville," *The Jewish Voice*, February 2021.

204 Adam Smith, *An Inquiry into the Nature and Causes of the Wealth of Nations* (New York: Random House, The Modern Library, Reprint, 1937).

205 Joseph Story, *A Familiar Exposition of the Constitution of the United States*, a reprint of the 1840 treatise (Lake Bluff: Regnery Books, 1986), 54.

206 The best study of this comes from Donald S. Lutz, "The Relative Influence of European Writers on Late Eighteenth-Century American Political Thought," *American Political Science Review 78*, no. 1 (March 1984): 189–197.

207 Story, *A Familiar Exposition of the Constitution of the United States*, 323.

208 Carol Berkin, *A Brilliant Solution: Inventing the American Constitution* (New York: Harcourt, Inc., 2002), 8.

209   Matthew 5:14: "You are the light of the world. A city that is set on a hill cannot be hid."

210   "Why They Asked Jefferson to Write The First Draft Of The Declaration of Independence," Varsity Tutors, https://www.varsitytutors.com/earlyamerica/freedom-documents/asked-jefferson-write-first-draft-declaration-independence.

211   Tony Williams, *America's Beginnings: The Dramatic Events that Shaped a Nation's Character* (Lanham: Rowman & Littlefield Publishers, Inc., 2010), 112–113.

212   "Before the Declaration of Independence, an Olive Branch Was Extended," New England Historical Society, https://www.newenglandhistoricalsociety.com/declaration-independence-olive-branch-extended/.

213   Williams, *America's Beginnings*, 113–114.

214   The Declaration of Independence, last paragraph. Language may have been suggested by Rev. John Witherspoon, delegate from New Jersey or Charles Pinckney, delegate from South Carolina.

215   Carol Berkin, *A Brilliant Solution*, 12.

216   Berkin, 16.

217   Berkin, 30–31.

218   Fred Rodell, *55 Men: The Story of the Constitution* (Harrisburg: Stackpole Books, 1936), 15–16.

219   John Eidsmoe, *Christianity and the Constitution: The Faith of Our Founding Fathers* (Grand Rapids: Baker Books, 1987), 57.

220   Eidsmoe, 331–332.

221   Rodell, *55 Men*, 89.

222   Richard T. Burress, *We the People: The Story of Our Constitutional Convention* (Stanford: Hoover Institution, 1987), 10.

223   Burress, *We the People*, 10.

224   Diane Rufino, "The Constitutional Convention of 1787: Prayer Served a Purpose Just as Prayer Always Serves a Purpose," *Tea In Politics* (blog), posted October 10, 2018, https://teainpolitics.wordpress.com/tag/ben-franklin/.

225   The youngest delegate to the convention at age twenty-six was Jonathan Dayton. He had enlisted in the New Jersey militia when his fifteen years old, fought in the New York and New Jersey campaigns under Washington, was captured and imprisoned by the British in New York, and reenlisted upon release, rising to the rank of captain. He took his New Jersey unit to Yorktown in 1781, where under the command of Alexander Hamilton, he led his company in a victorious perilous silent night bayonet attack on Redoubt 10, one of the last strongholds under General Cornwallis.

226   Rufino, "The Constitutional Convention of 1787."

227   Eidsmoe, *Christianity and the Constitution*, 346–347.

228 James Madison, *Notes of Debates in the Federal Convention of 1787 Reported by James Madison* (Athens: Ohio University Press, 1966), 309.

229 Madison, 311–312.

230 James Madison, *The Writings of James Madison*, 9 volumes (1787, The Journal of the Constitutional Convention) as cited by Carol Berkin, *A Brilliant Solution*, 121.

231 Madison, *Notes of Debates in the Federal Convention of 1787 Reported by James Madison*, 365.

232 Alexander Hamilton, The Federalist, No. 78.

233 Earl Starbuck, "Was Secession Treason?" Abbeville Institute Press blog, September 18, 2020, https://www.abbevilleinstitute.org/blog/was-secession-treason/.

234 Madison, *Notes of Debates in the Federal Convention of 1787, Reported by James Madison*.

235 "The Federalist Papers," Constitutional Rights Foundation, https://www.crf-usa.org/foundations-of-our-constitution/the-federalist-papers.html. See also: "After the Fact: Virginia, New York and 'The Federalist Papers,'" ushistory. org, https://www.ushistory.org/us/16d.asp.

236 Chuka Nwanazia, "Calvinism in the Netherlands: Why are the Dutch so Calvinist in Nature?" DutchReview, March 1, 2021, https://dutchreview.com/culture/society/calvinism-netherlands-dutch-calvinist-nature/.

237 Daily History.org, "What was the impact of John Knox, on Scotland and on religion?" https://dailyhistory.org/What_was_the_impact_of_John_Knox,_on_Scotland_and_on_religion.

238 Matthew 5:15–16. See also Meir Y. Soloveichik, Matthew Holbreich, Jonathan Silver, Stuart W. Halpern, *Proclaim Liberty Throughout the Land: The Hebrew Bible in the United States, A Sourcebook* (New Milford: The Toby Press LLC, 2019), 10–11. Emphasis added.

239 Lutz, "The Relative Influence of European Writers on Late Eighteenth Century American Political Thought," 189–197.

240 Jeff Desjardins, "Mapped: the World's Oldest Democracies," World Economic Forum, August 8, 2019, https://www.weforum.org/agenda/2019/08/countries-are-the-worlds-oldest-democracies.

241 Desjardins.

242 Douglas MacArthur, *Reminiscences* (New York: McGraw Hill, 1964), 311.

243 "Is it a scandal that Gen. MacArthur thought Christianity Would Help Japan?" Beliefnet, https://www.beliefnet.com/columnists/on_the_front_lines_of_the_culture_wars/2011/06/scandal-general-douglas-macarthur-thought-christianity-would-help-japan.html.

244 Masahiro Wakabayashi, "Democratization of the Taiwanese and South Korean Political Regimes: A Comparative Study," *The Developing Economies* 35, no. 4 (December 1997): 422–439.

245 For the best account, see Daniel Yergin and Joseph Stanislaw, *The Commanding Heights* (New York: Simon and Schuster, 1998, 2002).

246 History.com Editors, "First enslaved Africans arrive in Jamestown, setting the stage for slavery in North America," History, August 13, 2019, https://www.history.com/this-day-in-history/first-african-slave-ship-arrives-jamestown-colony. This account has it that Portuguese colonial forces involved in the slave trade captured members of the native Kongo and Ndongo kingdoms in what is now known as Angola in Africa. They were forcefully taken on a ship named *San Juan Bautista* sailing for Veracruz in the colony of New Spain, which is now Mexico. En route, that ship was attacked by two privateer ships, the *White Lion* and the *Treasurer*, whose crews took some of the *Bautista's* captives. It was the *White Lion* that arrived with some twenty African captives in the Jamestown colony on August 20, 1619, and there they were traded as indentured servants for food and water.

247 "African Americans at Jamestown," Historic Jamestowne. Technically, the black African captives were traded to the Jamestown colonists as indentured servants, a practice common in Britain and elsewhere at that time. In fact, many white Europeans came to America as indentured servants. Individuals typically became indentured servants to pay off debt that they owed another party. The contractual understanding of both parties was that the indentured servant would be taken care of in terms of room and board and work with no pay for the set amount of time, and would become free at the end of the contractual period. Historical records do indicate that some black African indentured servants did obtain their freedom, particularly in the Northern colonies. But with fewer white indentured servants arriving from England, a racial caste system developed in the Southern colonies in America, and African servants were increasingly held for life. In 1662, a Virginia court effectively codified slavery by ruling that children born to enslaved mothers were property of the mother's owner. With Virginia and the other Southern colonies being almost entirely agricultural—driven by the labor-intensive requirements of tobacco, cotton, and sugar farming—slavery became totally integrated into their economies.

248 US Const. art I, §9.

249 Boyd Cathey, "'A Sickness in the Public Mind,' The Battle Flag and the Attack on Western Culture" (blog) *Abbeville Institute Press*, August 4, 2015, https://

www.abbevilleinstitute.org/a-sickness-in-the-public-mind-the-battle-flag-and-the-attack-on-western-culture/.

250 Charles W. Ramsdell, "Lincoln and Fort Sumter," *The Journal of Southern History* 3, no. 3 (August 1937): 259–288.

251 Biblical reference from Galatians 3:26–28. Quote from Martin Luther King, Jr., "Letter from a Birmingham Jail," April 16, 1963. See https://www.africa.upenn.edu/Articles_Gen/Letter_Birmingham.html.

252 Proverbs 16:1–7.

253 See "Constitutional Amendments and Major Civil Rights Acts of Congress," U.S. House of Representatives: History, Art & Archives https://history.house.gov/Exhibitions-and-Publications/BAIC/Historical-Data/Constitutional-Amendments-and-Legislation/.

254 Research Center analysis of data from the Congressional Research Service. Katherine Schaeffer, "Racial, ethnic diversity increases yet again with the 117th Congress," Pew Research Center, January 28, 2021, https://www.pewresearch.org/fact-tank/2021/01/28/racial-ethnic-diversity-increases-yet-again-with-the-117th-congress/.

255 Schaeffer.

256 Serenah McKay, "Walmart Details its Report on Diversity," *Northwest Arkansas Democrat Gazette*, September 11, 2020, https://www.nwaonline.com/news/2020/sep/11/walmart-details-its-report-on-diversity/. People of color are defined in the report as "an aggregate composite of U.S. associates including African American/Black; Asian; Latino; Native American/Alaskan Native; Native Hawaiian/Pacific Islander; and individuals of two or more races."

257 Vinay Harpalani, "The Athletic Dominance of African Americans—Is there a Genetic Basis?" *Journal of African American Men* 2, no. 2/3(Fall 1996/Winter 1997), https://www.jstor.org/stable/41819304?seq=1.

258 "2020 Hollywood Diversity Report: A different story behind the scenes," News, UCLA College, https://www.college.ucla.edu/2020/02/06/2020-hollywood-diversity-report-a-different-story-behind-the-scenes/.

259 John Adams, letter to Abigail Adams, July 7, 1775, Founders Online, National Archives, https://founders.archives.gov/documents/Adams/04-01-02-0160#:~:text=Our%20Consolation%20must%20be%20this,once%20lost%20is%20lost%20forever.

260 Sam Adams, letter to James Warren, October 24, 1780, Revolutionary War and Beyond, https://www.revolutionary-war-and-beyond.com/Samuel-Adams-Letter-24Oct1780.html.

261 Lincoln's address to the Young Men's Lyceum of Springfield, Illinois, January 27, 1838.

262 Ephesians 6:11.
263 Isaiah 42:26.
264 Ephesians 5:8.
265 Matthew 5:14–6.

ACKNOWLEDGMENTS

Rediscovering America was years in the thinking and more than a year in the making. A heartfelt thank you is first due to my lovely wife, Faith, and precious daughter, Meriel, who supported the project while also begrudging it because of time lost with them. My two editors, Diana Carlyle and Mary Cantor, are national treasures in the literary field—truly remarkable.

Thanks also to my brother John and Stephen Post who were always there when I needed them, and to all those who were able to read and comment on the book manuscript or the prior "holiday" articles: Patricia Strong, Liane Mills, Michael O'Toole, Kathleen Wright, Harlan and Kathy Gephart, Rick and Valerie Chaples, Rock and Gina Daze, Alan McInally, Brian Dightman, Jim Macek, Phil Kirby, James Snyder, Terry Brown, Jonathan Buckley, Sandy Simmons, Terry Schran, Peter Davis, Henry Morriello, Cassy Wu, Gary Stump, Myles Brown, Kevin Thompson, Joseph and Laurel Saromines, and others who go unnamed but are greatly appreciated.

One of the book's prior published holiday articles that recounted the story of the Pilgrims and caused the editor of that magazine, Wlady Pleszczynski, to ask why, with all its diversity and essential elements of drama, the Thanksgiving story hadn't yet been made into a Hollywood movie. I also owe thanks to other professional editors, especially JR

Dunn, Stephen Gregory, and Judi McLeod who worked with me on publishing a number of different historical holiday articles prior to the book.

I am indebted to my colleagues at the Discovery Institute, notably Bruce Chapman, Steve Buri, John West, Erik Nutley, Steve Meyer, Jackson Meyer, and Kelly Unger who provided support and read and commented on my work in the midst of busy schedules.

I'd also like to thank Bill Wilson who, from the big sky state of Montana, tracked me down thirteen years ago after he had read my editorial on the financial collapse of 2008 in *Barron's Financial*, and has been a fan ever since. He provided special support and encouragement for my writing of this book, believing it would be an honest narrative that would slay the woke dragon intent on devouring American heritage. Across the country, from a town appropriately named Hope, in the state of Maine, friends Bradley and Lorinda Boyd deserve special recognition for their support. Thanks also to several other friends dating back to our junior high school roots, Hope Aldrich, Vytas Simas, and Tim and Robin Beck. Thanks also to Jim Conroy in Connecticut for his support and reading parts of the manuscript, and his insight on Roger Sherman, the remarkable Connecticut delegate whose equanimity and Great Compromise helped save the Constitutional Convention in 1787. Victor Sperandeo, the busiest guy I know from Texas, also made time for my work over the years.

Among supporters of the project, there are three to whom I owe special thanks because of their unique distinction of putting up with me twice, having read and commented on chapters of this book and a previous book: Eugenia Campbell, Virginia Hurt, and Andrew Hruska.

There seems to be no greater concentration of American patriots than in the state of Virginia, which may explain why the state and its institutions, such as VMI, UVA, and Monument Avenue in Richmond, are in the crosshairs of the enemy. In addition to fielding more Founding Fathers than any other state, Virginia raised up four out of the first five presidents of the United States. Thanks go to Jane Stidham, James Stansberry III, George McCall, Pat and Mary Hendy, Melissa Sharpley, Bob Raynor, and Dave Brat for their interest and support. Ann McLean deserves special recognition for her indefatigable patriotism and her commitment—in the midst of her efforts to save historic statues in Richmond and save her alma mater, UVA, from Marxist takeover—to read and comment on nearly half the manuscript. I also owe thanks to her, and particularly Doc Garnett, Bo Traywick, and Marshall DeRosa who all took the time to fill the gaps in my knowledge about the history of the South.

Peter Halasz came to my rescue in directing me to patriot scholars of the Jewish tradition who opened my eyes to a deeper understanding of the Hebraic roots of the Christian faith of both the Pilgrims and the Puritans. Those sources also led me to discover the little-known story of the talented Jewish financier immigrant from Poland, Haym Salomon, who arrived in America in 1775 just in the nick of time to play the pivotal role in financing the Revolutionary War.

Late stage support came from Nick Adams, an Australian immigrant turned American superpatriot and founder of FLAG, who introduced me to the founder of my publisher Post Hill Press; and from John Cote who designed the book's cover and Tisa Christiana Spraul whose talents are in social media. John White chimed in from Australia, while Annette Eliot and Mary Anderson like what they see for their women's clubs in California and Louisiana. Locally, Rob Pacienza, Frank Wright, Jerry Newcombe, Audrey DePodesta, Rosane Cooper, Pat Cohen, Howard Stoller, Narei Leavitt, and Chuck Tiedje are all enthusiastic promoters of *Rediscovering America*.

With the biblical admonition that the last shall be first, a special thanks goes to William Yavelak, a remarkable patriot from Ohio with a calling for and delivery of a Christian counseling ministry to US presidents. Bill made *Rediscovering America* his priority during the two weeks before submission to the publisher, providing insight and editorial commentary on the entire manuscript.